# MOON LAKE

by

# Terry Moore

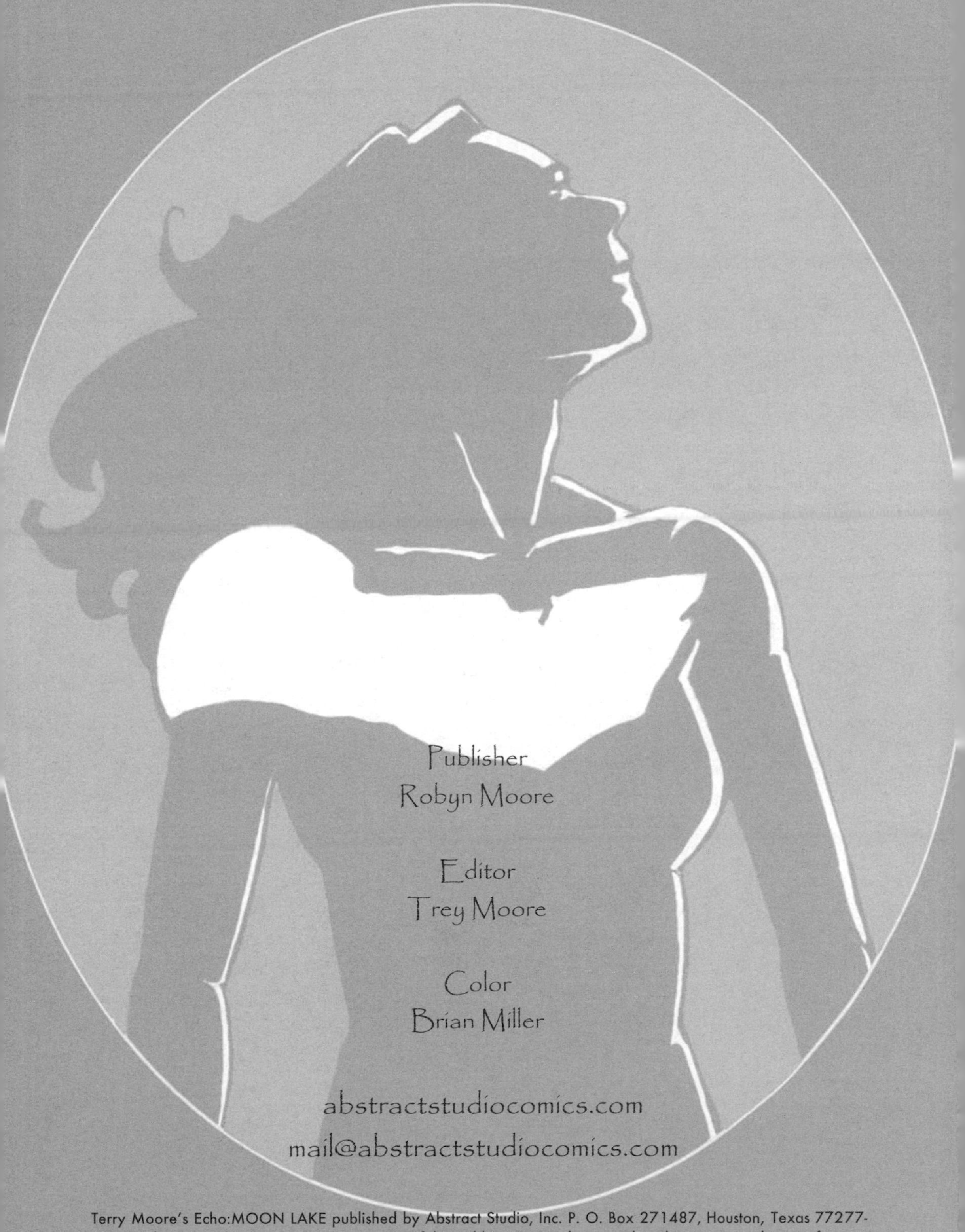

Publisher
Robyn Moore

Editor
Trey Moore

Color
Brian Miller

abstractstudiocomics.com
mail@abstractstudiocomics.com

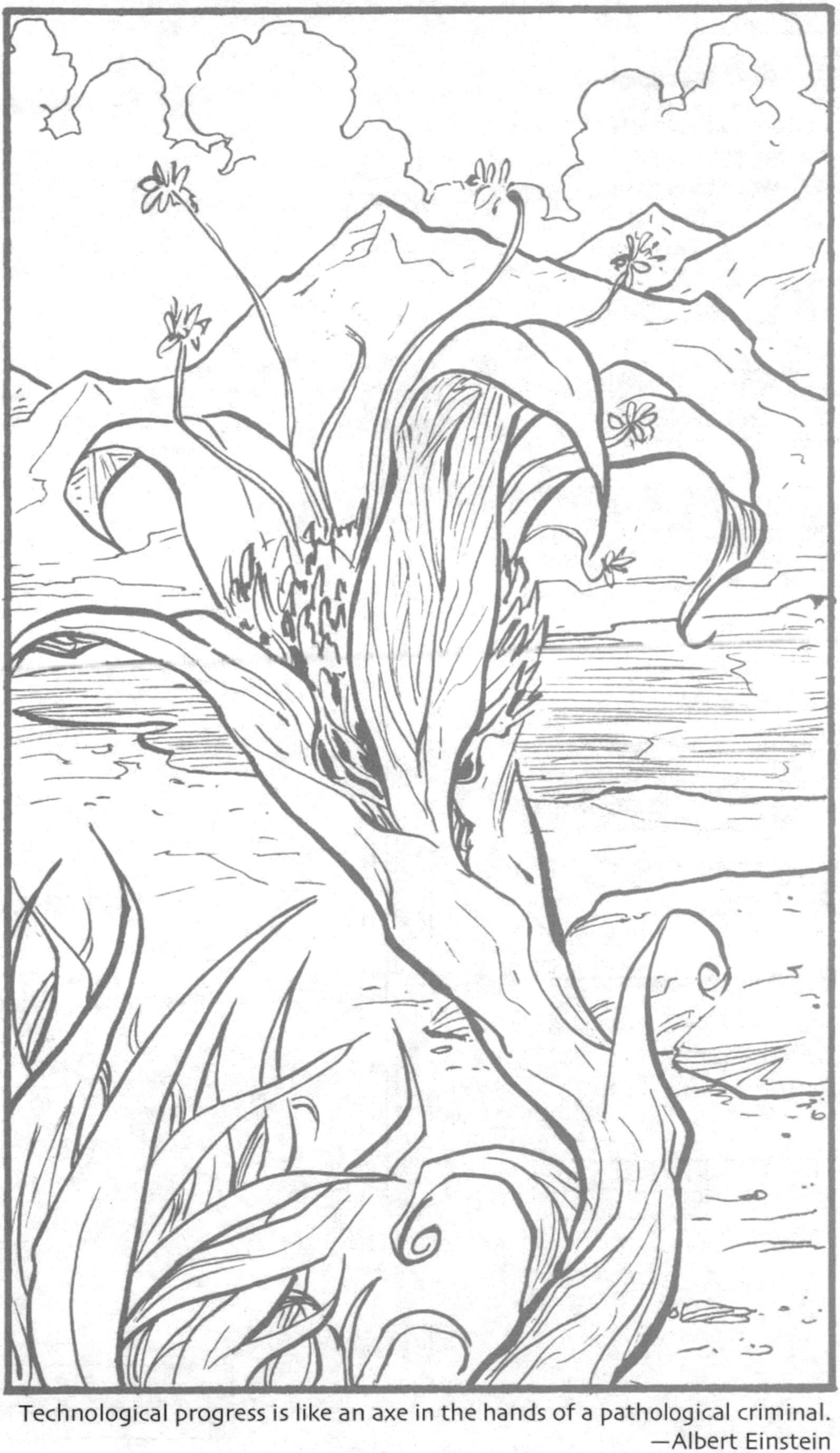

Technological progress is like an axe in the hands of a pathological criminal.
—Albert Einstein

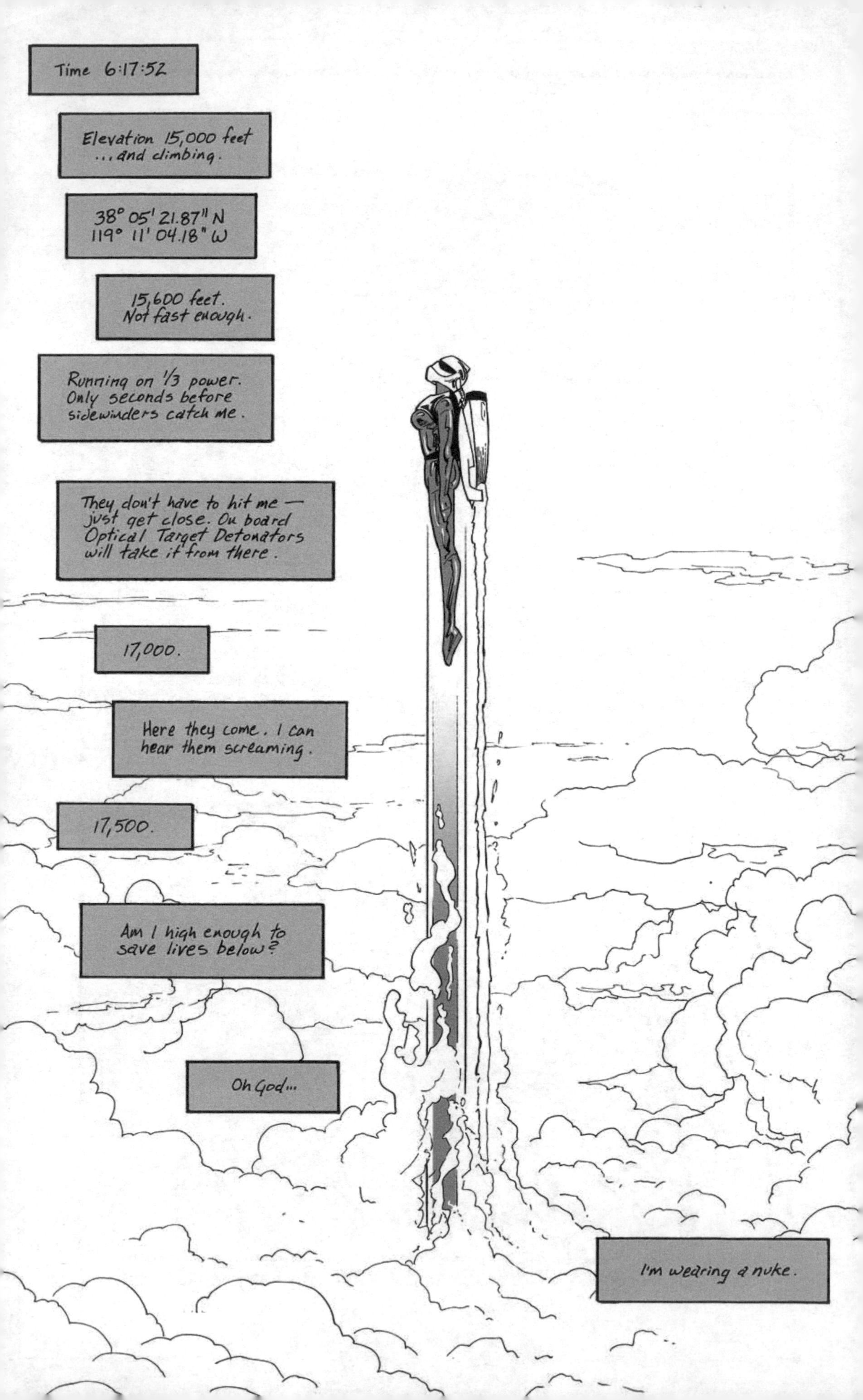
Time 6:17:52
Elevation 15,000 feet ...and climbing.
38° 05' 21.87" N 119° 11' 04.18" W
15,600 feet. Not fast enough.
Running on 1/3 power. Only seconds before sidewinders catch me.
They don't have to hit me — just get close. On board Optical Target Detonators will take it from there.
17,000.
Here they come. I can hear them screaming.
17,500.
Am I high enough to save lives below?
Oh God...
I'm wearing a nuke.

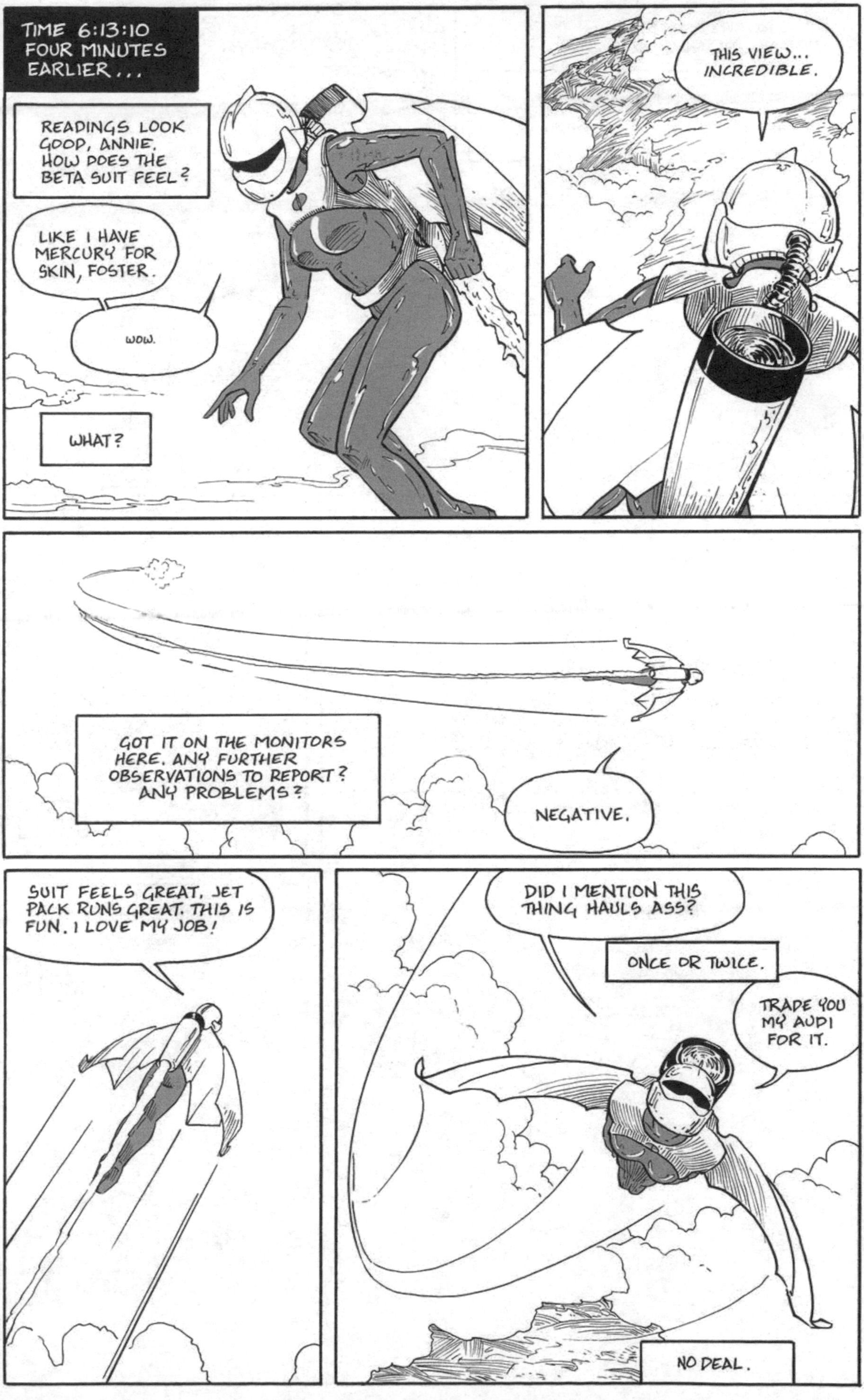
TIME 6:13:10 FOUR MINUTES EARLIER...
READINGS LOOK GOOD, ANNIE. HOW DOES THE BETA SUIT FEEL?
LIKE I HAVE MERCURY FOR SKIN, FOSTER.
WOW.
WHAT?
THIS VIEW... INCREDIBLE.
GOT IT ON THE MONITORS HERE. ANY FURTHER OBSERVATIONS TO REPORT? ANY PROBLEMS?
NEGATIVE.
SUIT FEELS GREAT. JET PACK RUNS GREAT. THIS IS FUN. I LOVE MY JOB!
DID I MENTION THIS THING HAULS ASS?
ONCE OR TWICE.
TRADE YOU MY AUDI FOR IT.
NO DEAL.

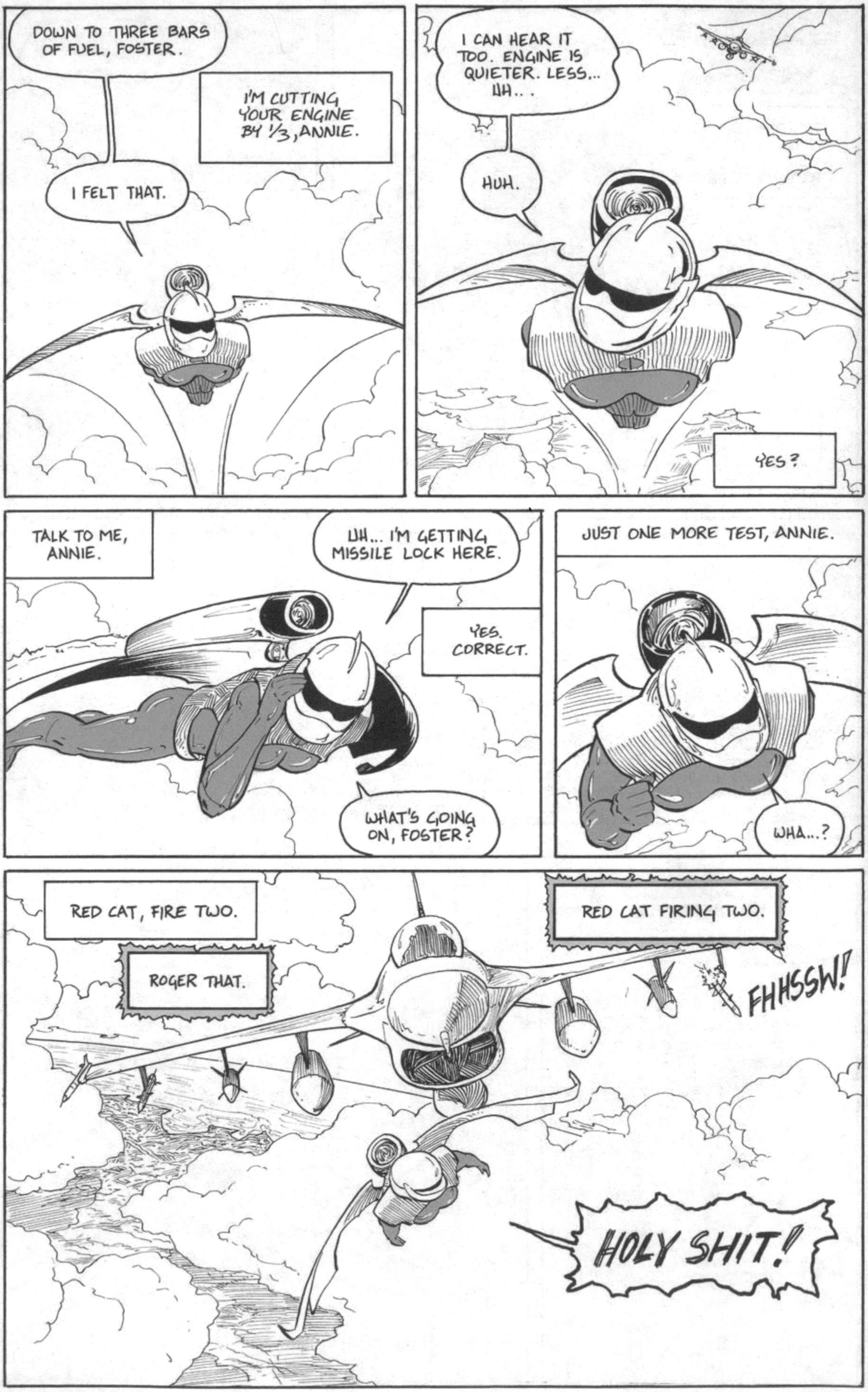
DOWN TO THREE BARS OF FUEL, FOSTER.
I'M CUTTING YOUR ENGINE BY 1/3, ANNIE.
I FELT THAT.
I CAN HEAR IT TOO. ENGINE IS QUIETER. LESS... UH...
HUH.
YES?
TALK TO ME, ANNIE.
UH... I'M GETTING MISSILE LOCK HERE.
YES. CORRECT.
WHAT'S GOING ON, FOSTER?
JUST ONE MORE TEST, ANNIE.
WHA...?
RED CAT, FIRE TWO.
ROGER THAT.
RED CAT FIRING TWO.
FHHSSW!
HOLY SHIT!

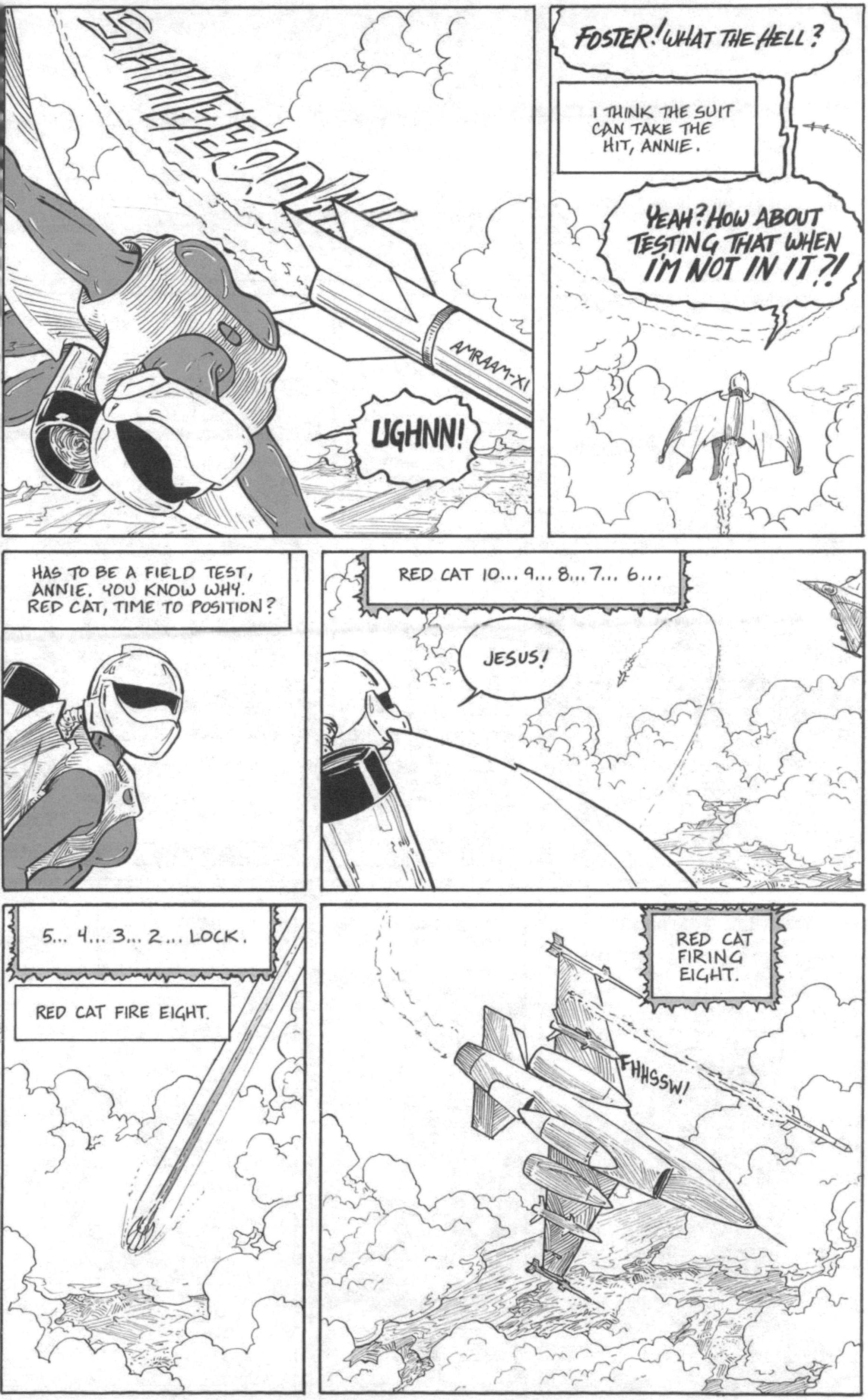
SHHEEEOOWWW
AMRAAM-XI
UGHNN!
FOSTER! WHAT THE HELL?
I THINK THE SUIT CAN TAKE THE HIT, ANNIE.
YEAH? HOW ABOUT TESTING THAT WHEN I'M NOT IN IT?!
HAS TO BE A FIELD TEST, ANNIE. YOU KNOW WHY. RED CAT, TIME TO POSITION?
RED CAT 10... 9... 8... 7... 6...
JESUS!
5... 4... 3... 2... LOCK.
RED CAT FIRE EIGHT.
RED CAT FIRING EIGHT.
FHHSSW!

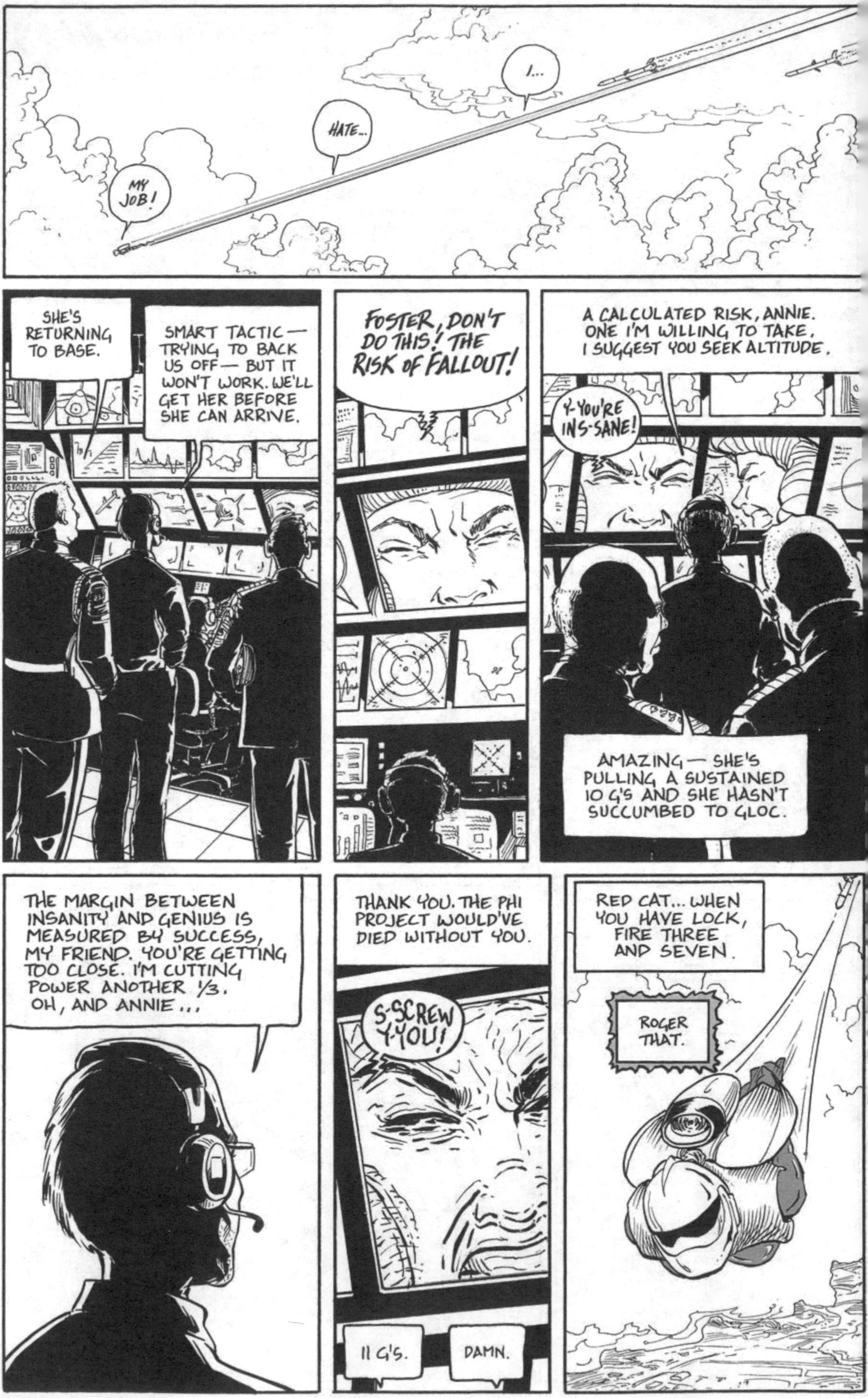
MY JOB!
HATE...
I...
SHE'S RETURNING TO BASE.
SMART TACTIC— TRYING TO BACK US OFF— BUT IT WON'T WORK. WE'LL GET HER BEFORE SHE CAN ARRIVE.
FOSTER, DON'T DO THIS! THE RISK OF FALLOUT!
A CALCULATED RISK, ANNIE. ONE I'M WILLING TO TAKE. I SUGGEST YOU SEEK ALTITUDE.
Y-YOU'RE INS-SANE!
AMAZING— SHE'S PULLING A SUSTAINED 10 G'S AND SHE HASN'T SUCCUMBED TO GLOC.
THE MARGIN BETWEEN INSANITY AND GENIUS IS MEASURED BY SUCCESS, MY FRIEND. YOU'RE GETTING TOO CLOSE. I'M CUTTING POWER ANOTHER 1/3. OH, AND ANNIE...
THANK YOU. THE PHI PROJECT WOULD'VE DIED WITHOUT YOU.
S-SCREW Y-YOU!
11 G'S.
DAMN.
RED CAT... WHEN YOU HAVE LOCK, FIRE THREE AND SEVEN.
ROGER THAT.

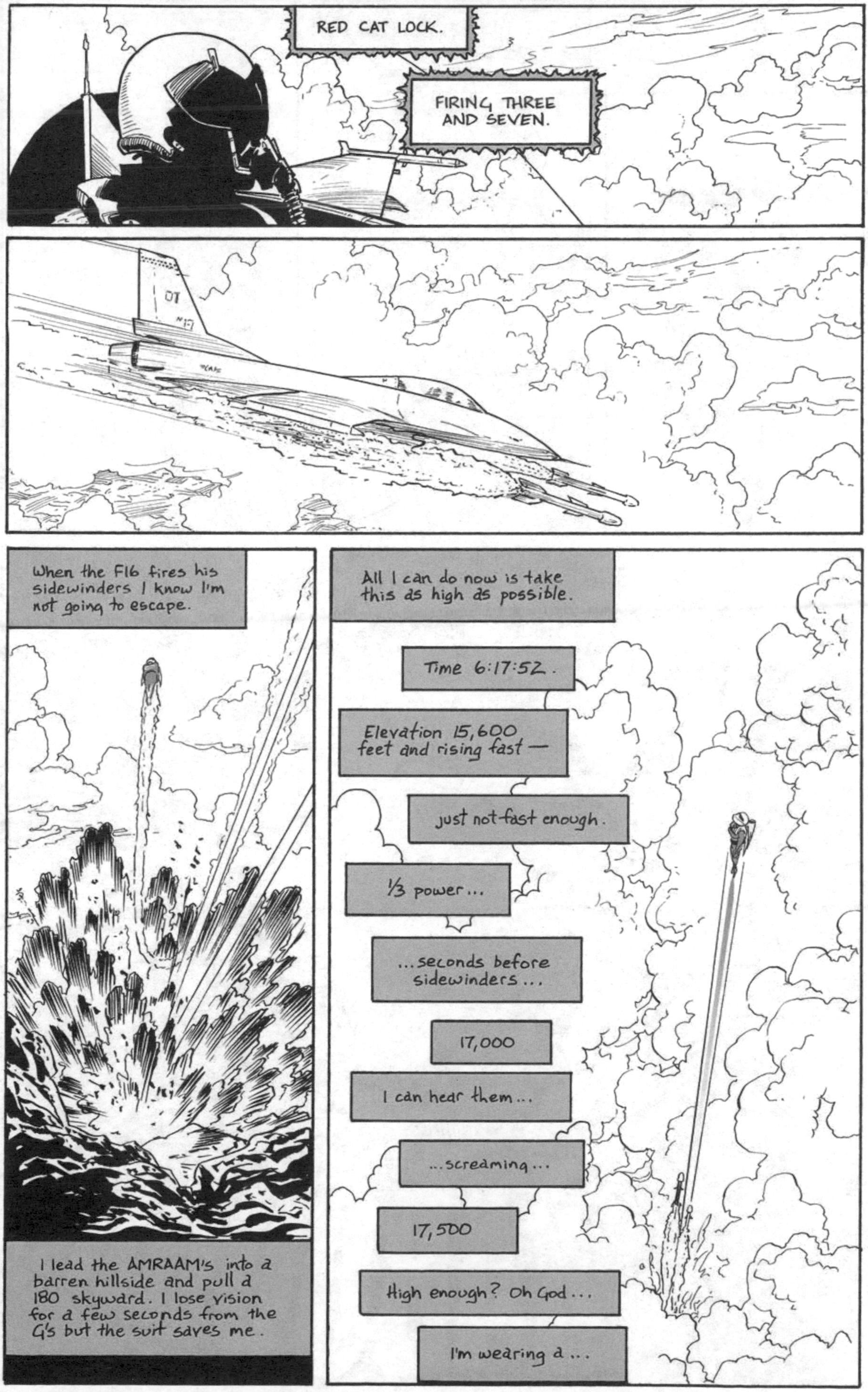
RED CAT LOCK.
FIRING THREE AND SEVEN.
When the F16 fires his sidewinders I know I'm not going to escape.
I lead the AMRAAM's into a barren hillside and pull a 180 skyward. I lose vision for a few seconds from the G's but the suit saves me.
All I can do now is take this as high as possible.
Time 6:17:52.
Elevation 15,600 feet and rising fast —
just not fast enough.
1/3 power...
...seconds before sidewinders...
17,000
I can hear them...
...screaming...
17,500
High enough? Oh God...
I'm wearing a...

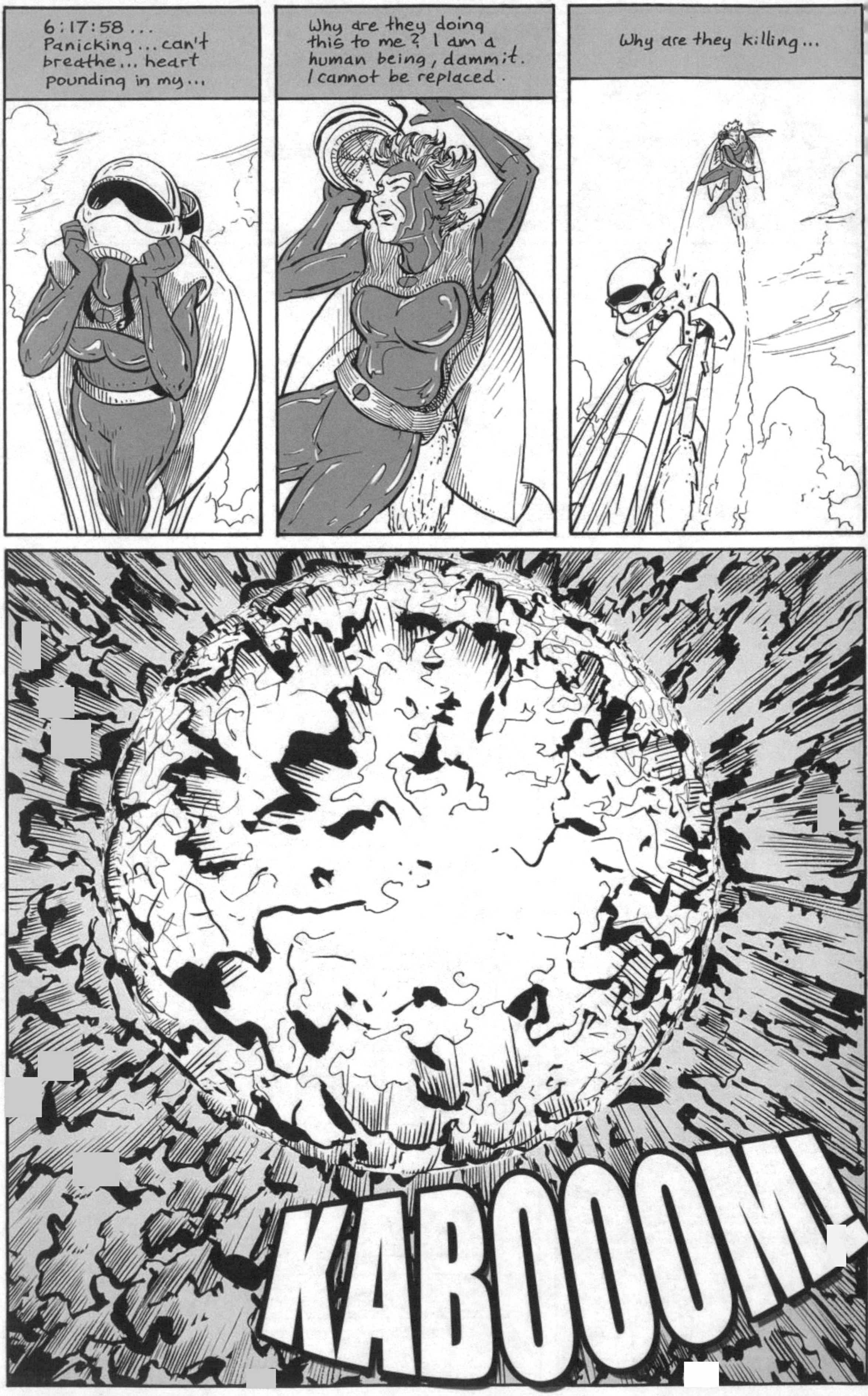
6:17:58...
Panicking... can't breathe... heart pounding in my...
Why are they doing this to me? I am a human being, dammit. I cannot be replaced.
Why are they killing...
KABOOOOM!

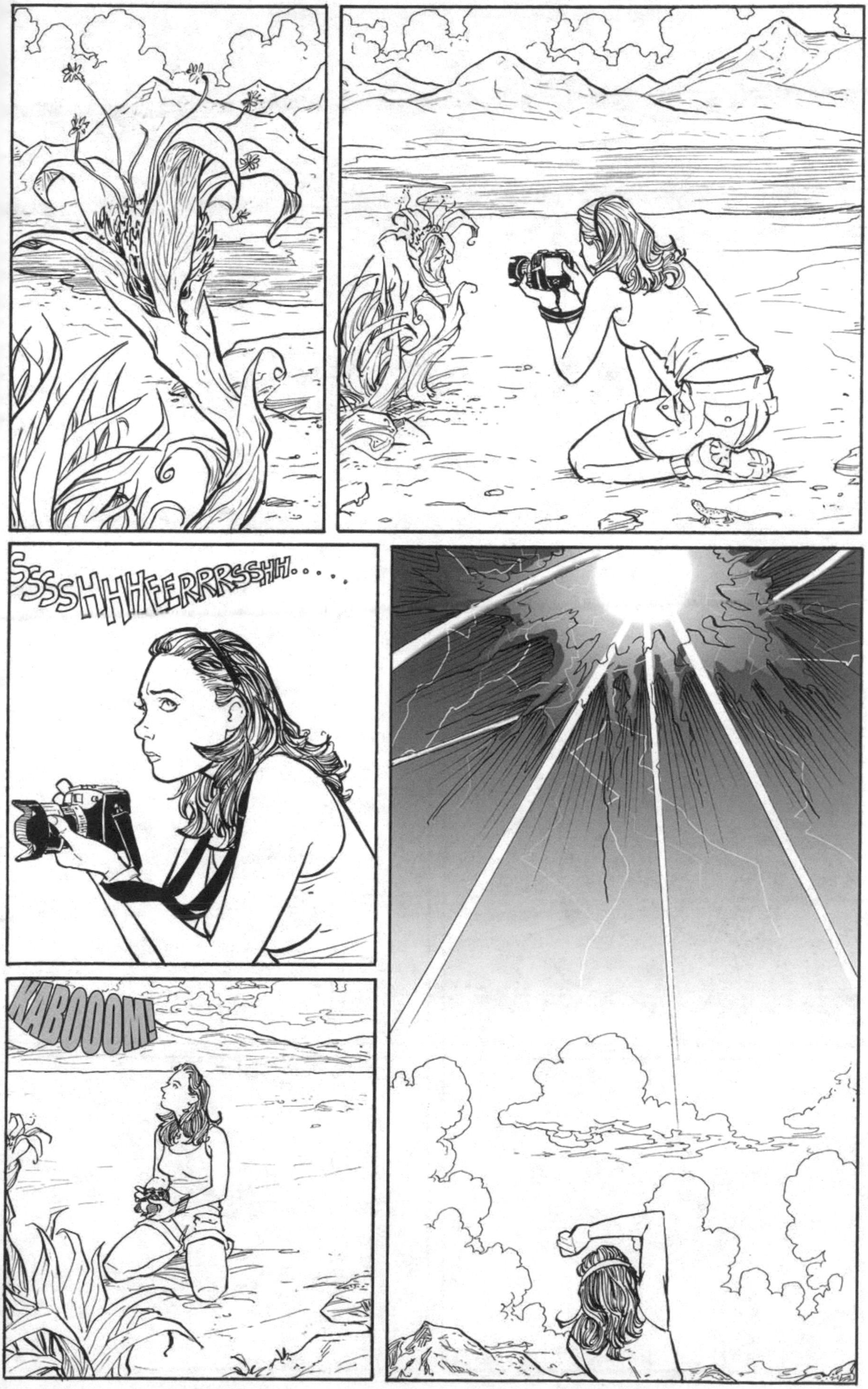
SSSSHHHEERRRSSHH.....
KABOOOM!

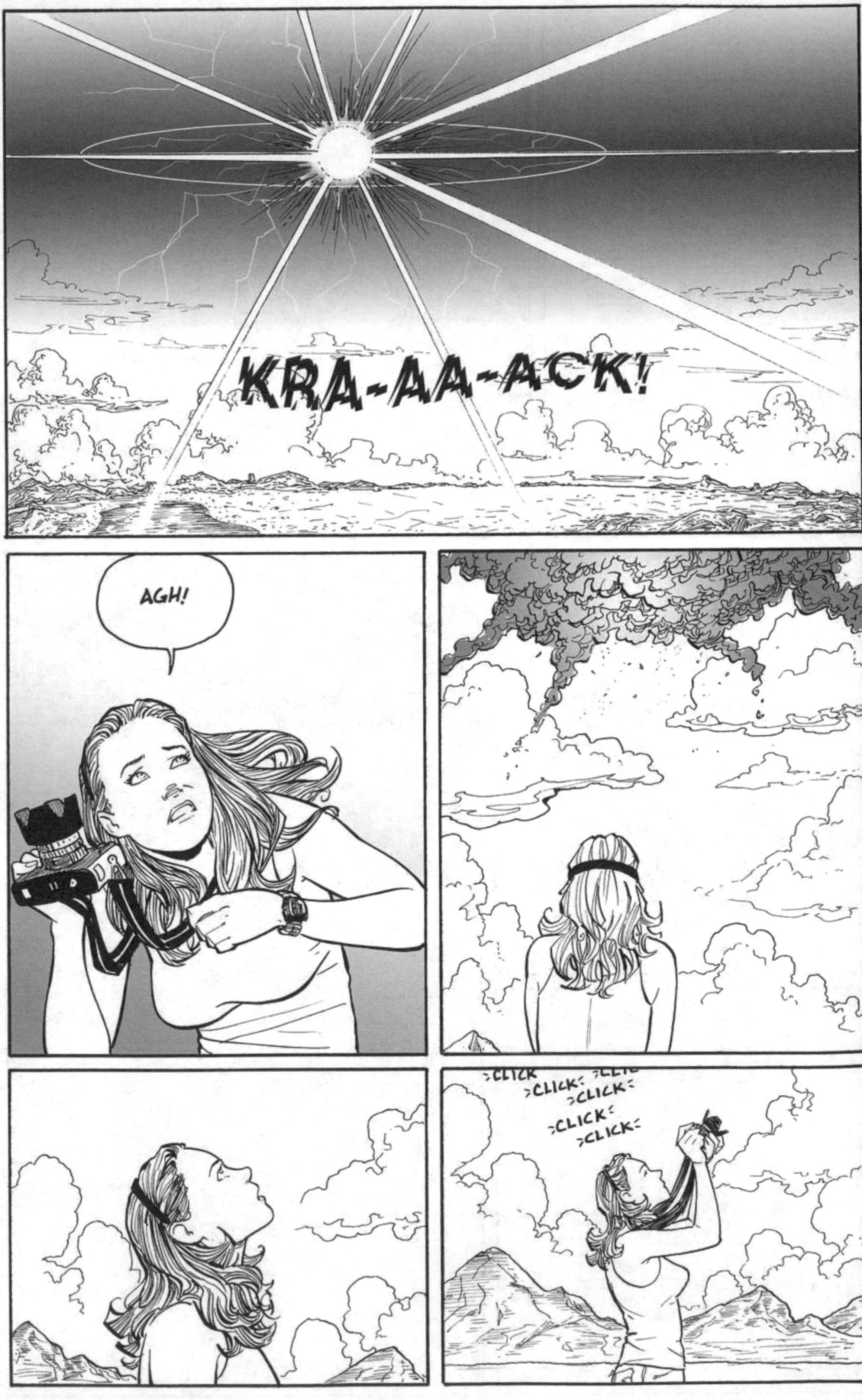
KRA-AA-ACK!
AGH!
CLICK
CLICK
CLICK
CLICK
CLICK

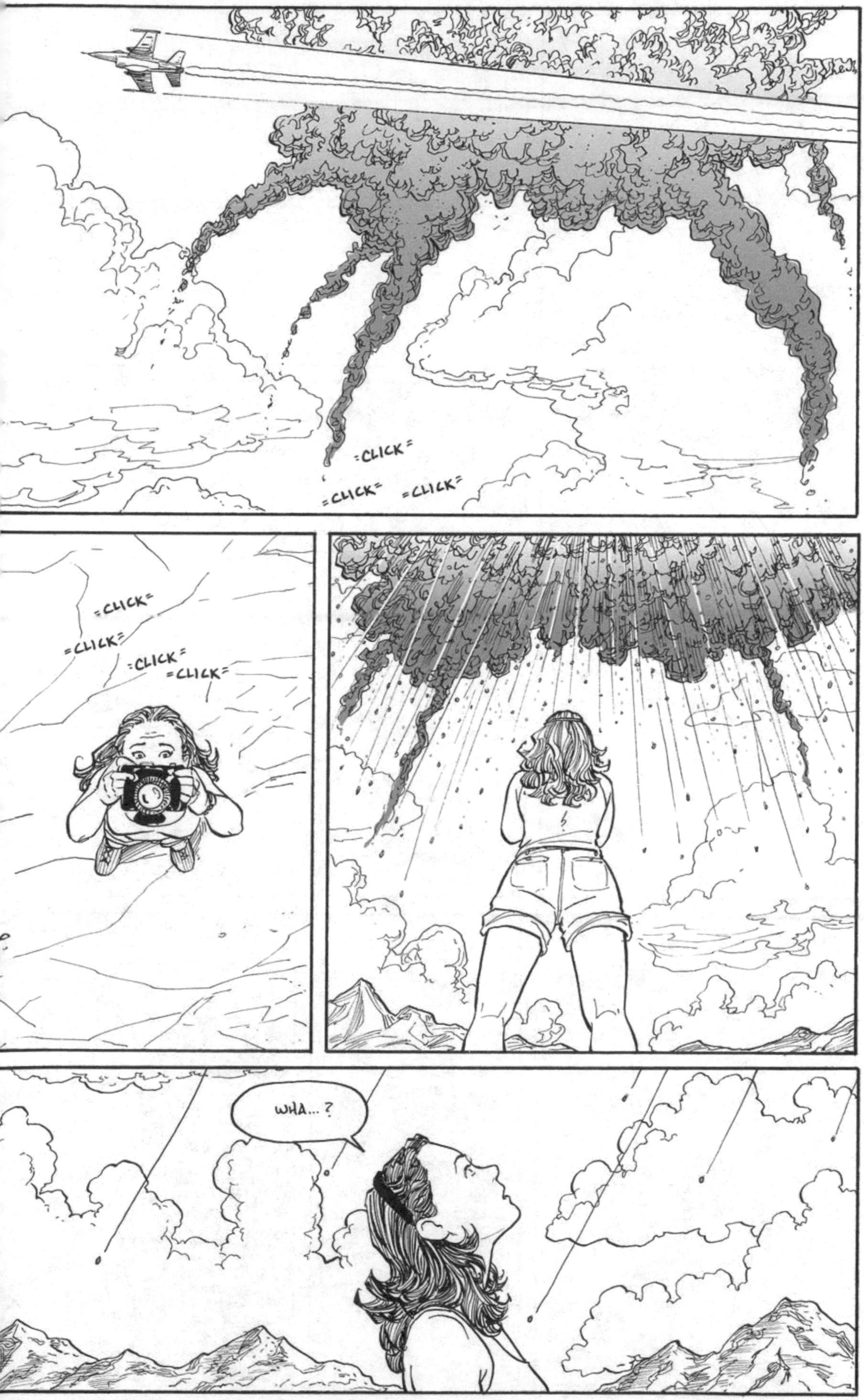
=CLICK=
=CLICK=
=CLICK=
=CLICK=
=CLICK=
=CLICK=
=CLICK=
WHA... ?

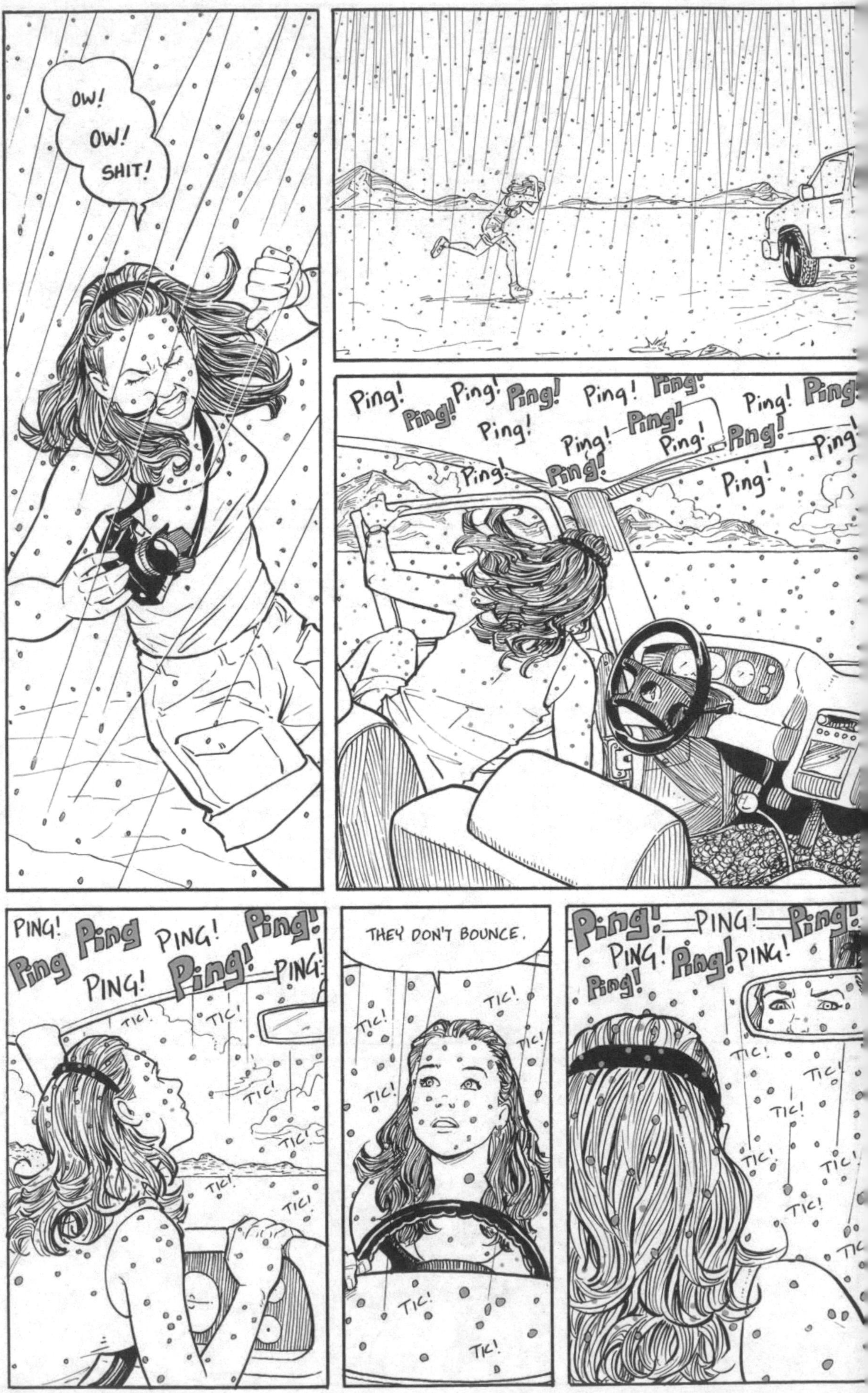
OW!
OW!
SHIT!
Ping! Ping! Ping! Ping! Ping! Ping! Ping! Ping! Ping! Ping! Ping! Ping! Ping! Ping! Ping! Ping!
PING! Ping PING! Ping! Ping PING! Ping! PING!
TIC! TIC! TIC! TIC! TIC! TIC!
THEY DON'T BOUNCE.
TIC! TIC! TIC! TIC! TIC! TK!
Ping! PING! Ping! PING! Ping! PING! Ping!
TIC! TIC! TIC! TIC! TIC! TIC!

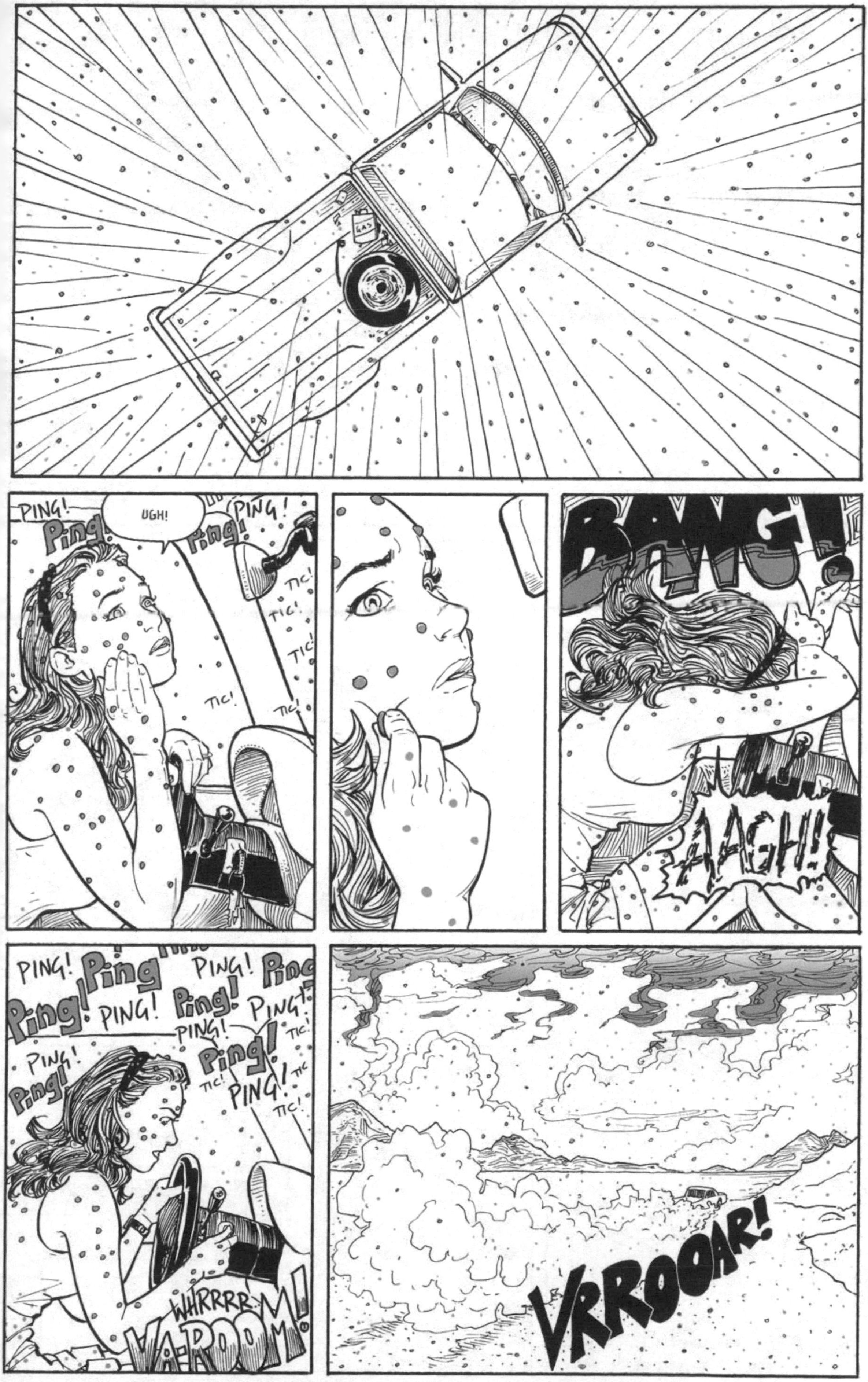
PING!
Ping!
UGH!
PING!
Ping!
TIC!
TIC!
TIC!
TIC!
TIC!
BANG!
AAGH!
PING! Ping!
PING! Ping!
Ping! PING! Ping! PING!
PING!
PING!
Ping!
Ping!
TIC!
PING!
TIC!
WHRRRR
VA-ROOM!
VRROOAR!

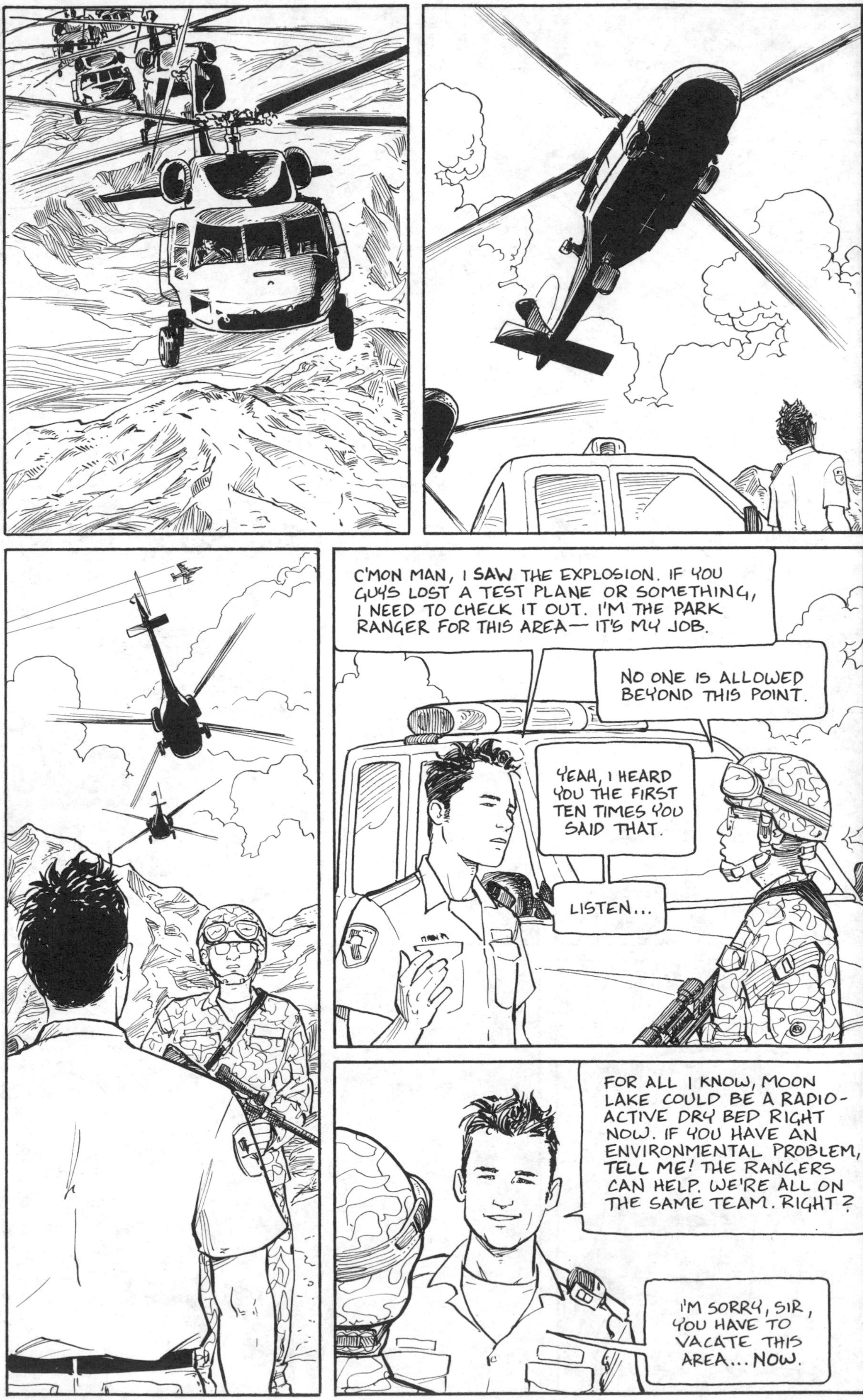
C'MON MAN, I SAW THE EXPLOSION. IF YOU GUYS LOST A TEST PLANE OR SOMETHING, I NEED TO CHECK IT OUT. I'M THE PARK RANGER FOR THIS AREA— IT'S MY JOB.
NO ONE IS ALLOWED BEYOND THIS POINT.
YEAH, I HEARD YOU THE FIRST TEN TIMES YOU SAID THAT.
LISTEN...
FOR ALL I KNOW, MOON LAKE COULD BE A RADIO-ACTIVE DRY BED RIGHT NOW. IF YOU HAVE AN ENVIRONMENTAL PROBLEM, TELL ME! THE RANGERS CAN HELP. WE'RE ALL ON THE SAME TEAM. RIGHT?
I'M SORRY, SIR, YOU HAVE TO VACATE THIS AREA... NOW.

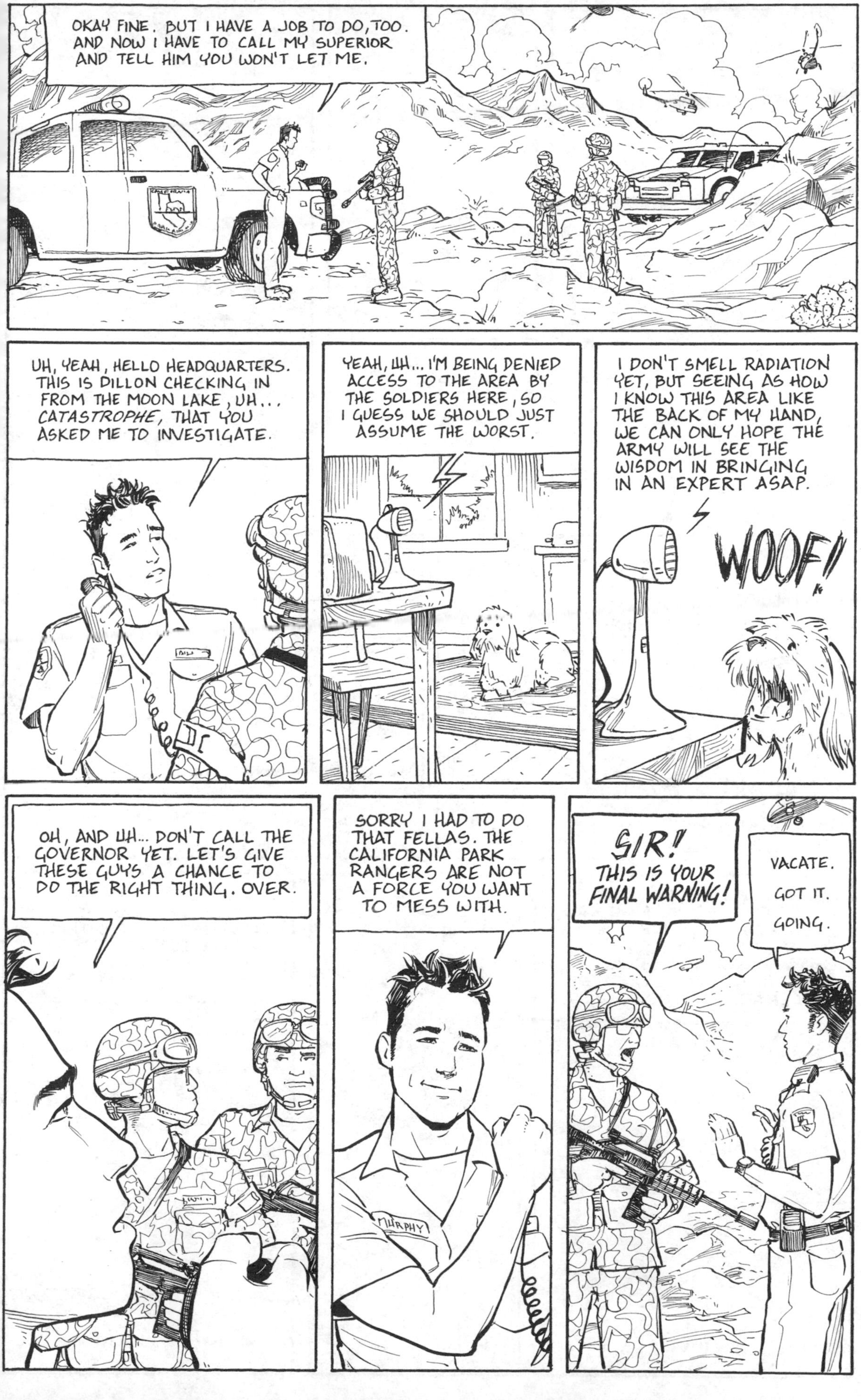
OKAY FINE. BUT I HAVE A JOB TO DO, TOO. AND NOW I HAVE TO CALL MY SUPERIOR AND TELL HIM YOU WON'T LET ME.
UH, YEAH, HELLO HEADQUARTERS. THIS IS DILLON CHECKING IN FROM THE MOON LAKE, UH... *CATASTROPHE*, THAT YOU ASKED ME TO INVESTIGATE.
YEAH, UH... I'M BEING DENIED ACCESS TO THE AREA BY THE SOLDIERS HERE, SO I GUESS WE SHOULD JUST ASSUME THE WORST.
I DON'T SMELL RADIATION YET, BUT SEEING AS HOW I KNOW THIS AREA LIKE THE BACK OF MY HAND, WE CAN ONLY HOPE THE ARMY WILL SEE THE WISDOM IN BRINGING IN AN EXPERT ASAP.
WOOF!
OH, AND UH... DON'T CALL THE GOVERNOR YET. LET'S GIVE THESE GUYS A CHANCE TO DO THE RIGHT THING. OVER.
SORRY I HAD TO DO THAT FELLAS. THE CALIFORNIA PARK RANGERS ARE NOT A FORCE YOU WANT TO MESS WITH.
MURPHY
SIR! THIS IS YOUR FINAL WARNING!
VACATE.
GOT IT.
GOING.

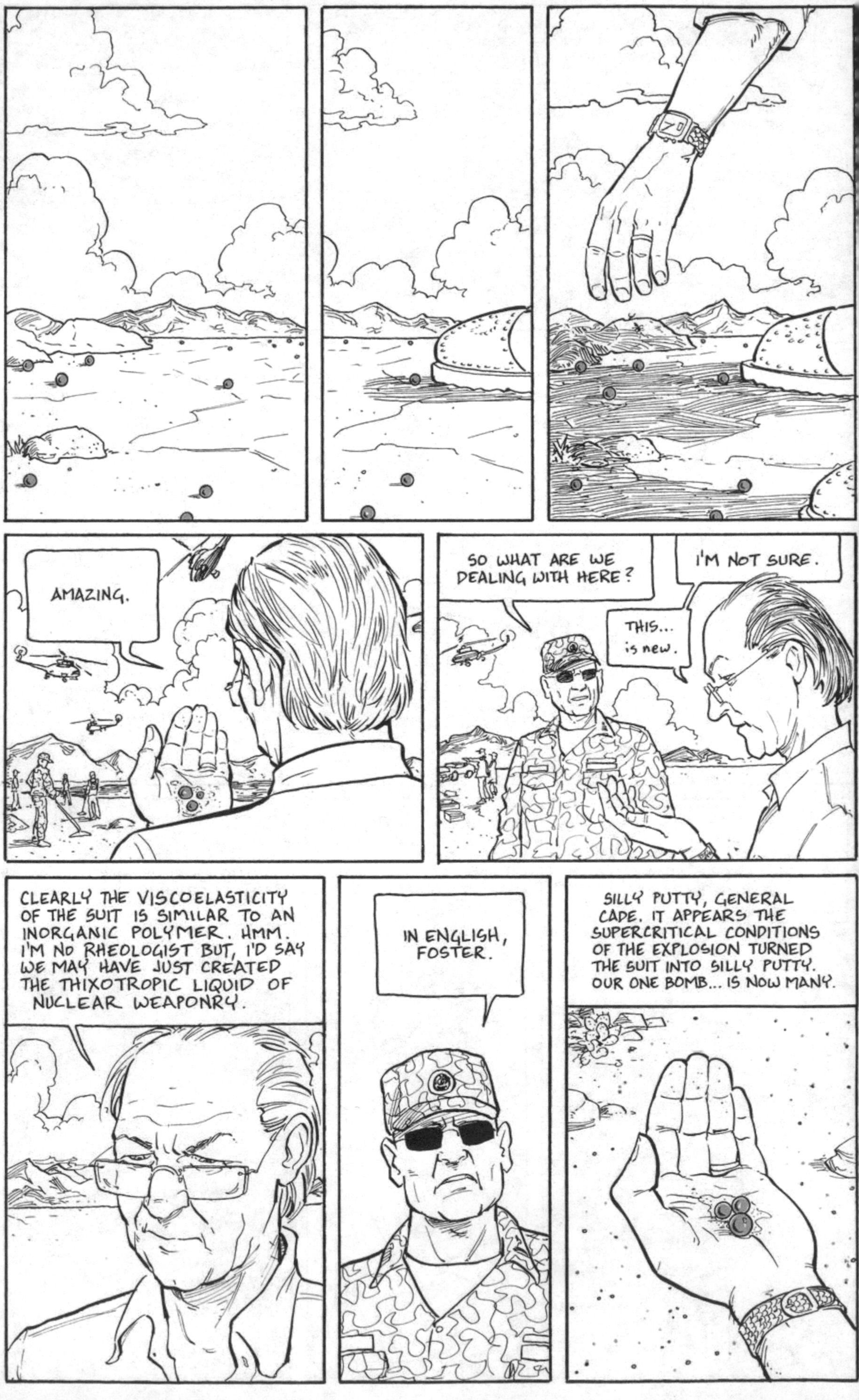
AMAZING.
SO WHAT ARE WE DEALING WITH HERE?
I'M NOT SURE.
THIS... is new.
CLEARLY THE VISCOELASTICITY OF THE SUIT IS SIMILAR TO AN INORGANIC POLYMER. HMM. I'M NO RHEOLOGIST BUT, I'D SAY WE MAY HAVE JUST CREATED THE THIXOTROPIC LIQUID OF NUCLEAR WEAPONRY.
IN ENGLISH, FOSTER.
SILLY PUTTY, GENERAL CADE. IT APPEARS THE SUPERCRITICAL CONDITIONS OF THE EXPLOSION TURNED THE SUIT INTO SILLY PUTTY. OUR ONE BOMB... IS NOW MANY.

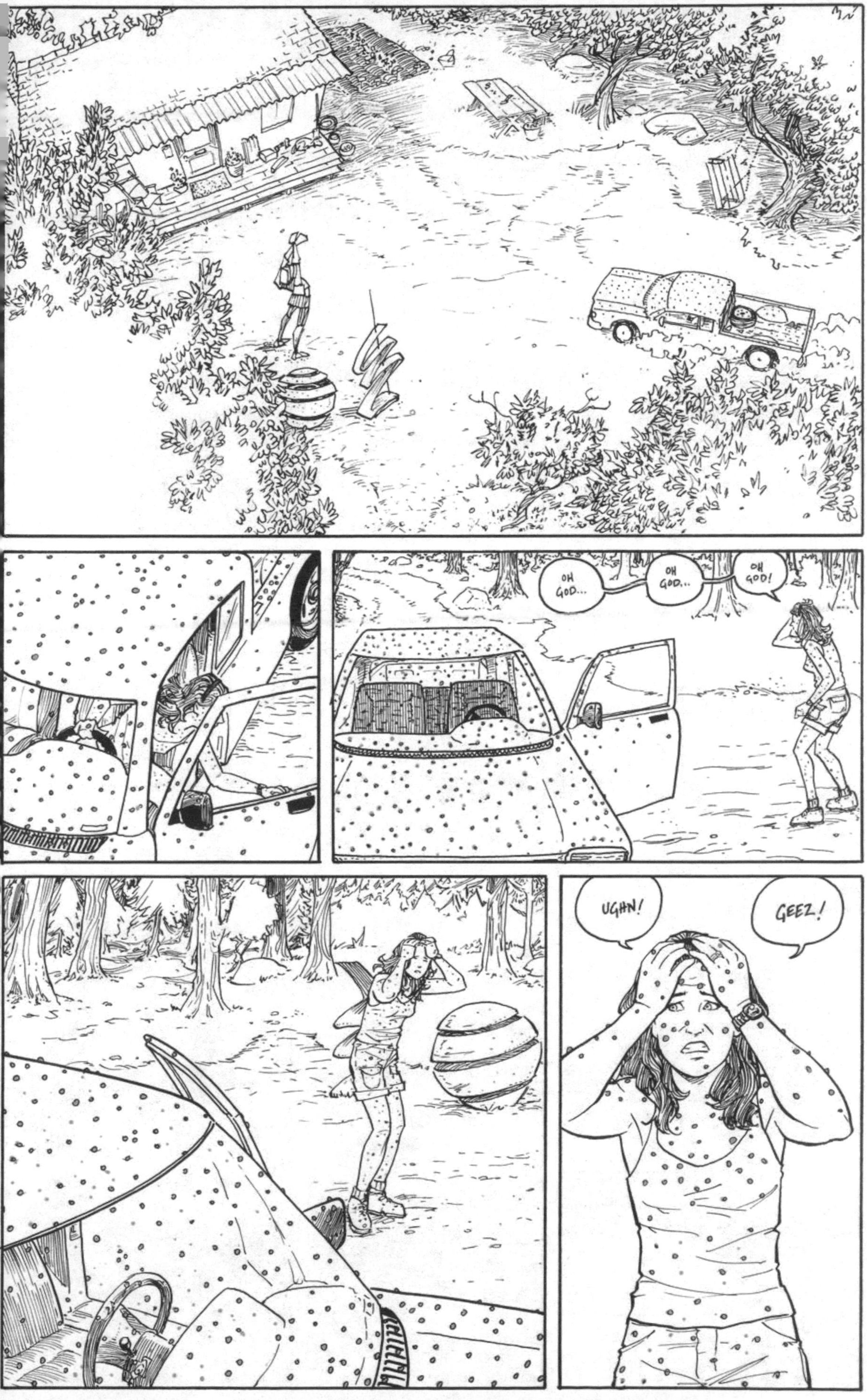
OH GOD...
OH GOD...
OH GOD!
UGHN!
GEEZ!

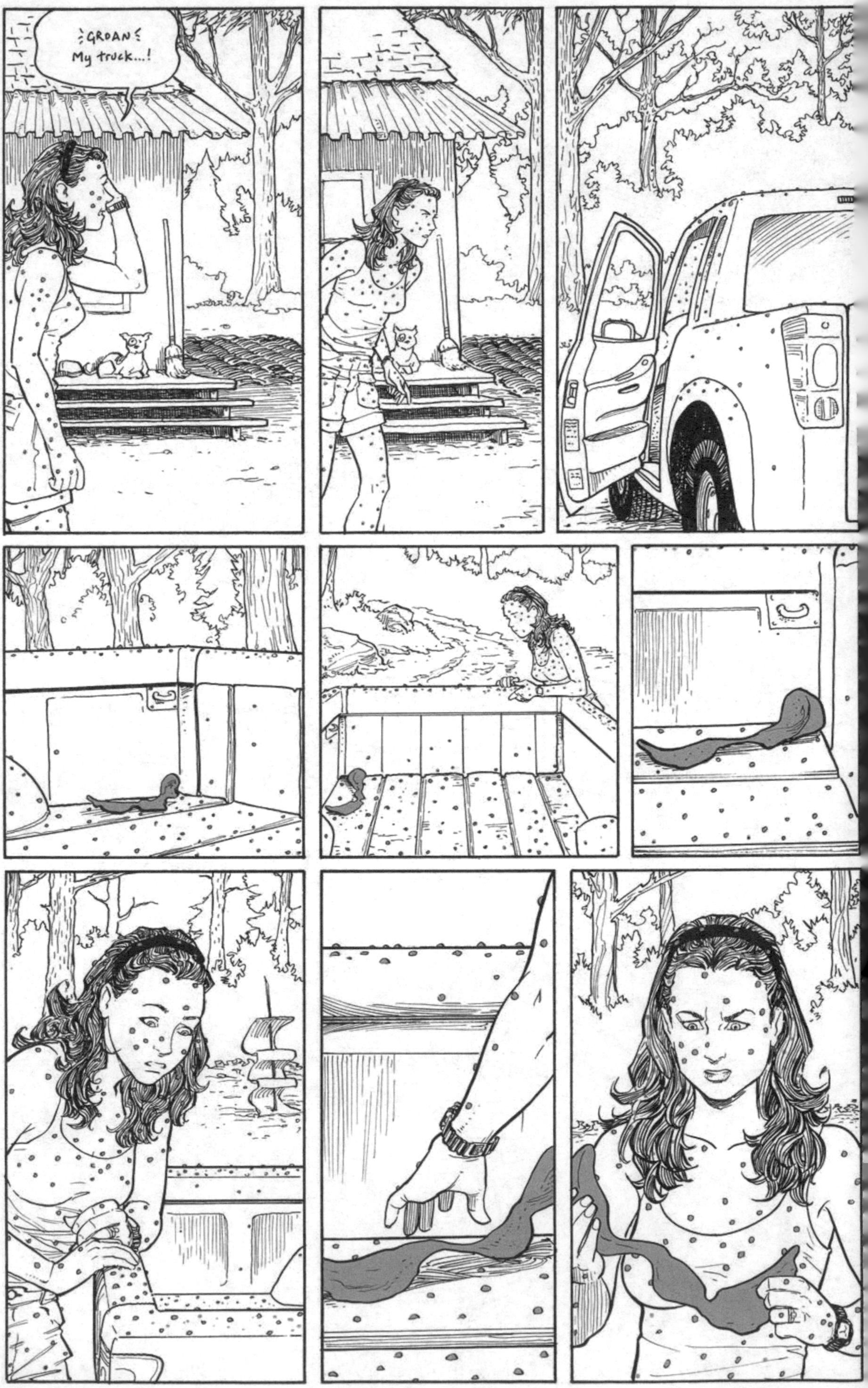
GROAN
My truck...!

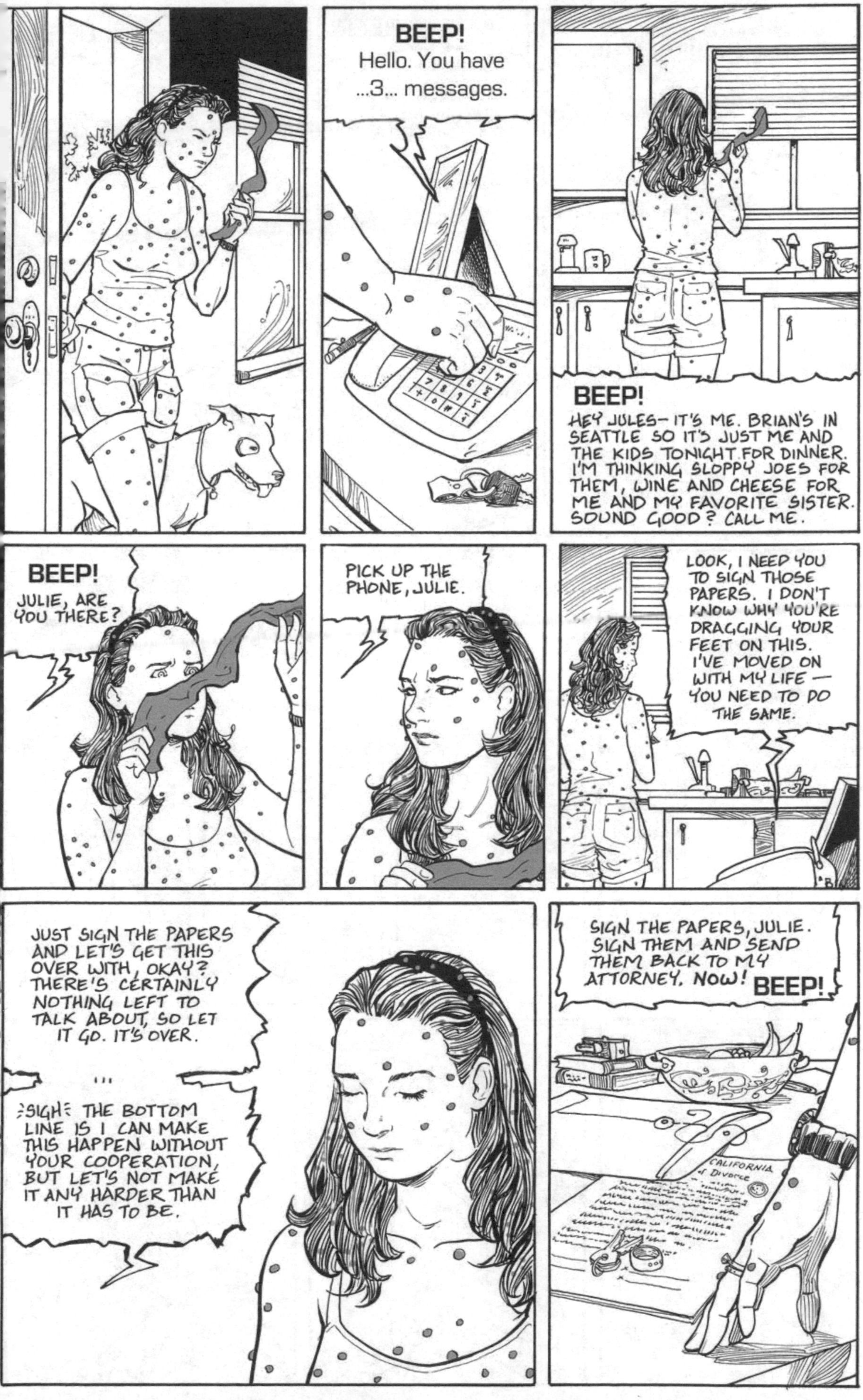
BEEP!
Hello. You have ...3... messages.
BEEP!
HEY JULES– IT'S ME. BRIAN'S IN SEATTLE SO IT'S JUST ME AND THE KIDS TONIGHT FOR DINNER. I'M THINKING SLOPPY JOES FOR THEM, WINE AND CHEESE FOR ME AND MY FAVORITE SISTER. SOUND GOOD? CALL ME.
BEEP!
JULIE, ARE YOU THERE?
PICK UP THE PHONE, JULIE.
LOOK, I NEED YOU TO SIGN THOSE PAPERS. I DON'T KNOW WHY YOU'RE DRAGGING YOUR FEET ON THIS. I'VE MOVED ON WITH MY LIFE — YOU NEED TO DO THE SAME.
JUST SIGN THE PAPERS AND LET'S GET THIS OVER WITH, OKAY? THERE'S CERTAINLY NOTHING LEFT TO TALK ABOUT, SO LET IT GO. IT'S OVER.
...
:SIGH: THE BOTTOM LINE IS I CAN MAKE THIS HAPPEN WITHOUT YOUR COOPERATION, BUT LET'S NOT MAKE IT ANY HARDER THAN IT HAS TO BE.
SIGN THE PAPERS, JULIE. SIGN THEM AND SEND THEM BACK TO MY ATTORNEY. NOW!
BEEP!
CALIFORNIA
Divorce

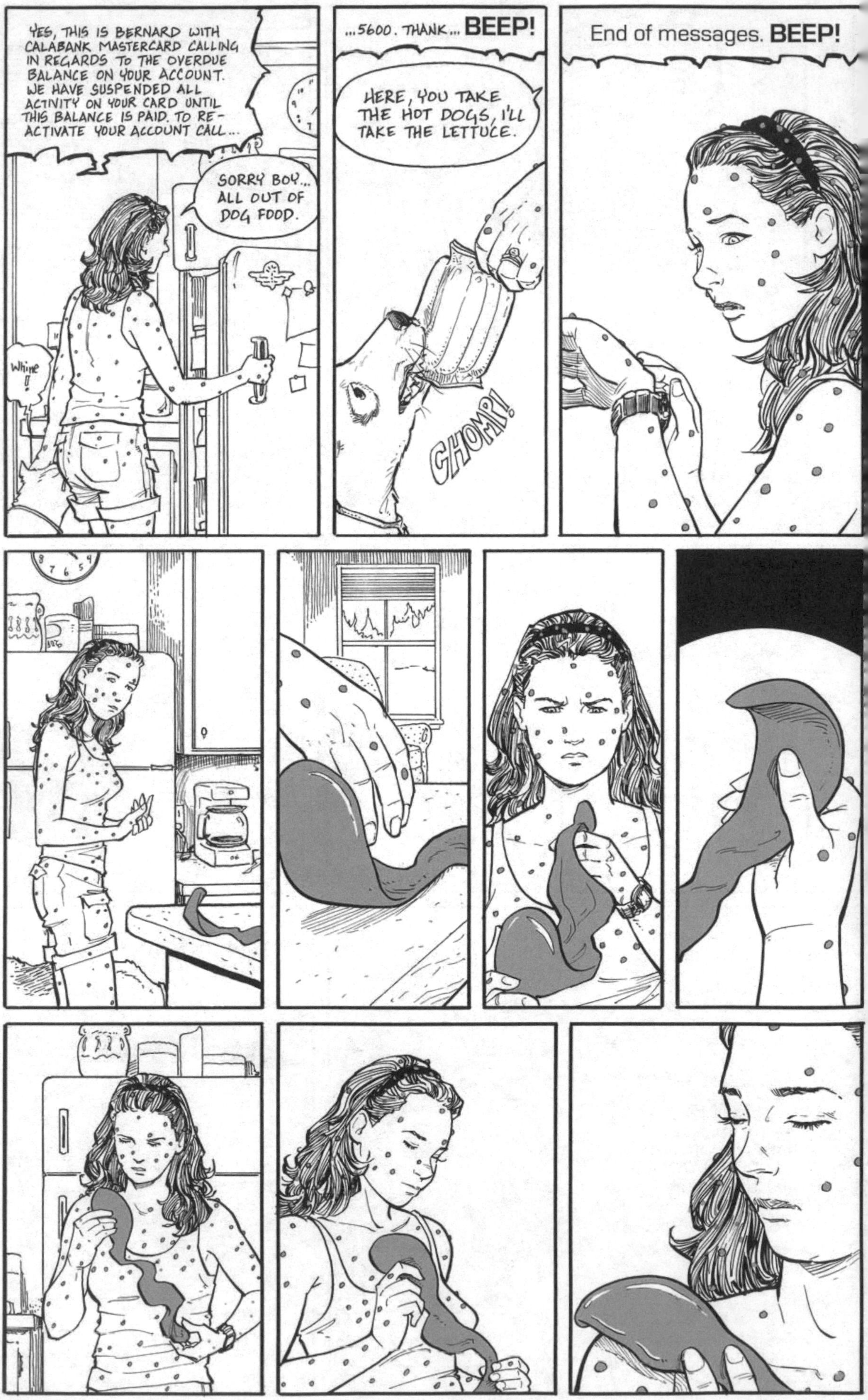
YES, THIS IS BERNARD WITH CALABANK MASTERCARD CALLING IN REGARDS TO THE OVERDUE BALANCE ON YOUR ACCOUNT. WE HAVE SUSPENDED ALL ACTIVITY ON YOUR CARD UNTIL THIS BALANCE IS PAID. TO RE-ACTIVATE YOUR ACCOUNT CALL...
SORRY BOY... ALL OUT OF DOG FOOD.
Whine!
...5600. THANK... BEEP!
HERE, YOU TAKE THE HOT DOGS, I'LL TAKE THE LETTUCE.
CHOMP!
End of messages. BEEP!

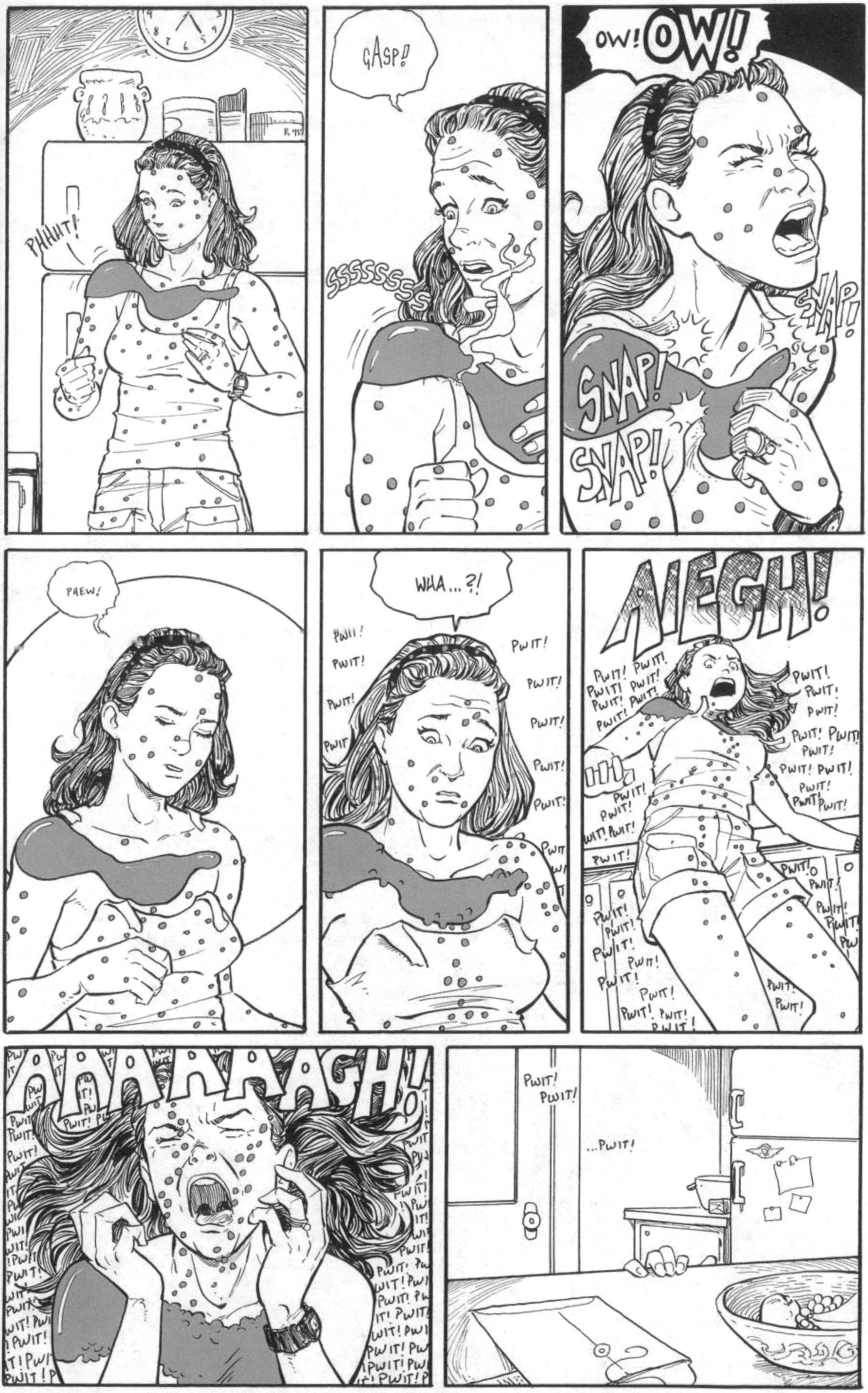
PHHWIT!
GASP!
SSSSSSSSS
OW! OW!
SNAP!
SNAP!
SNAP!
PHEW!
WHA...?!
PWIT! PWIT! PWIT! PWIT! PWIT! PWIT! PWIT! PWIT! PWIT! PWIT!
AIEGH!
PWIT! PWIT! PWIT! PWIT! PWIT! PWIT! PWIT! PWIT! PWIT! PWIT!
AAAAAACH!
PWIT! PWIT! PWIT! PWIT! PWIT!
PWIT!
PWIT!
...PWIT!

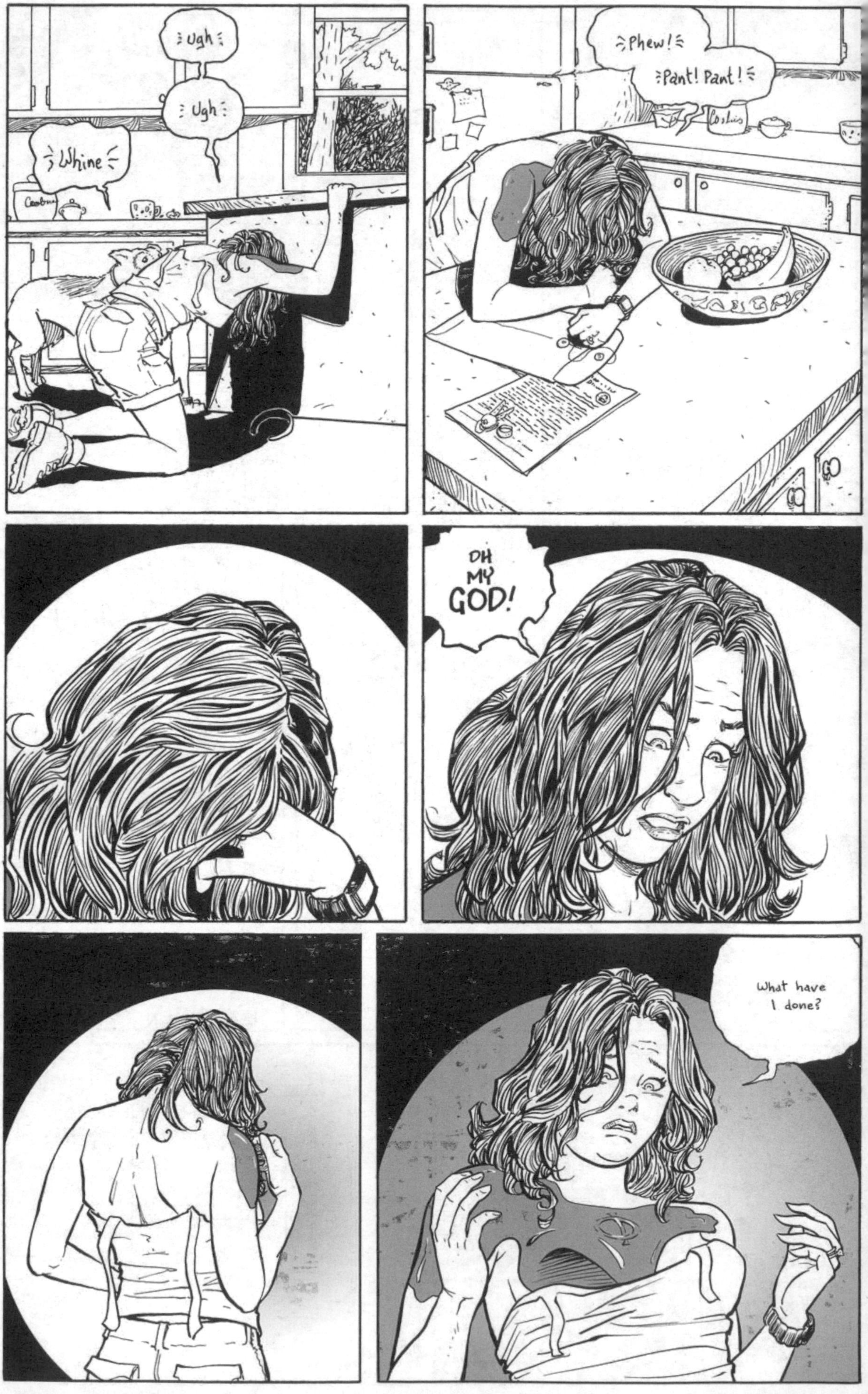
Ugh
Ugh
Whine
Phew!
Pant! Pant!
OH MY GOD!
What have I done?

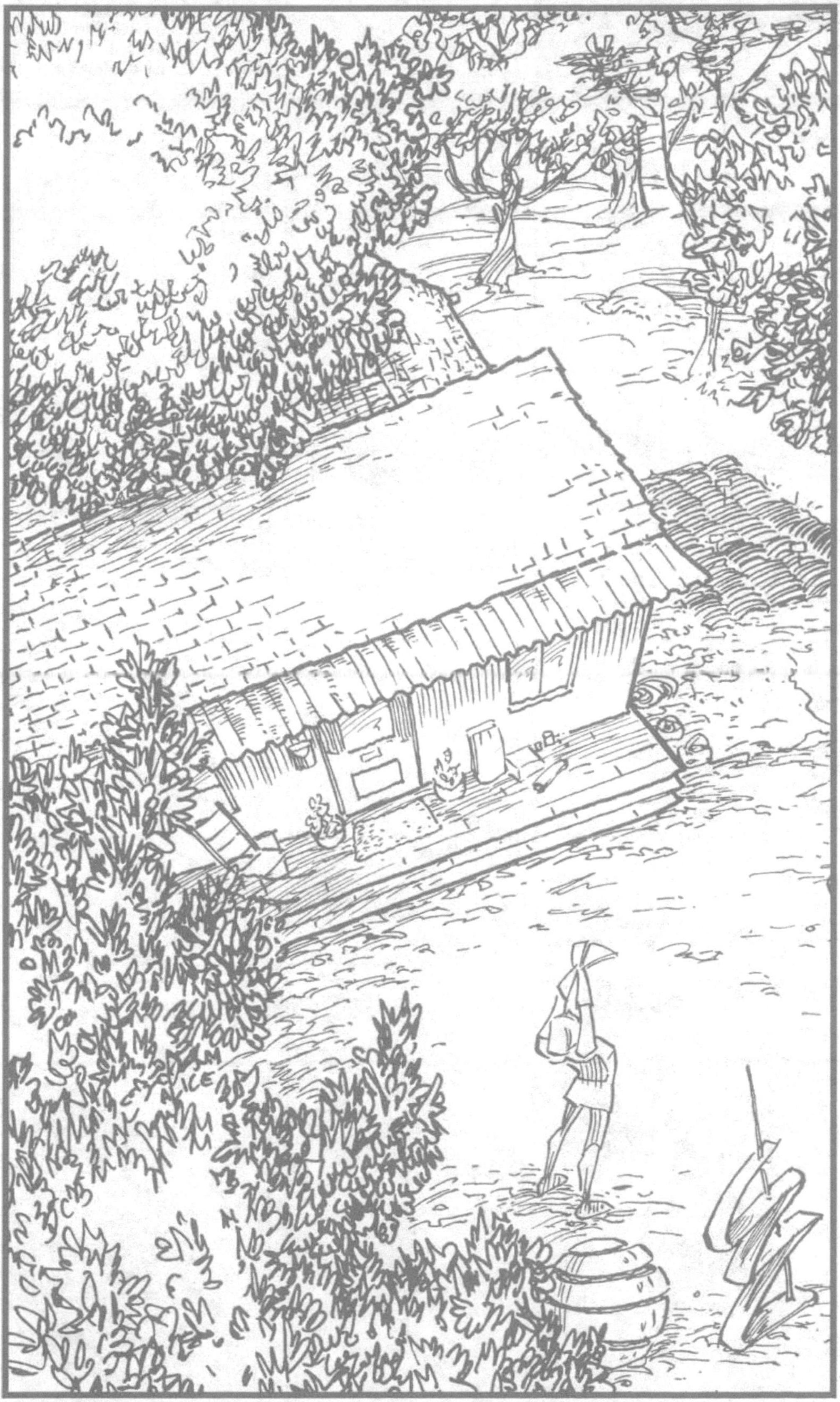

The release of atom power has changed everything except our way of thinking... the solution to this problem lies in the heart of mankind. If only I had known, I should have become a watchmaker.
—Albert Einstein

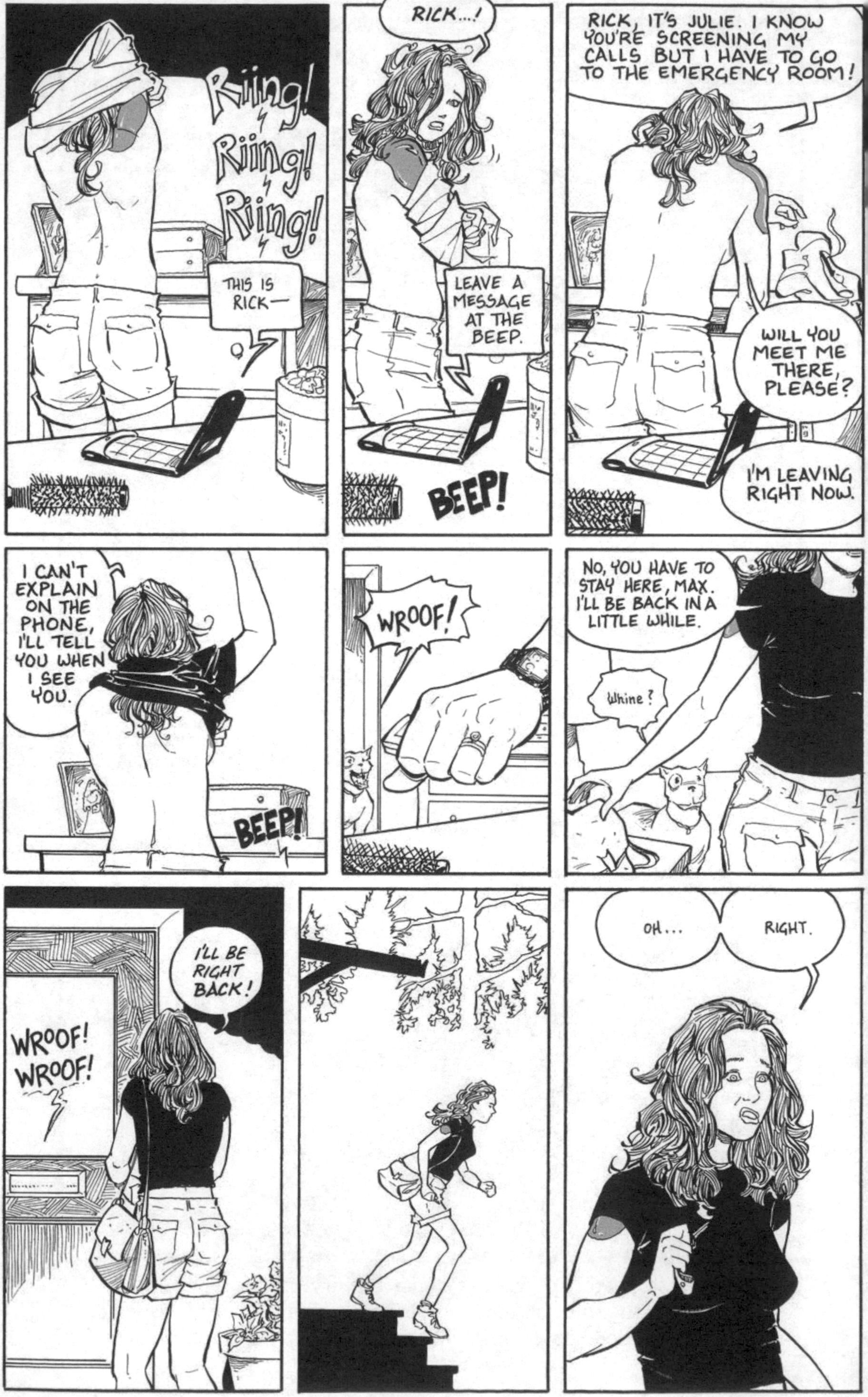
Riing!
Riing!
Riing!
THIS IS RICK—
RICK...!
LEAVE A MESSAGE AT THE BEEP.
BEEP!
RICK, IT'S JULIE. I KNOW YOU'RE SCREENING MY CALLS BUT I HAVE TO GO TO THE EMERGENCY ROOM!
WILL YOU MEET ME THERE, PLEASE?
I'M LEAVING RIGHT NOW.
I CAN'T EXPLAIN ON THE PHONE, I'LL TELL YOU WHEN I SEE YOU.
BEEP!
WROOF!
NO, YOU HAVE TO STAY HERE, MAX. I'LL BE BACK IN A LITTLE WHILE.
Whine?
I'LL BE RIGHT BACK!
WROOF! WROOF!
OH...
RIGHT.

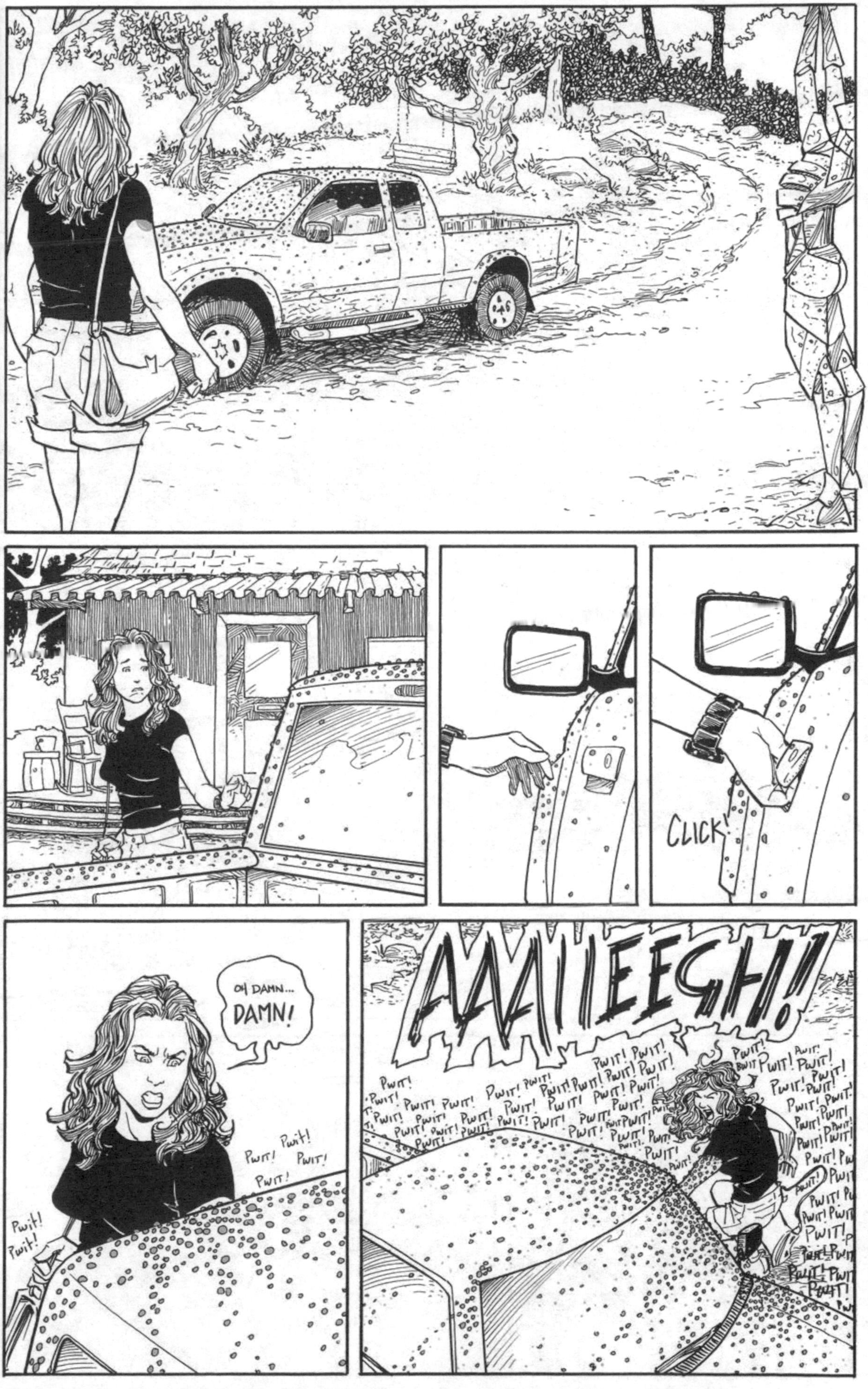
CLICK!
OH DAMN... DAMN!
Pwit! Pwit!
Pwit! Pwit!
Pwit!
AAIIEEGH!

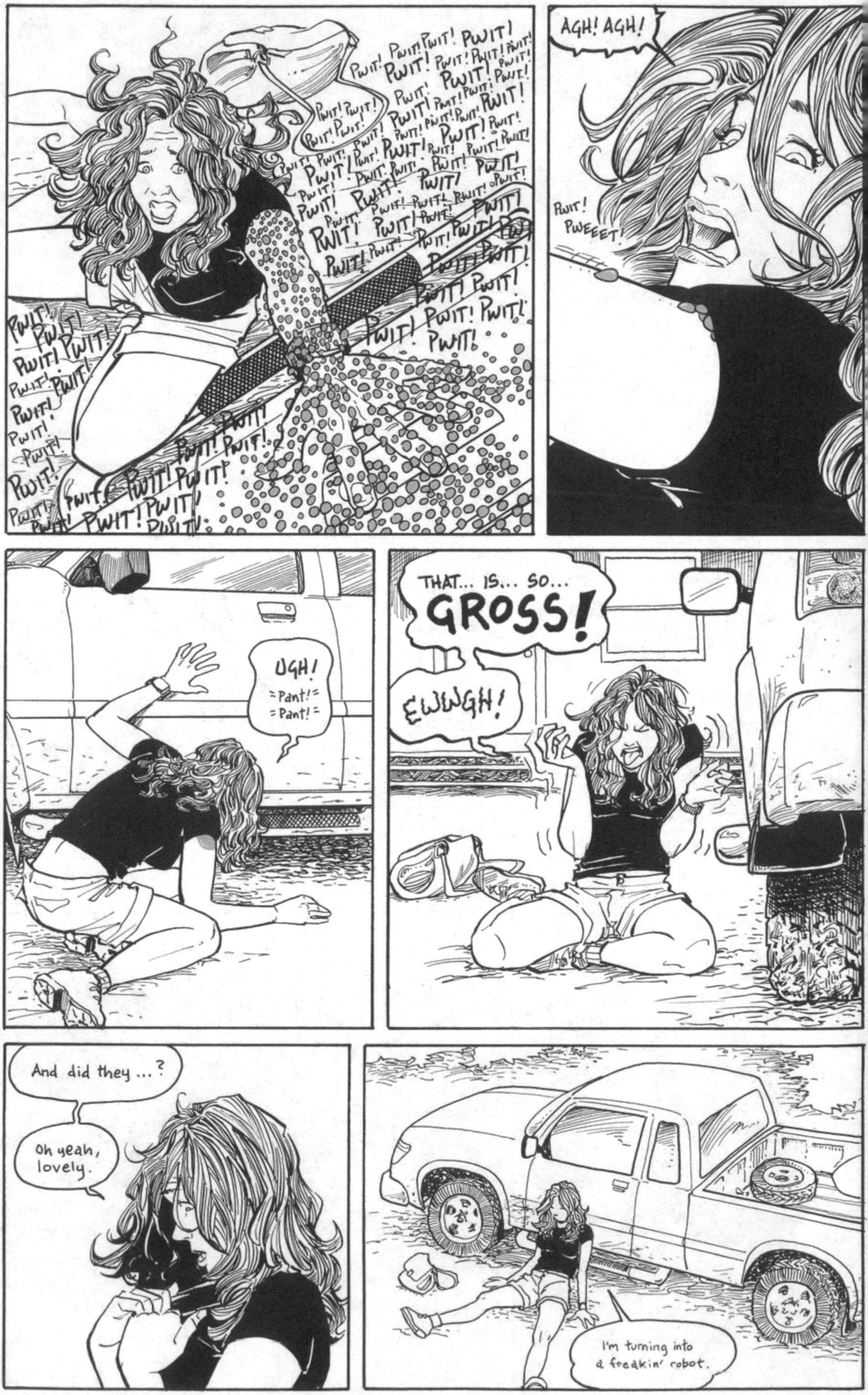

PWIT! PWIT! PWIT!
AGH! AGH!
PWIT!
PWEEET!
UGH!
=Pant!=
=Pant!=
THAT... IS... SO...
GROSS!
EWNGH!
And did they ...?
Oh yeah, lovely.
I'm turning into a freakin' robot.

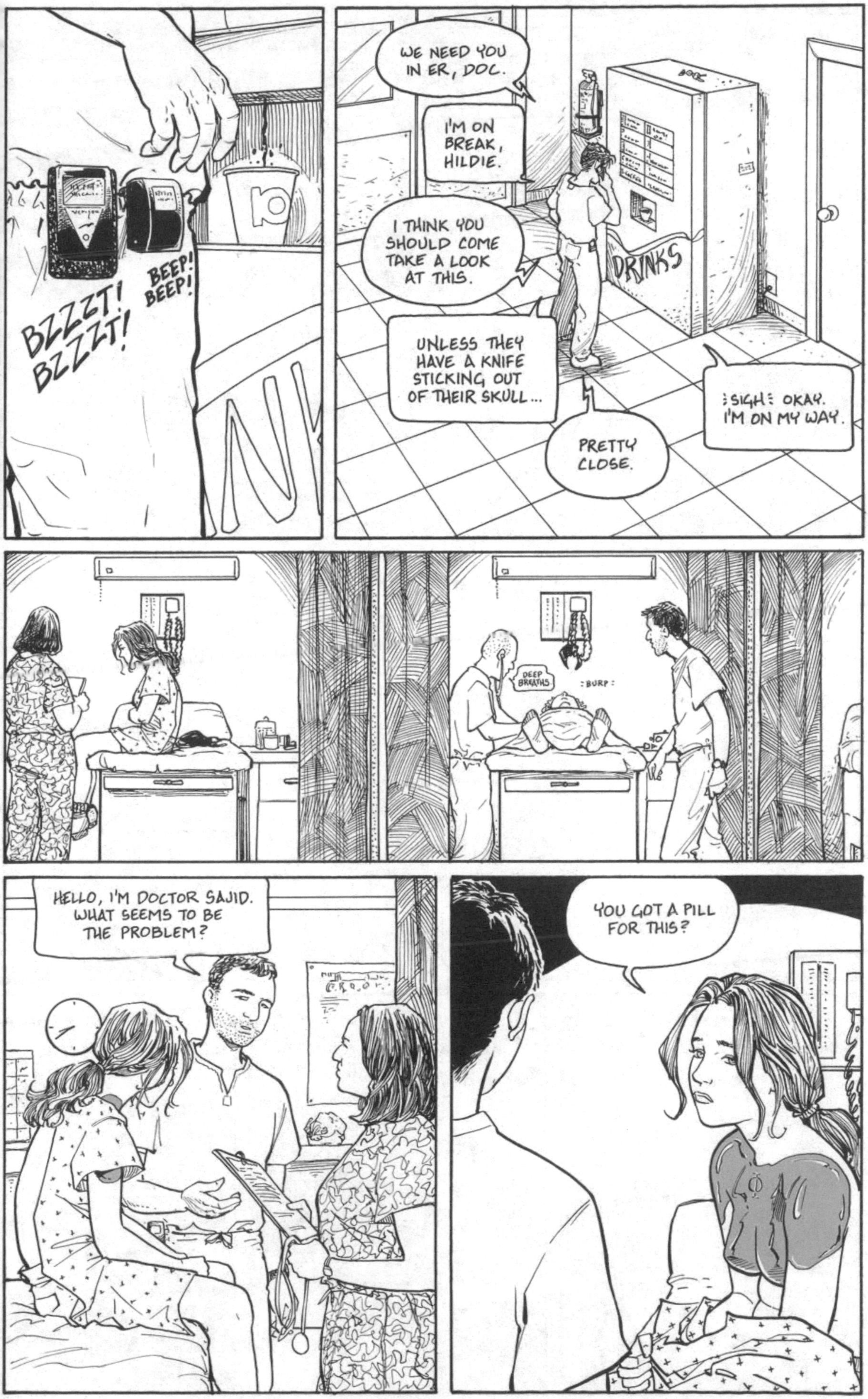
BEEP! BEEP!
BZZZT! BZZZT!
WE NEED YOU IN ER, DOC.
I'M ON BREAK, HILDIE.
I THINK YOU SHOULD COME TAKE A LOOK AT THIS.
UNLESS THEY HAVE A KNIFE STICKING OUT OF THEIR SKULL...
PRETTY CLOSE.
:SIGH: OKAY. I'M ON MY WAY.
DRINKS
DEEP BREATHS.
:BURP:
HELLO, I'M DOCTOR SAJID. WHAT SEEMS TO BE THE PROBLEM?
YOU GOT A PILL FOR THIS?

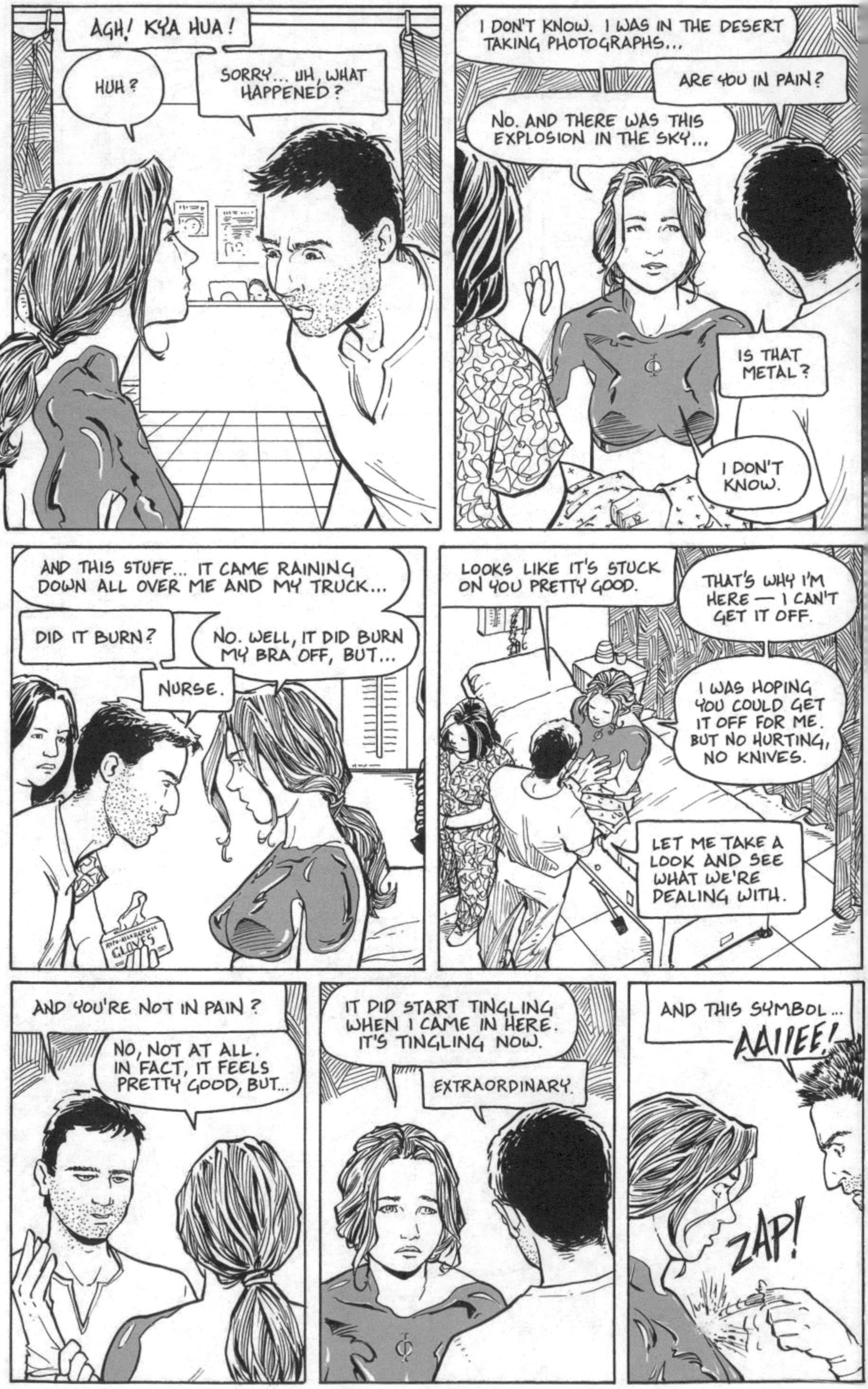
AGH! KYA HUA!
HUH?
SORRY... UH, WHAT HAPPENED?
I DON'T KNOW. I WAS IN THE DESERT TAKING PHOTOGRAPHS...
ARE YOU IN PAIN?
NO. AND THERE WAS THIS EXPLOSION IN THE SKY...
IS THAT METAL?
I DON'T KNOW.
AND THIS STUFF... IT CAME RAINING DOWN ALL OVER ME AND MY TRUCK...
DID IT BURN?
NO. WELL, IT DID BURN MY BRA OFF, BUT...
NURSE.
GLOVES
LOOKS LIKE IT'S STUCK ON YOU PRETTY GOOD.
THAT'S WHY I'M HERE — I CAN'T GET IT OFF.
I WAS HOPING YOU COULD GET IT OFF FOR ME. BUT NO HURTING, NO KNIVES.
LET ME TAKE A LOOK AND SEE WHAT WE'RE DEALING WITH.
AND YOU'RE NOT IN PAIN?
NO, NOT AT ALL. IN FACT, IT FEELS PRETTY GOOD, BUT...
IT DID START TINGLING WHEN I CAME IN HERE. IT'S TINGLING NOW.
EXTRAORDINARY.
AND THIS SYMBOL...
AAIIEE!
ZAP!

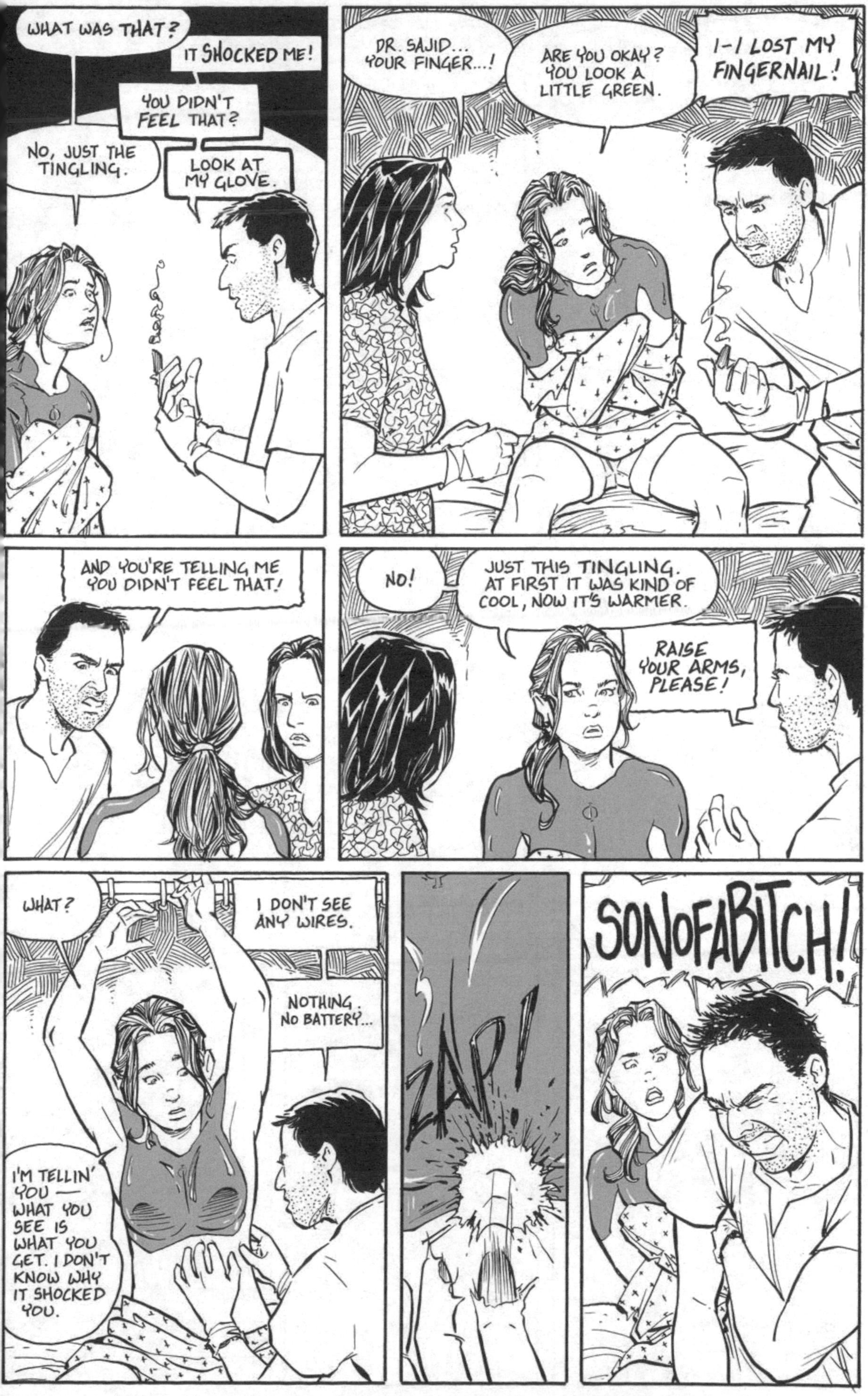
WHAT WAS THAT?
IT SHOCKED ME!
YOU DIDN'T FEEL THAT?
NO, JUST THE TINGLING.
LOOK AT MY GLOVE.
DR. SAJID... YOUR FINGER...!
ARE YOU OKAY? YOU LOOK A LITTLE GREEN.
I-I LOST MY FINGERNAIL!
AND YOU'RE TELLING ME YOU DIDN'T FEEL THAT!
NO!
JUST THIS TINGLING. AT FIRST IT WAS KIND OF COOL, NOW IT'S WARMER.
RAISE YOUR ARMS, PLEASE!
WHAT?
I DON'T SEE ANY WIRES.
NOTHING. NO BATTERY...
I'M TELLIN' YOU — WHAT YOU SEE IS WHAT YOU GET. I DON'T KNOW WHY IT SHOCKED YOU.
ZAP!
SONOFABITCH!

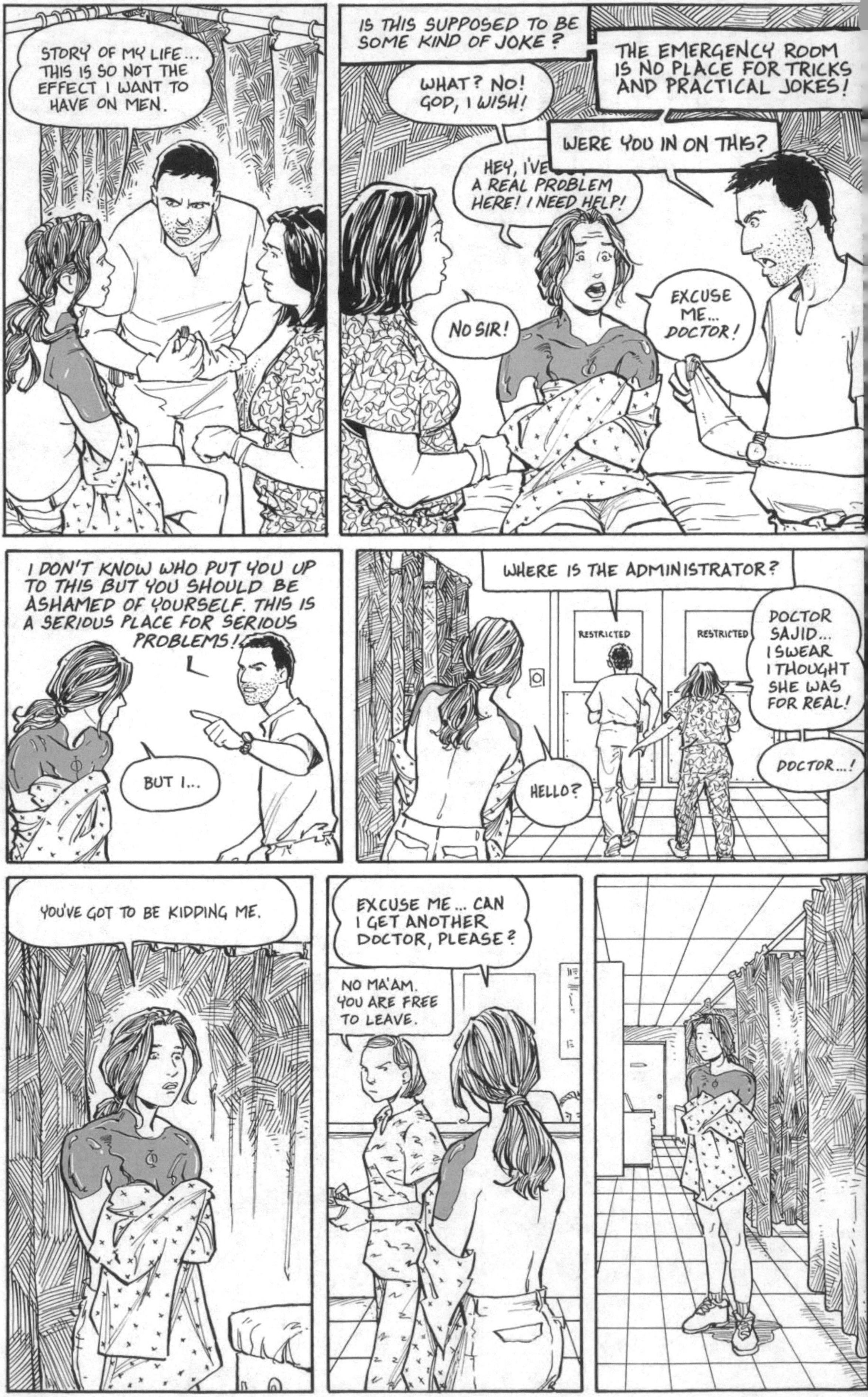
STORY OF MY LIFE... THIS IS SO NOT THE EFFECT I WANT TO HAVE ON MEN.
IS THIS SUPPOSED TO BE SOME KIND OF JOKE?
THE EMERGENCY ROOM IS NO PLACE FOR TRICKS AND PRACTICAL JOKES!
WHAT? NO! GOD, I WISH!
WERE YOU IN ON THIS?
HEY, I'VE A REAL PROBLEM HERE! I NEED HELP!
NO SIR!
EXCUSE ME... DOCTOR!
I DON'T KNOW WHO PUT YOU UP TO THIS BUT YOU SHOULD BE ASHAMED OF YOURSELF. THIS IS A SERIOUS PLACE FOR SERIOUS PROBLEMS!
BUT I...
WHERE IS THE ADMINISTRATOR?
RESTRICTED
RESTRICTED
DOCTOR SAJID... I SWEAR I THOUGHT SHE WAS FOR REAL!
HELLO?
DOCTOR...!
YOU'VE GOT TO BE KIDDING ME.
EXCUSE ME... CAN I GET ANOTHER DOCTOR, PLEASE?
NO MA'AM. YOU ARE FREE TO LEAVE.

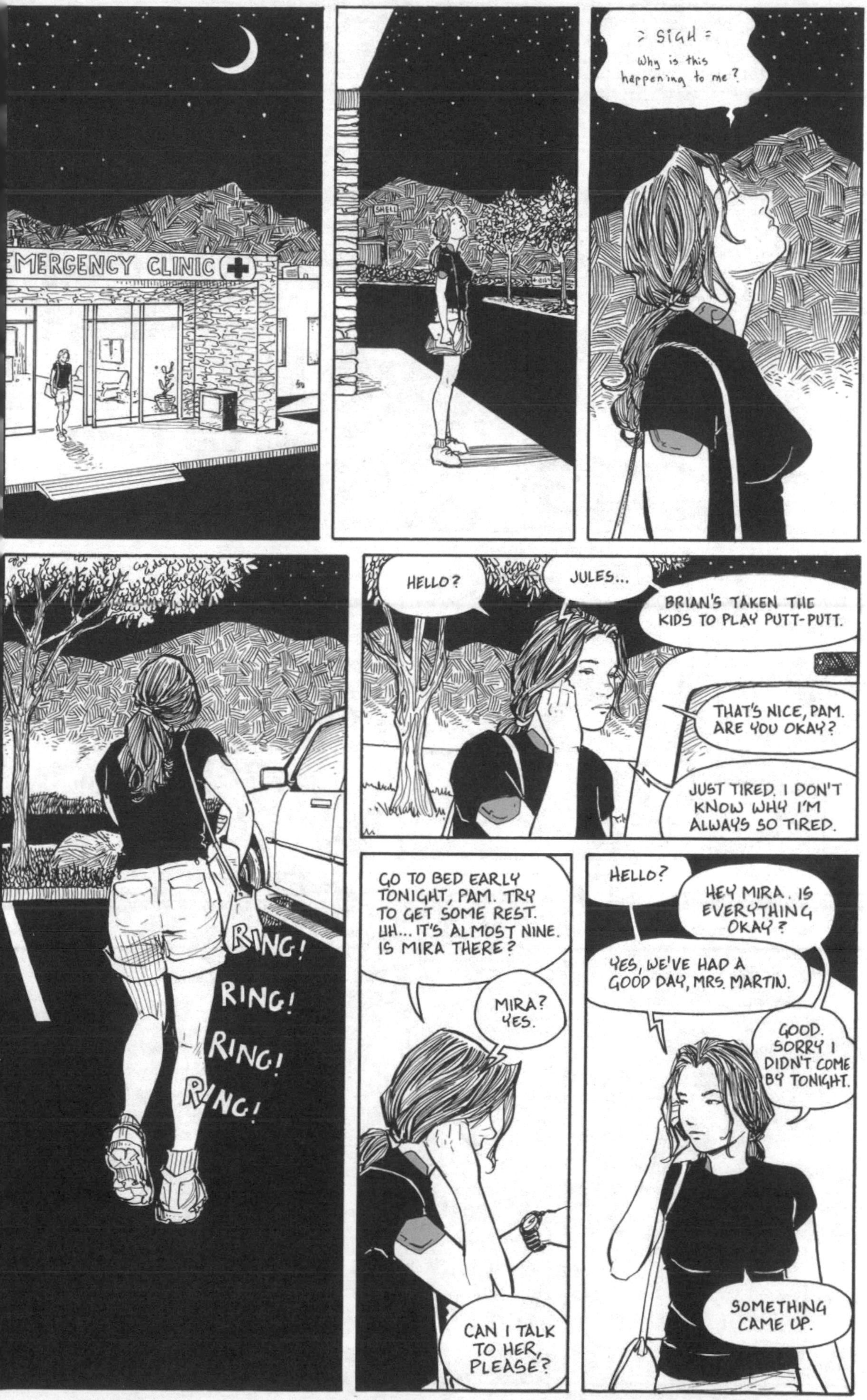
EMERGENCY CLINIC
SHELL
= SIGH =
Why is this happening to me?
RING!
RING!
RING!
RING!
HELLO?
JULES...
BRIAN'S TAKEN THE KIDS TO PLAY PUTT-PUTT.
THAT'S NICE, PAM. ARE YOU OKAY?
JUST TIRED. I DON'T KNOW WHY I'M ALWAYS SO TIRED.
GO TO BED EARLY TONIGHT, PAM. TRY TO GET SOME REST. UH... IT'S ALMOST NINE. IS MIRA THERE?
MIRA? YES.
CAN I TALK TO HER, PLEASE?
HELLO?
HEY MIRA. IS EVERYTHING OKAY?
YES, WE'VE HAD A GOOD DAY, MRS. MARTIN.
GOOD. SORRY I DIDN'T COME BY TONIGHT.
SOMETHING CAME UP.

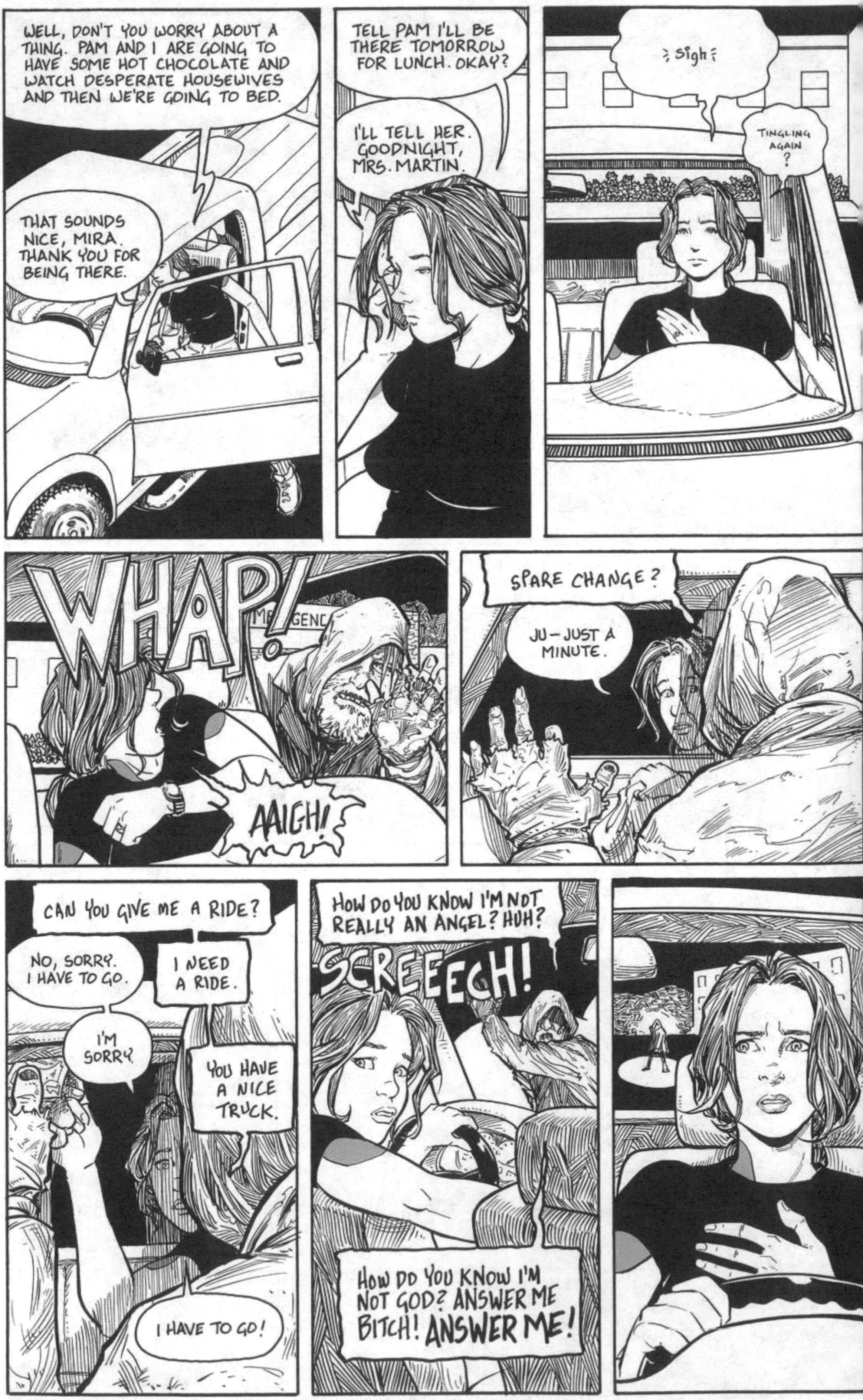
WELL, DON'T YOU WORRY ABOUT A THING. PAM AND I ARE GOING TO HAVE SOME HOT CHOCOLATE AND WATCH DESPERATE HOUSEWIVES AND THEN WE'RE GOING TO BED.
THAT SOUNDS NICE, MIRA. THANK YOU FOR BEING THERE.
TELL PAM I'LL BE THERE TOMORROW FOR LUNCH. OKAY?
I'LL TELL HER. GOODNIGHT, MRS. MARTIN.
Sigh
TINGLING AGAIN?
WHAP!
AAIGH!
SPARE CHANGE?
JU—JUST A MINUTE.
CAN YOU GIVE ME A RIDE?
NO, SORRY. I HAVE TO GO.
I NEED A RIDE.
I'M SORRY.
YOU HAVE A NICE TRUCK.
I HAVE TO GO!
HOW DO YOU KNOW I'M NOT REALLY AN ANGEL? HUH?
SCREEECH!
HOW DO YOU KNOW I'M NOT GOD? ANSWER ME BITCH! ANSWER ME!

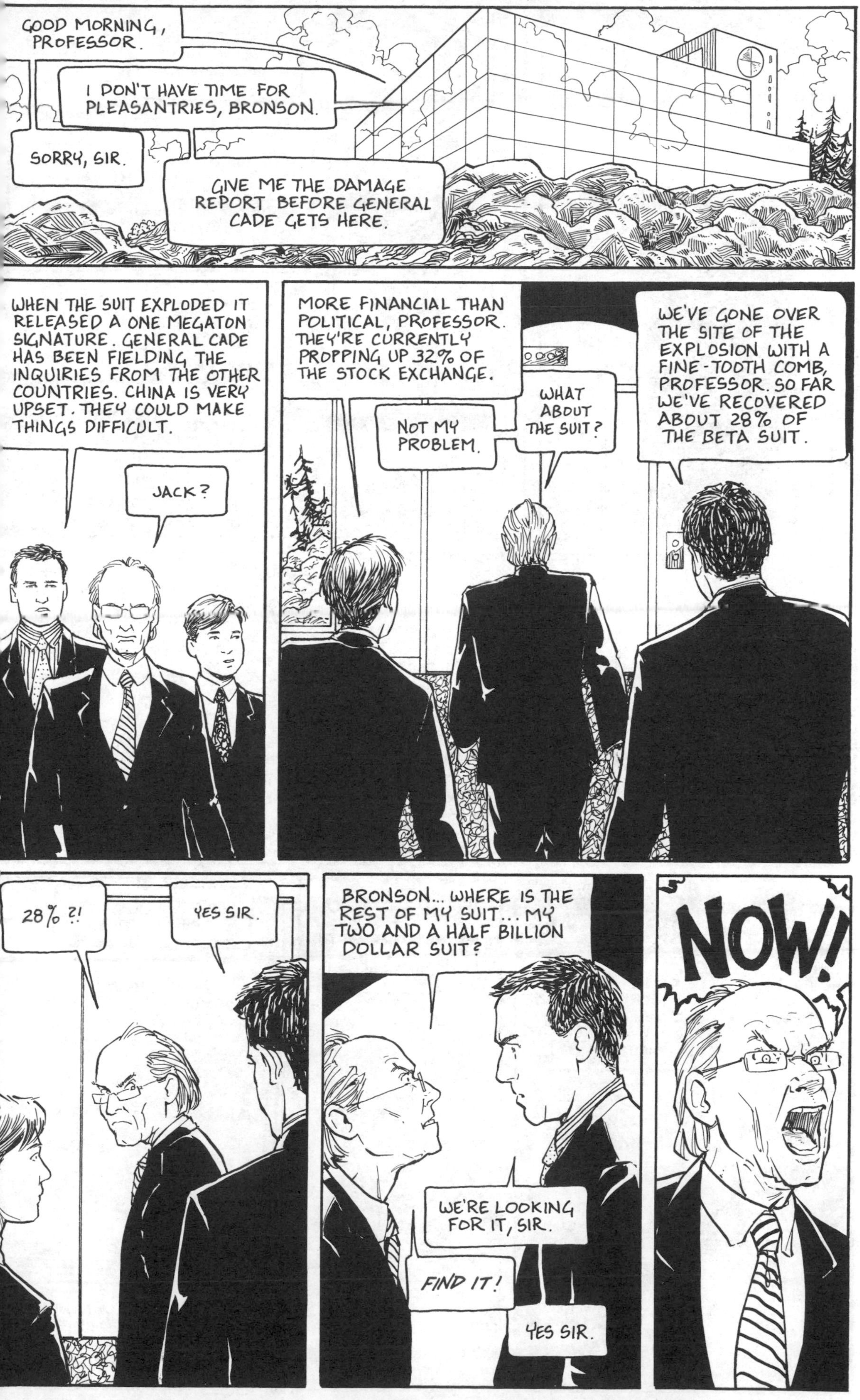
GOOD MORNING, PROFESSOR.
I DON'T HAVE TIME FOR PLEASANTRIES, BRONSON.
SORRY, SIR.
GIVE ME THE DAMAGE REPORT BEFORE GENERAL CADE GETS HERE.
WHEN THE SUIT EXPLODED IT RELEASED A ONE MEGATON SIGNATURE. GENERAL CADE HAS BEEN FIELDING THE INQUIRIES FROM THE OTHER COUNTRIES. CHINA IS VERY UPSET. THEY COULD MAKE THINGS DIFFICULT.
JACK?
MORE FINANCIAL THAN POLITICAL, PROFESSOR. THEY'RE CURRENTLY PROPPING UP 32% OF THE STOCK EXCHANGE.
NOT MY PROBLEM.
WHAT ABOUT THE SUIT?
WE'VE GONE OVER THE SITE OF THE EXPLOSION WITH A FINE-TOOTH COMB, PROFESSOR. SO FAR WE'VE RECOVERED ABOUT 28% OF THE BETA SUIT.
28% ?!
YES SIR.
BRONSON... WHERE IS THE REST OF MY SUIT... MY TWO AND A HALF BILLION DOLLAR SUIT?
WE'RE LOOKING FOR IT, SIR.
FIND IT!
YES SIR.
NOW!

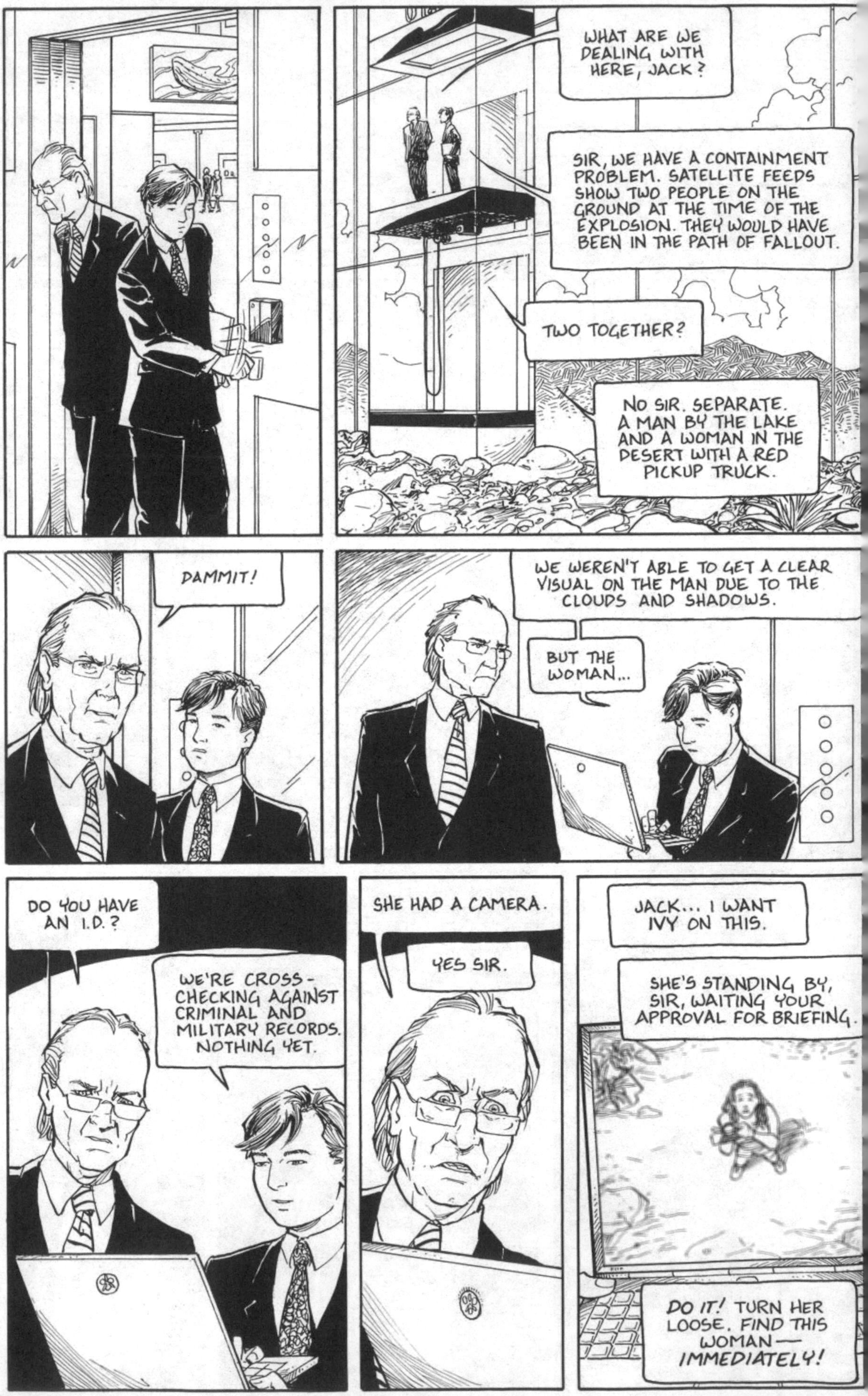
WHAT ARE WE DEALING WITH HERE, JACK?
SIR, WE HAVE A CONTAINMENT PROBLEM. SATELLITE FEEDS SHOW TWO PEOPLE ON THE GROUND AT THE TIME OF THE EXPLOSION. THEY WOULD HAVE BEEN IN THE PATH OF FALLOUT.
TWO TOGETHER?
NO SIR. SEPARATE. A MAN BY THE LAKE AND A WOMAN IN THE DESERT WITH A RED PICKUP TRUCK.
DAMMIT!
WE WEREN'T ABLE TO GET A CLEAR VISUAL ON THE MAN DUE TO THE CLOUDS AND SHADOWS.
BUT THE WOMAN...
DO YOU HAVE AN I.D.?
WE'RE CROSS-CHECKING AGAINST CRIMINAL AND MILITARY RECORDS. NOTHING YET.
SHE HAD A CAMERA.
YES SIR.
JACK... I WANT IVY ON THIS.
SHE'S STANDING BY, SIR, WAITING YOUR APPROVAL FOR BRIEFING.
DO IT! TURN HER LOOSE. FIND THIS WOMAN— IMMEDIATELY!

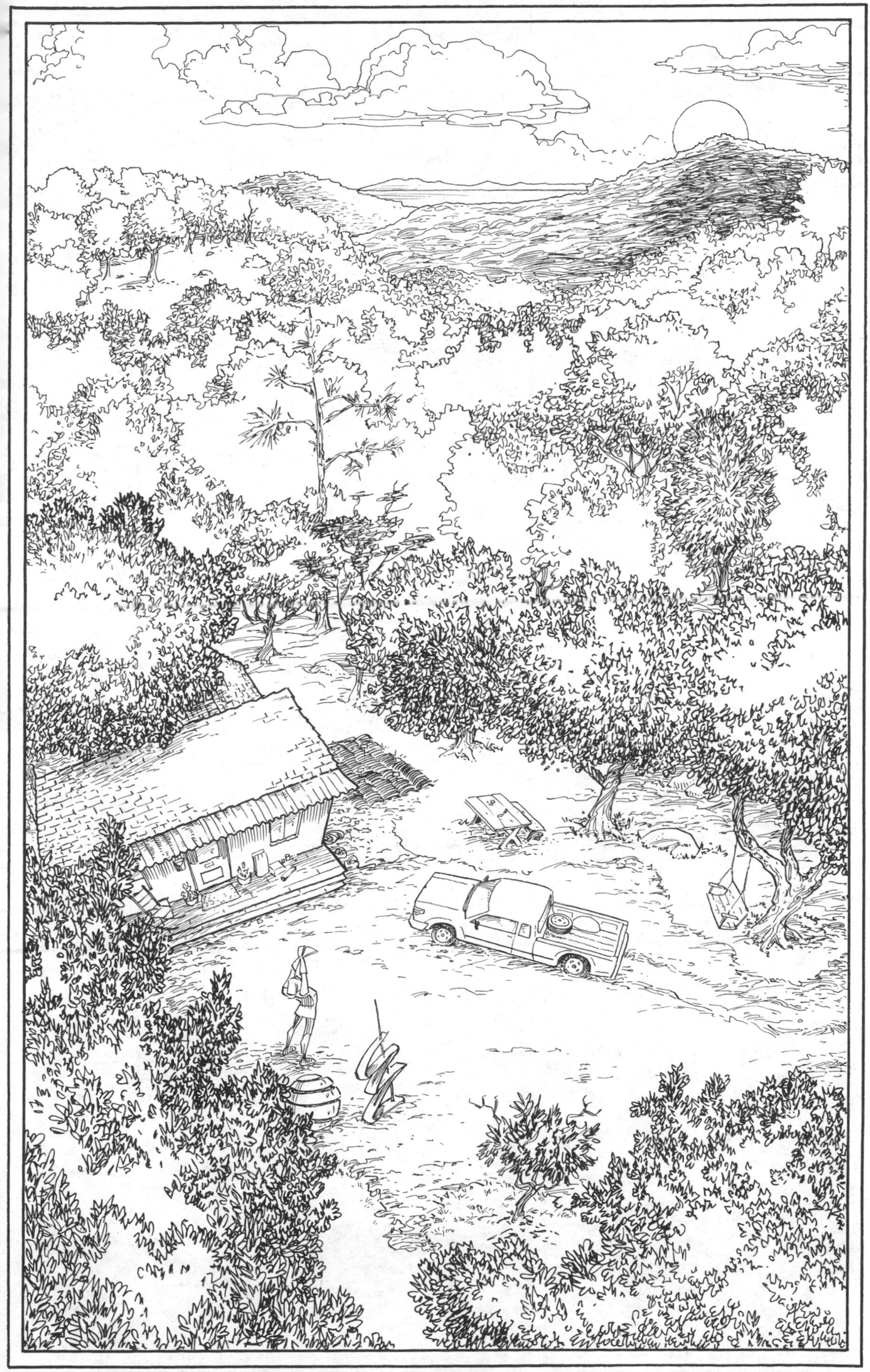

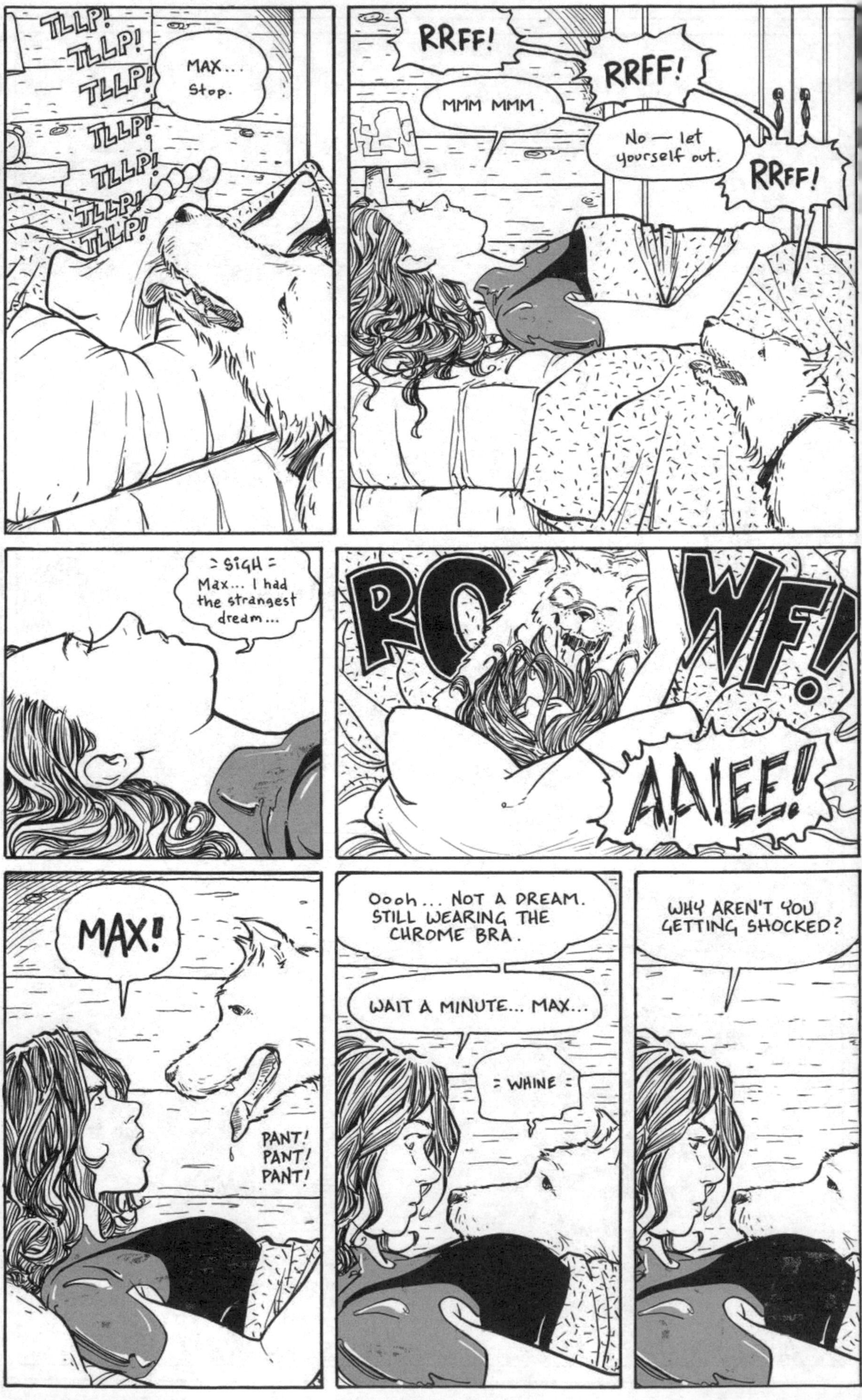
TLLP! TLLP! TLLP! TLLP! TLLP! TLLP! TLLP!
MAX... Stop.
RRFF!
RRFF!
MMM MMM.
No — let yourself out.
RRFF!
= SIGH =
Max... I had the strangest dream...
ROWF!
AAIEE!
MAX!
PANT! PANT! PANT!
Oooh... NOT A DREAM. STILL WEARING THE CHROME BRA.
WAIT A MINUTE... MAX...
= WHINE =
WHY AREN'T YOU GETTING SHOCKED?

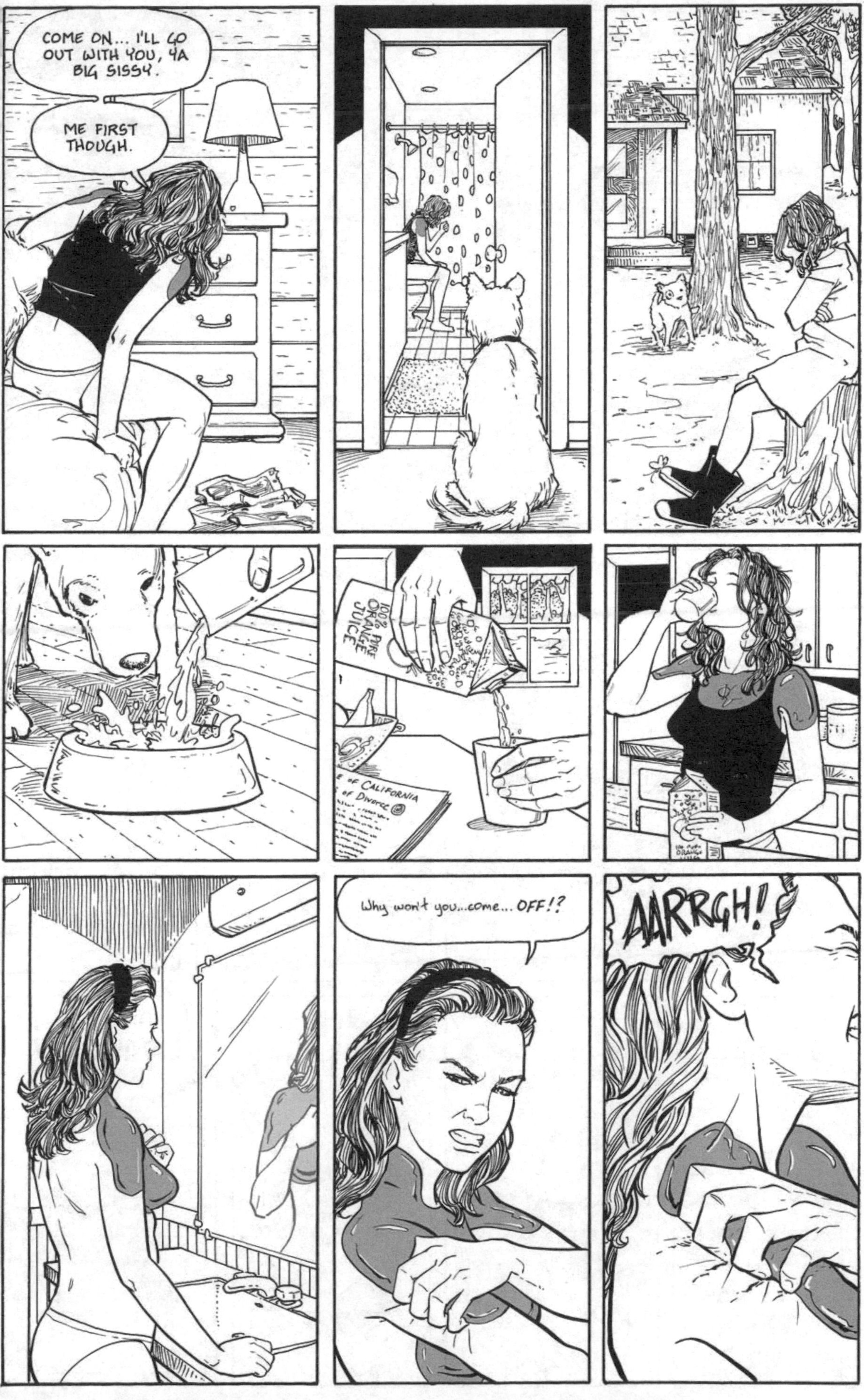
COME ON... I'LL GO OUT WITH YOU, YA BIG SISSY.
ME FIRST THOUGH.
100% PURE ORANGE JUICE
CALIFORNIA
of Divorce
Why won't you...come... OFF!?
AARRGH!

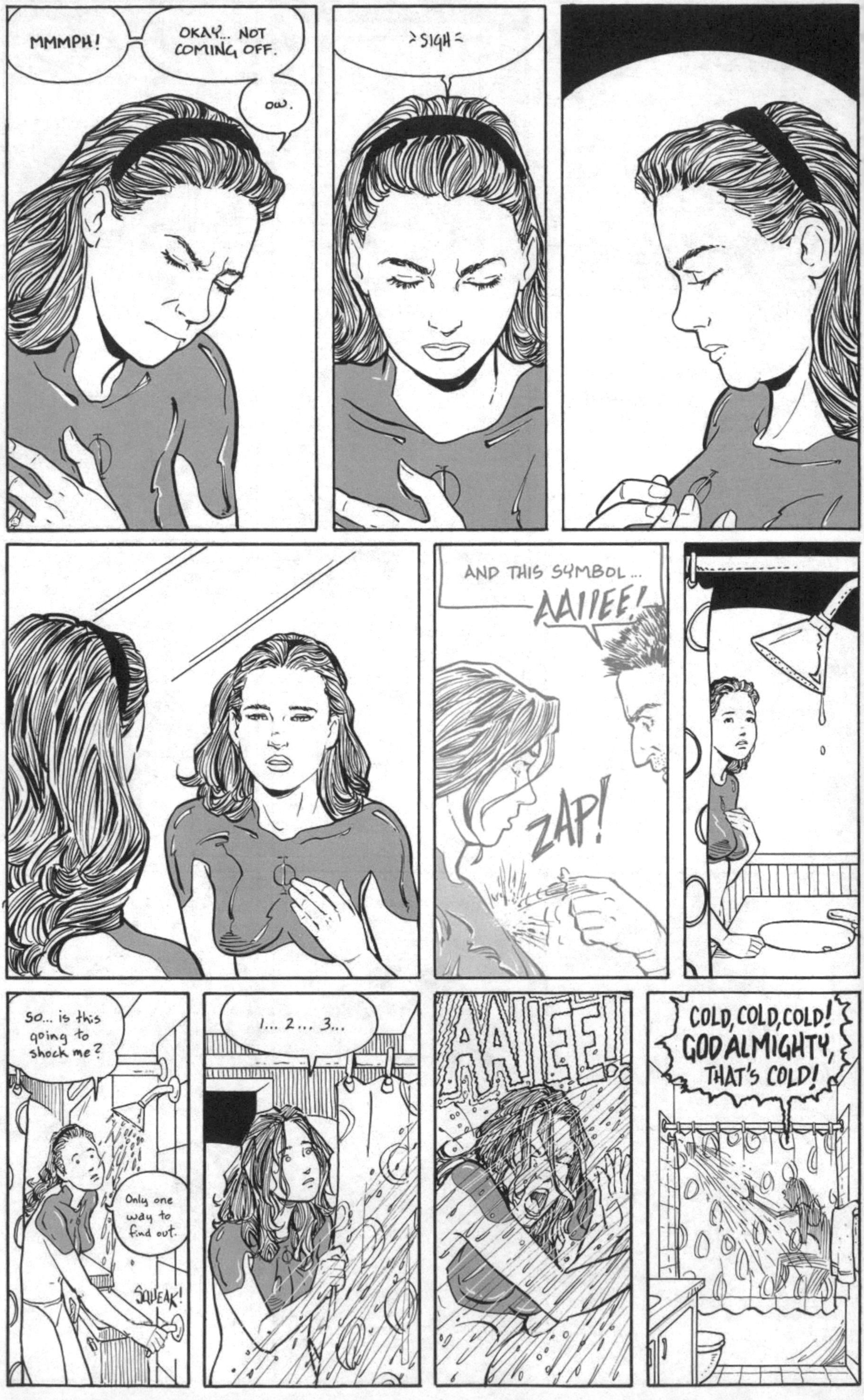
MMMPH!
OKAY... NOT COMING OFF.
OW.
~SIGH~
AND THIS SYMBOL...
AAIIEE!
ZAP!
SO... IS THIS GOING TO SHOCK ME?
Only one way to find out.
SQUEAK!
1... 2... 3...
AAIEEE!!
COLD, COLD, COLD! GOD ALMIGHTY, THAT'S COLD!

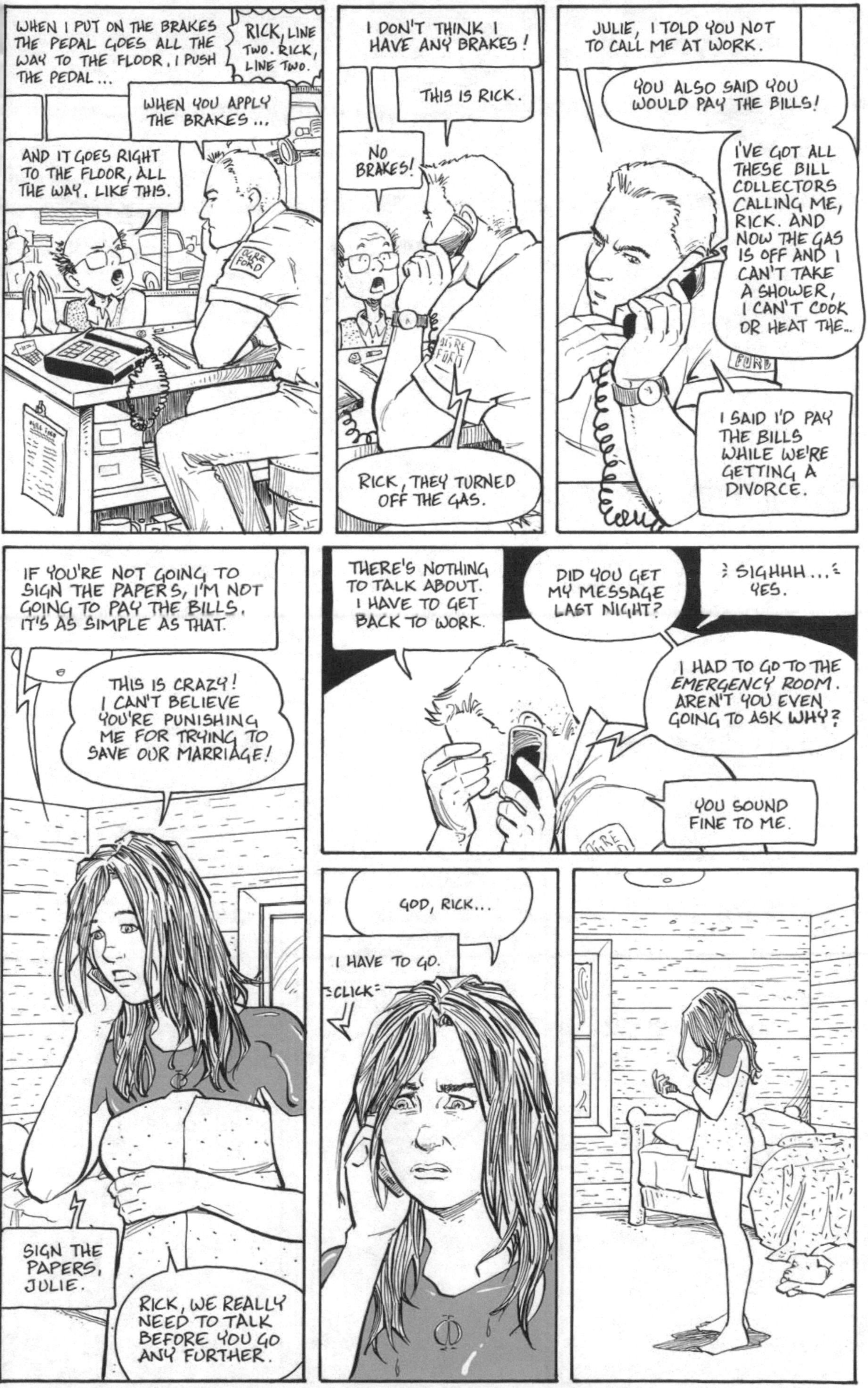
WHEN I PUT ON THE BRAKES THE PEDAL GOES ALL THE WAY TO THE FLOOR. I PUSH THE PEDAL...
RICK, LINE TWO. RICK, LINE TWO.
WHEN YOU APPLY THE BRAKES...
AND IT GOES RIGHT TO THE FLOOR, ALL THE WAY. LIKE THIS.
OGRE FORD
I DON'T THINK I HAVE ANY BRAKES!
THIS IS RICK.
NO BRAKES!
RICK, THEY TURNED OFF THE GAS.
JULIE, I TOLD YOU NOT TO CALL ME AT WORK.
YOU ALSO SAID YOU WOULD PAY THE BILLS!
I'VE GOT ALL THESE BILL COLLECTORS CALLING ME, RICK. AND NOW THE GAS IS OFF AND I CAN'T TAKE A SHOWER, I CAN'T COOK OR HEAT THE..
I SAID I'D PAY THE BILLS WHILE WE'RE GETTING A DIVORCE.
IF YOU'RE NOT GOING TO SIGN THE PAPERS, I'M NOT GOING TO PAY THE BILLS. IT'S AS SIMPLE AS THAT.
THIS IS CRAZY! I CAN'T BELIEVE YOU'RE PUNISHING ME FOR TRYING TO SAVE OUR MARRIAGE!
SIGN THE PAPERS, JULIE.
RICK, WE REALLY NEED TO TALK BEFORE YOU GO ANY FURTHER.
THERE'S NOTHING TO TALK ABOUT. I HAVE TO GET BACK TO WORK.
DID YOU GET MY MESSAGE LAST NIGHT?
SIGHHH... YES.
I HAD TO GO TO THE EMERGENCY ROOM. AREN'T YOU EVEN GOING TO ASK WHY?
YOU SOUND FINE TO ME.
GOD, RICK...
I HAVE TO GO.
CLICK

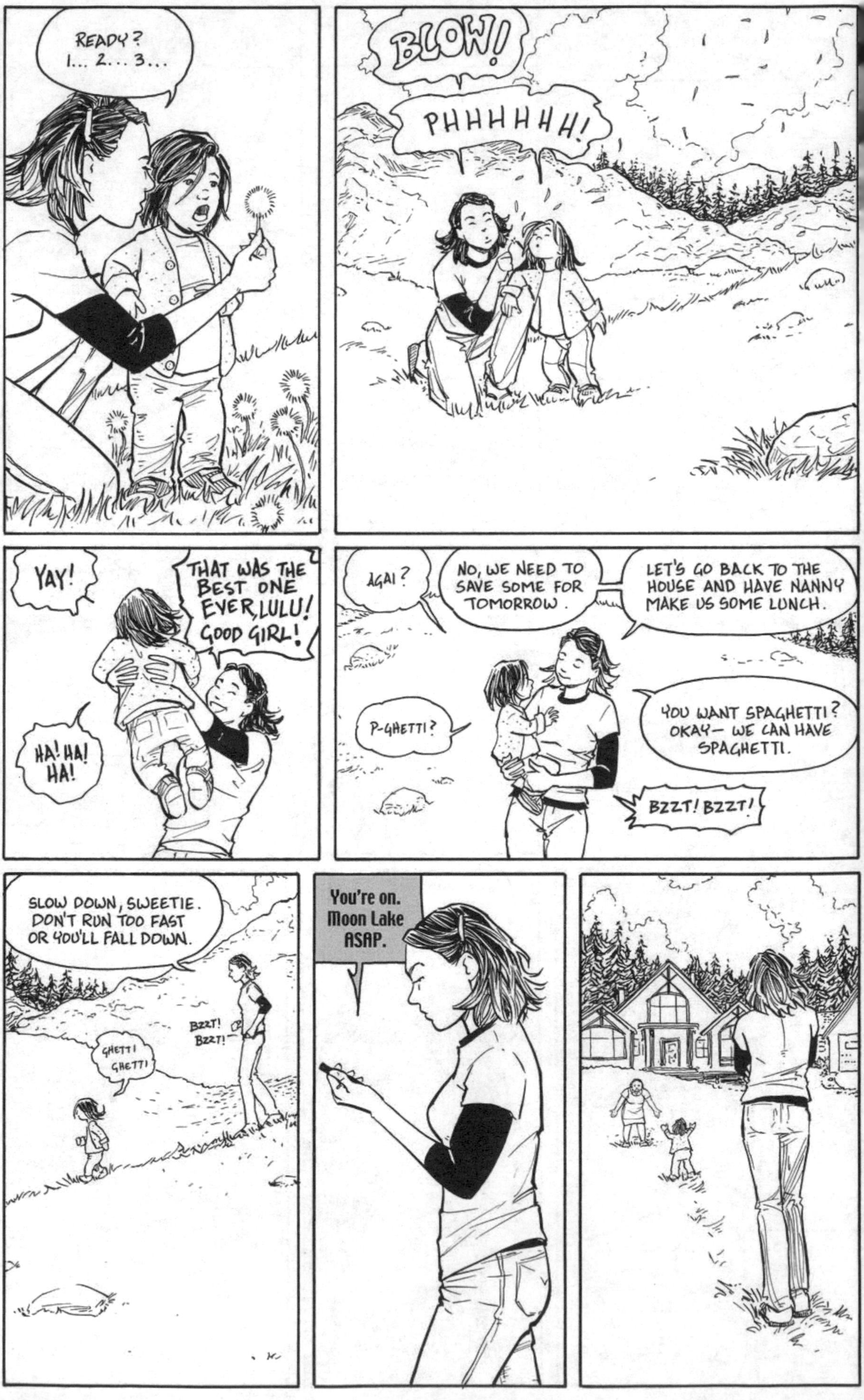
READY? 1... 2... 3...
BLOW!
PHHHHHH!
YAY!
THAT WAS THE BEST ONE EVER, LULU! GOOD GIRL!
HA! HA! HA!
AGAI?
NO, WE NEED TO SAVE SOME FOR TOMORROW.
LET'S GO BACK TO THE HOUSE AND HAVE NANNY MAKE US SOME LUNCH.
P-GHETTI?
YOU WANT SPAGHETTI? OKAY— WE CAN HAVE SPAGHETTI.
BZZT! BZZT!
SLOW DOWN, SWEETIE. DON'T RUN TOO FAST OR YOU'LL FALL DOWN.
GHETTI GHETTI
BZZT! BZZT!
You're on. Moon Lake ASAP.

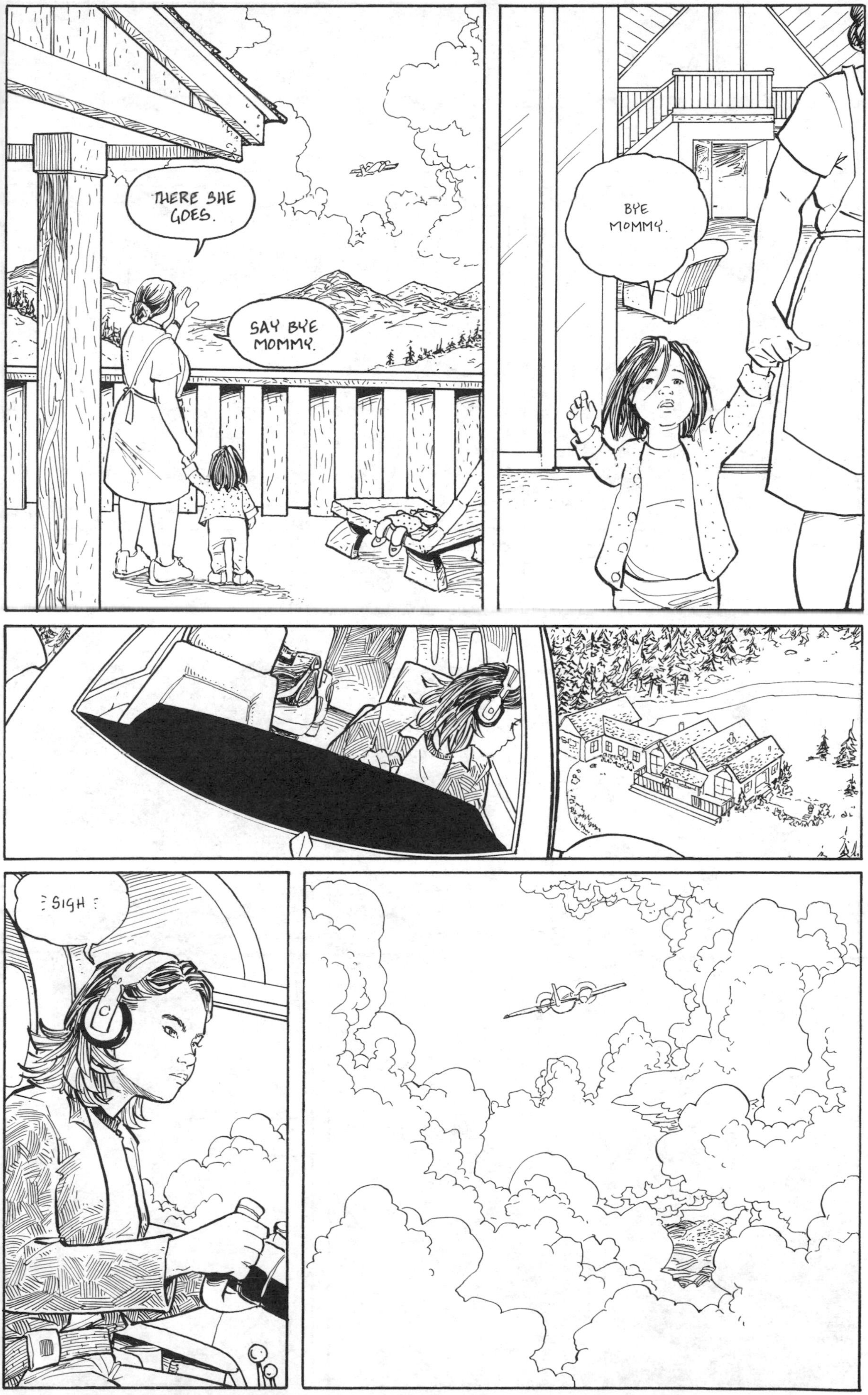
THERE SHE GOES.
SAY BYE MOMMY.
BYE MOMMY.
SIGH

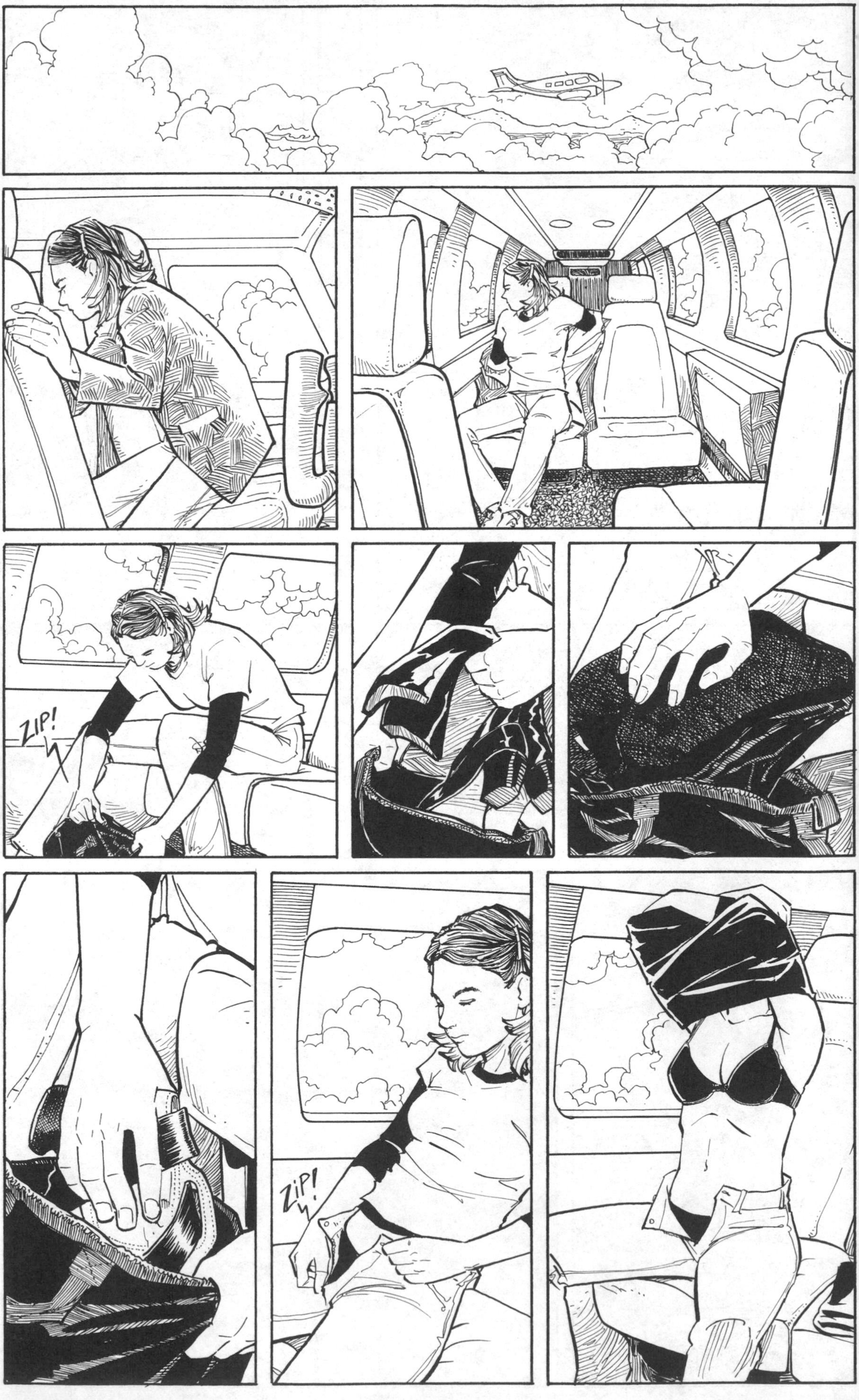
ZIP!
ZIP!

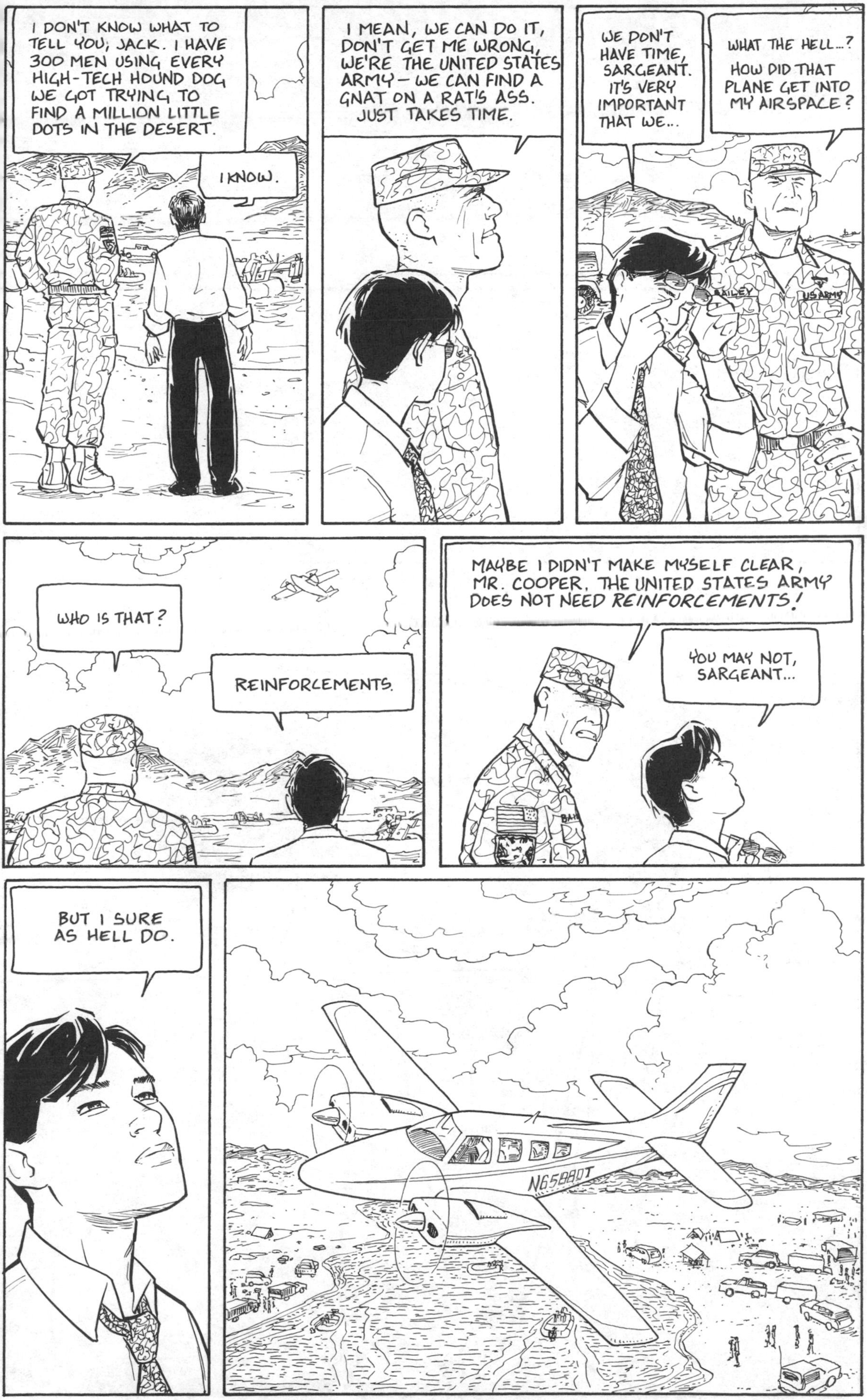
I DON'T KNOW WHAT TO TELL YOU, JACK. I HAVE 300 MEN USING EVERY HIGH-TECH HOUND DOG WE GOT TRYING TO FIND A MILLION LITTLE DOTS IN THE DESERT.
I KNOW.
I MEAN, WE CAN DO IT, DON'T GET ME WRONG, WE'RE THE UNITED STATES ARMY— WE CAN FIND A GNAT ON A RAT'S ASS. JUST TAKES TIME.
WE DON'T HAVE TIME, SARGEANT. IT'S VERY IMPORTANT THAT WE...
WHAT THE HELL...? HOW DID THAT PLANE GET INTO MY AIRSPACE?
BAILEY
US ARMY
WHO IS THAT?
REINFORCEMENTS.
MAYBE I DIDN'T MAKE MYSELF CLEAR, MR. COOPER. THE UNITED STATES ARMY DOES NOT NEED *REINFORCEMENTS!*
YOU MAY NOT, SARGEANT...
BUT I SURE AS HELL DO.
N65880T

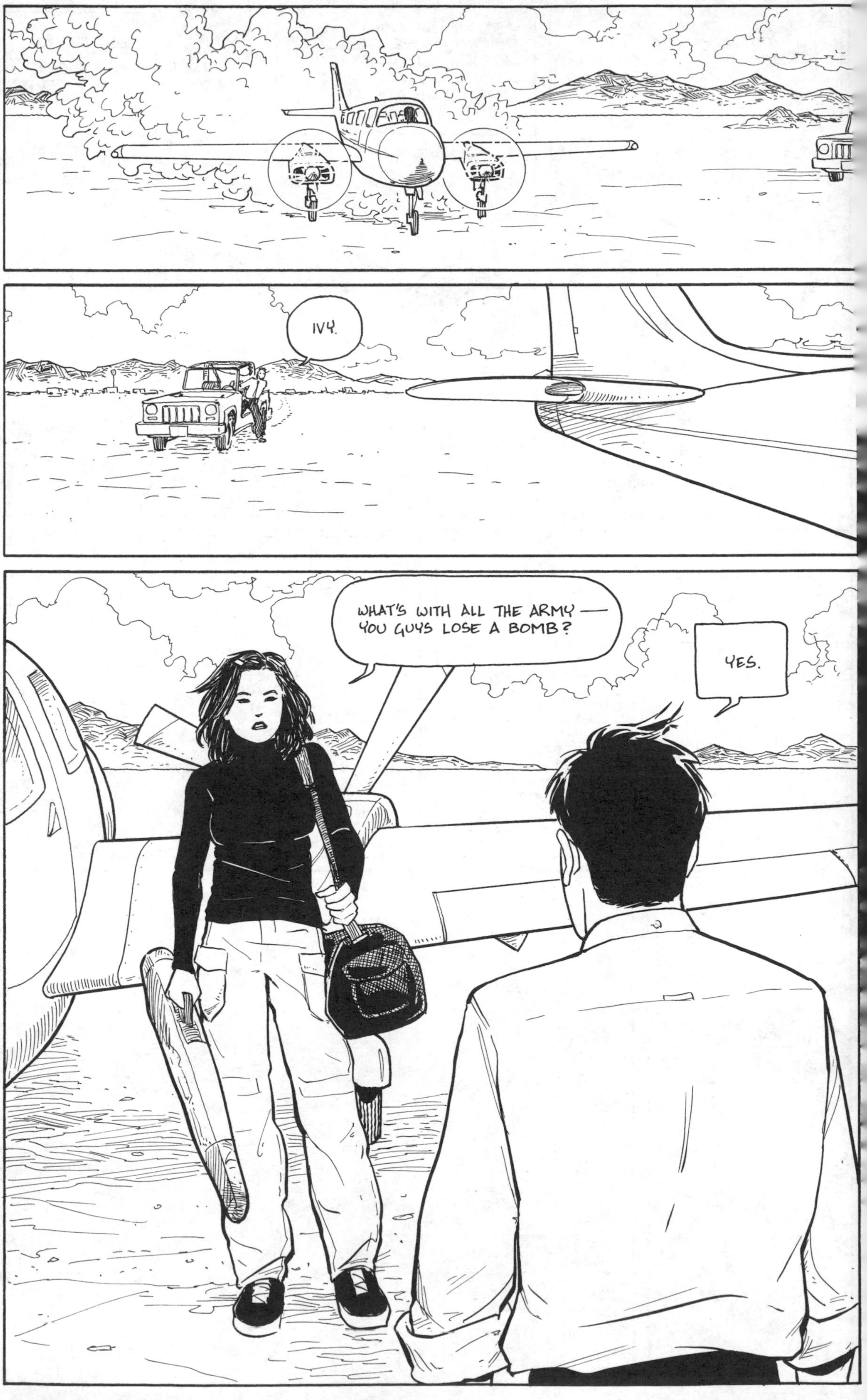
IVY.
WHAT'S WITH ALL THE ARMY — YOU GUYS LOSE A BOMB?
YES.

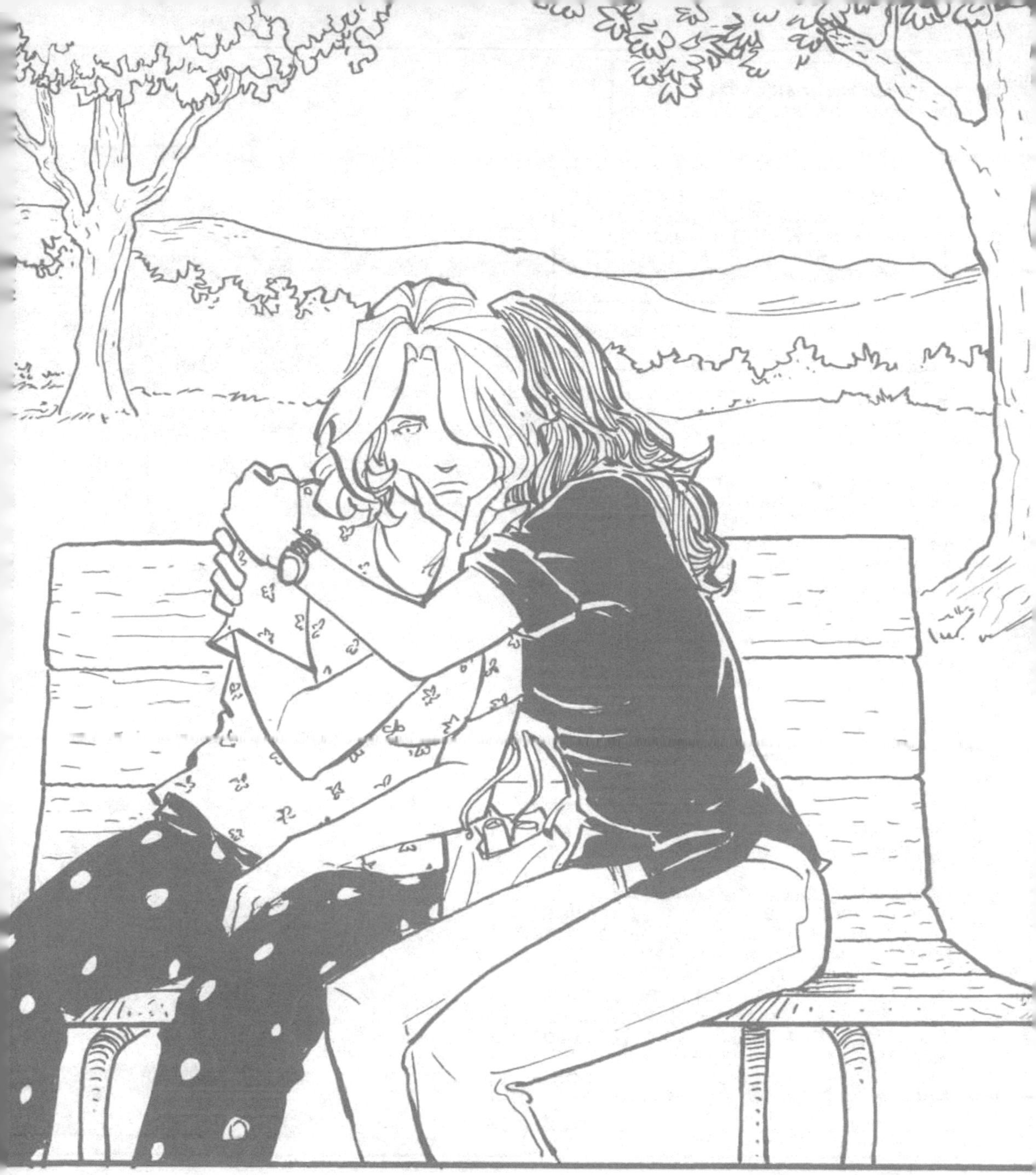

I know not with what weapons World War III will be fought,
but World War IV will be fought with sticks and stones.
—Albert Einstein

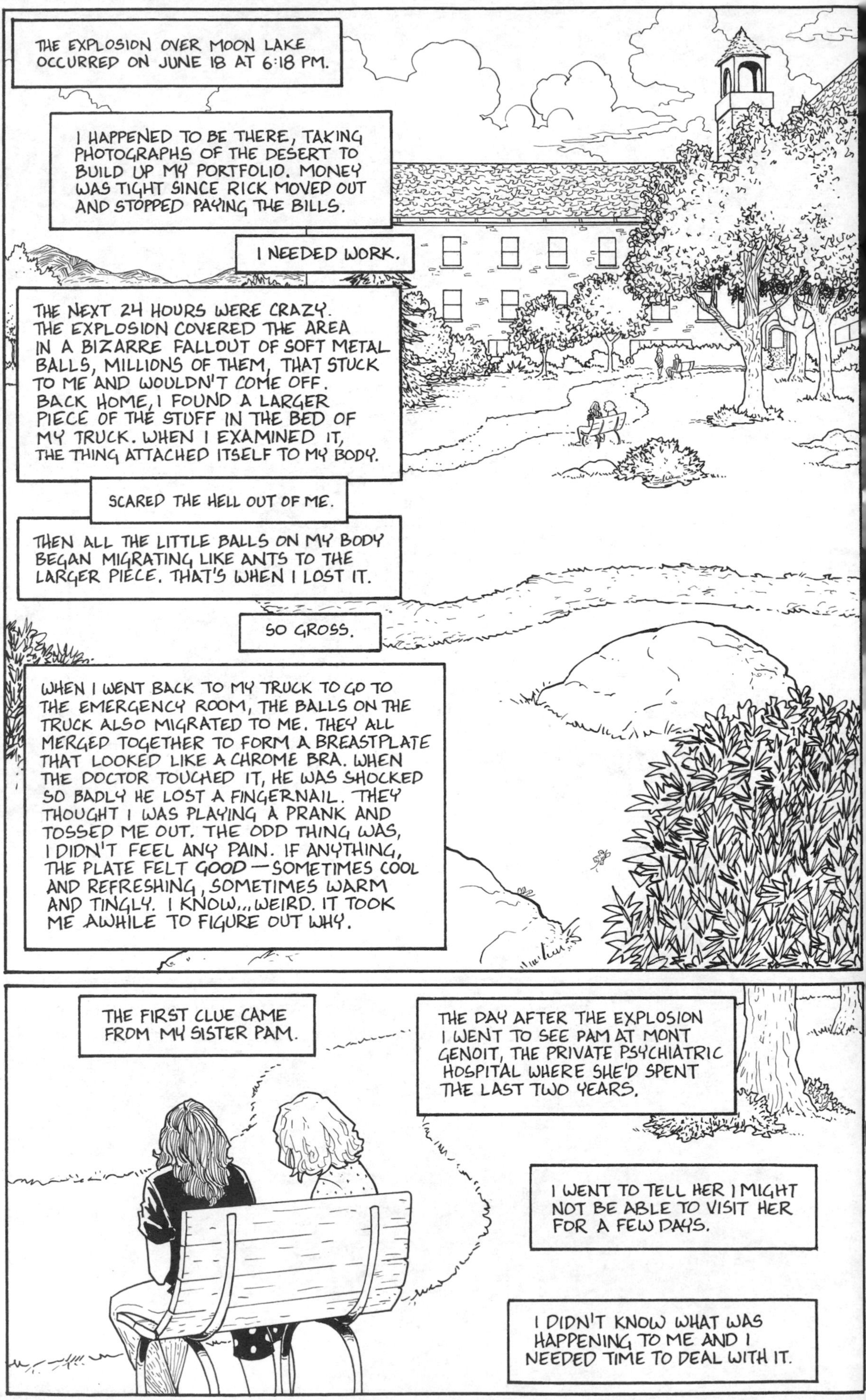
THE EXPLOSION OVER MOON LAKE OCCURRED ON JUNE 18 AT 6:18 PM.
I HAPPENED TO BE THERE, TAKING PHOTOGRAPHS OF THE DESERT TO BUILD UP MY PORTFOLIO. MONEY WAS TIGHT SINCE RICK MOVED OUT AND STOPPED PAYING THE BILLS.
I NEEDED WORK.
THE NEXT 24 HOURS WERE CRAZY. THE EXPLOSION COVERED THE AREA IN A BIZARRE FALLOUT OF SOFT METAL BALLS, MILLIONS OF THEM, THAT STUCK TO ME AND WOULDN'T COME OFF. BACK HOME, I FOUND A LARGER PIECE OF THE STUFF IN THE BED OF MY TRUCK. WHEN I EXAMINED IT, THE THING ATTACHED ITSELF TO MY BODY.
SCARED THE HELL OUT OF ME.
THEN ALL THE LITTLE BALLS ON MY BODY BEGAN MIGRATING LIKE ANTS TO THE LARGER PIECE. THAT'S WHEN I LOST IT.
SO GROSS.
WHEN I WENT BACK TO MY TRUCK TO GO TO THE EMERGENCY ROOM, THE BALLS ON THE TRUCK ALSO MIGRATED TO ME. THEY ALL MERGED TOGETHER TO FORM A BREASTPLATE THAT LOOKED LIKE A CHROME BRA. WHEN THE DOCTOR TOUCHED IT, HE WAS SHOCKED SO BADLY HE LOST A FINGERNAIL. THEY THOUGHT I WAS PLAYING A PRANK AND TOSSED ME OUT. THE ODD THING WAS, I DIDN'T FEEL ANY PAIN. IF ANYTHING, THE PLATE FELT *GOOD*—SOMETIMES COOL AND REFRESHING, SOMETIMES WARM AND TINGLY. I KNOW... WEIRD. IT TOOK ME AWHILE TO FIGURE OUT WHY.
THE FIRST CLUE CAME FROM MY SISTER PAM.
THE DAY AFTER THE EXPLOSION I WENT TO SEE PAM AT MONT GENOIT, THE PRIVATE PSYCHIATRIC HOSPITAL WHERE SHE'D SPENT THE LAST TWO YEARS.
I WENT TO TELL HER I MIGHT NOT BE ABLE TO VISIT HER FOR A FEW DAYS.
I DIDN'T KNOW WHAT WAS HAPPENING TO ME AND I NEEDED TIME TO DEAL WITH IT.

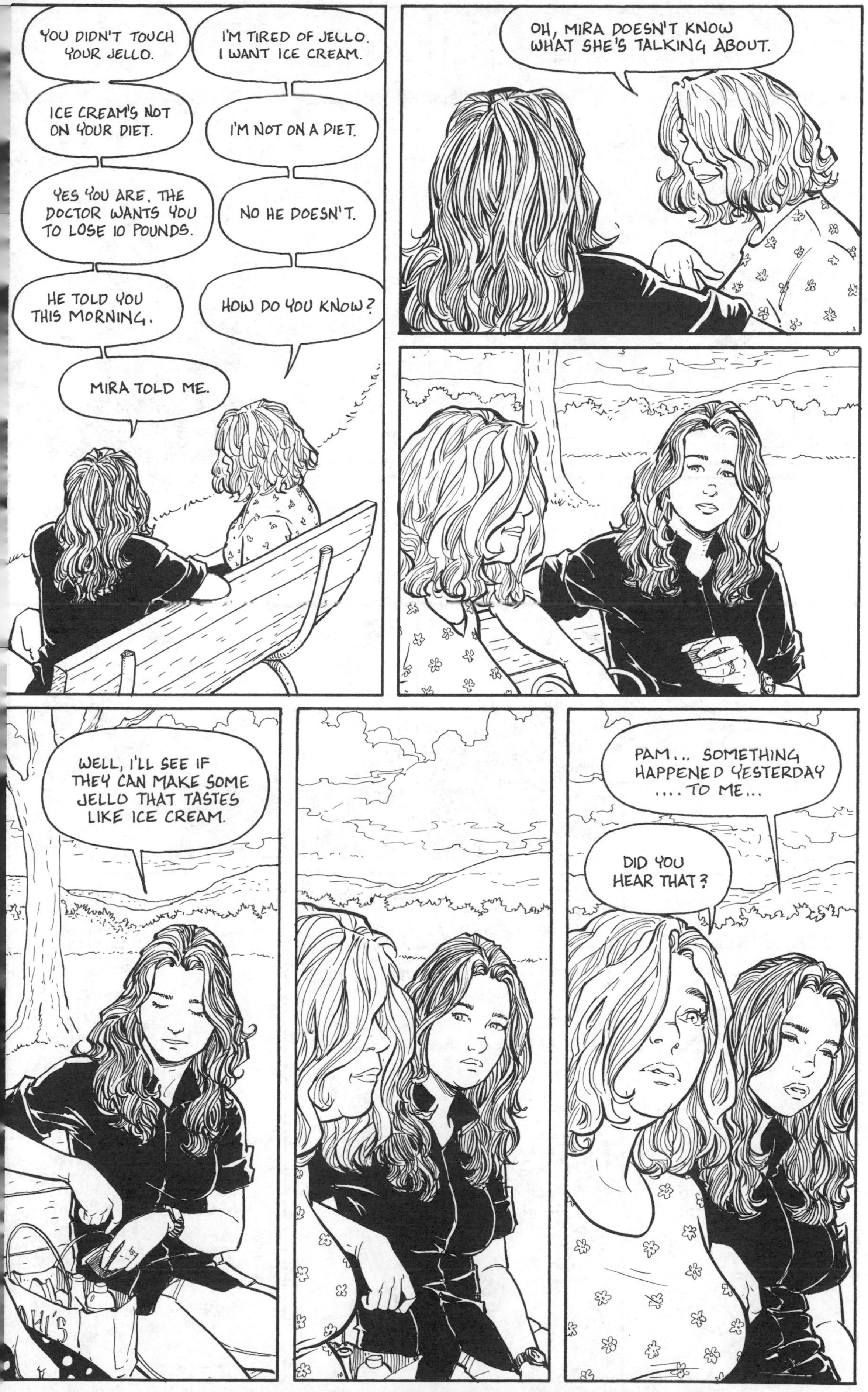
YOU DIDN'T TOUCH YOUR JELLO.
I'M TIRED OF JELLO. I WANT ICE CREAM.
ICE CREAM'S NOT ON YOUR DIET.
I'M NOT ON A DIET.
YES YOU ARE. THE DOCTOR WANTS YOU TO LOSE 10 POUNDS.
NO HE DOESN'T.
HE TOLD YOU THIS MORNING.
HOW DO YOU KNOW?
MIRA TOLD ME.
OH, MIRA DOESN'T KNOW WHAT SHE'S TALKING ABOUT.
WELL, I'LL SEE IF THEY CAN MAKE SOME JELLO THAT TASTES LIKE ICE CREAM.
PAM... SOMETHING HAPPENED YESTERDAY .... TO ME...
DID YOU HEAR THAT?

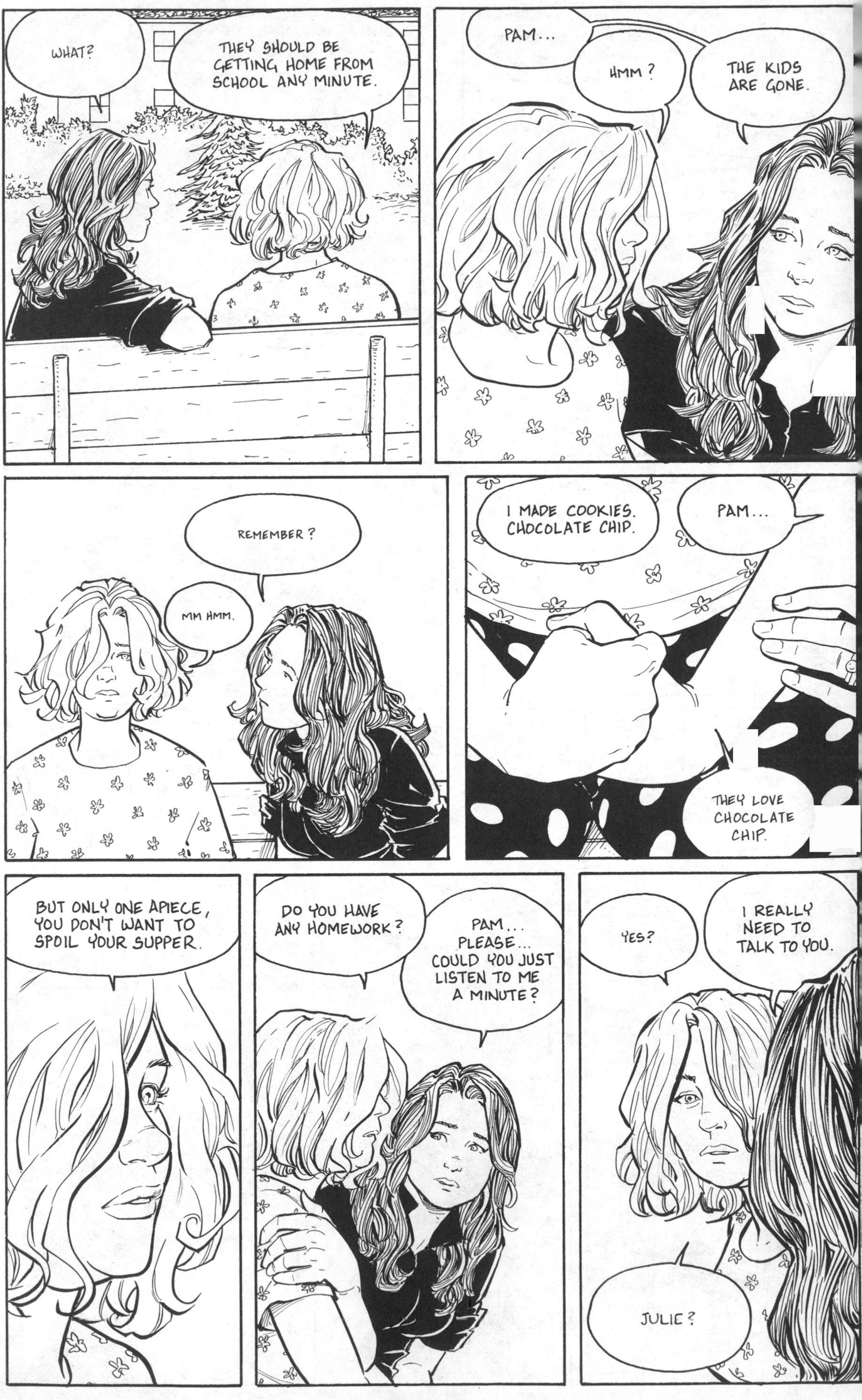
WHAT?
THEY SHOULD BE GETTING HOME FROM SCHOOL ANY MINUTE.
PAM...
HMM?
THE KIDS ARE GONE.
REMEMBER?
MM HMM.
I MADE COOKIES. CHOCOLATE CHIP.
PAM...
THEY LOVE CHOCOLATE CHIP.
BUT ONLY ONE APIECE, YOU DON'T WANT TO SPOIL YOUR SUPPER.
DO YOU HAVE ANY HOMEWORK?
PAM... PLEASE... COULD YOU JUST LISTEN TO ME A MINUTE?
YES?
I REALLY NEED TO TALK TO YOU.
JULIE?

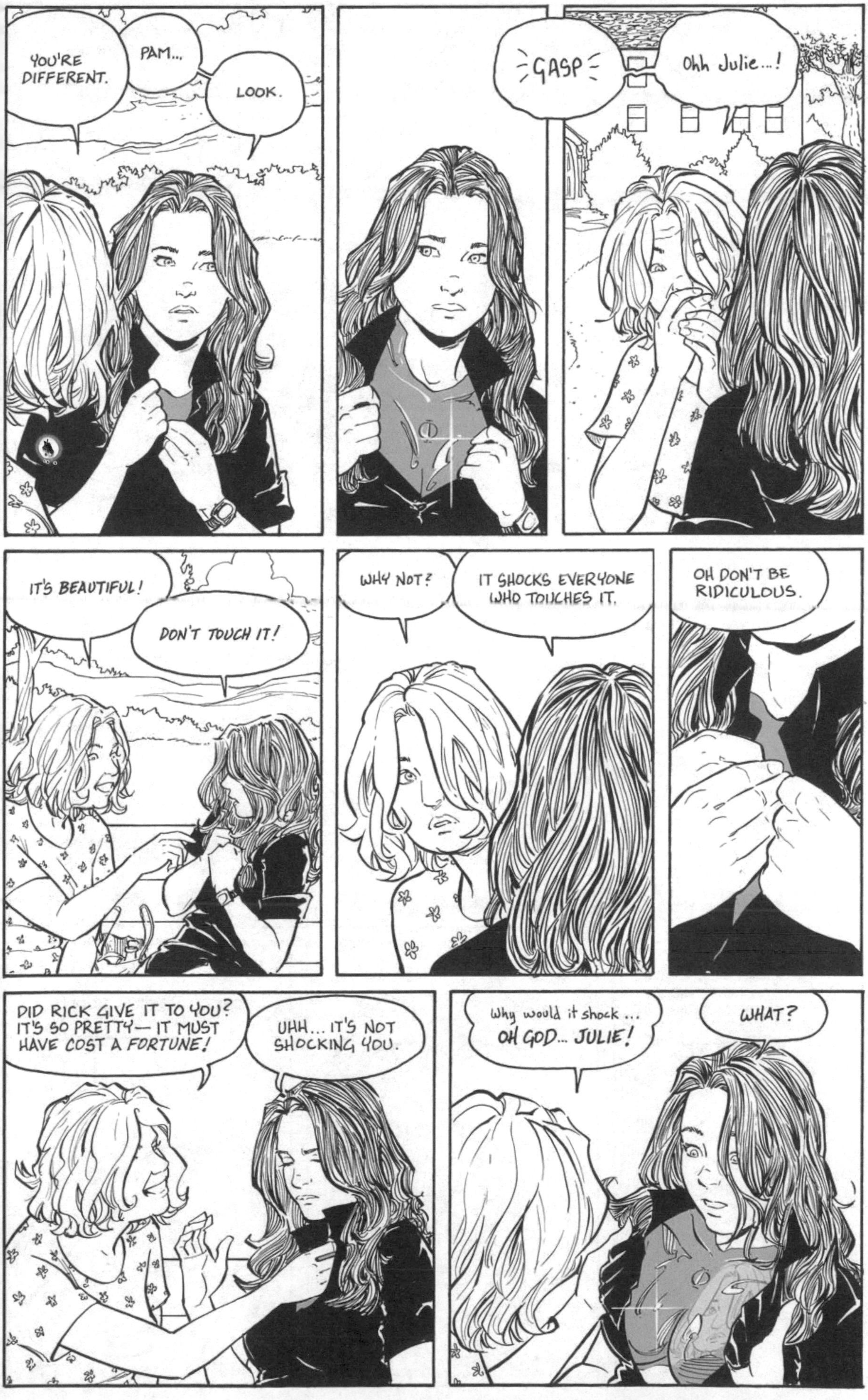
YOU'RE DIFFERENT.
PAM...
LOOK.
GASP
Ohh Julie...!
IT'S BEAUTIFUL!
DON'T TOUCH IT!
WHY NOT?
IT SHOCKS EVERYONE WHO TOUCHES IT.
OH DON'T BE RIDICULOUS.
DID RICK GIVE IT TO YOU? IT'S SO PRETTY— IT MUST HAVE COST A FORTUNE!
UHH... IT'S NOT SHOCKING YOU.
Why would it shock ... OH GOD... JULIE!
WHAT?

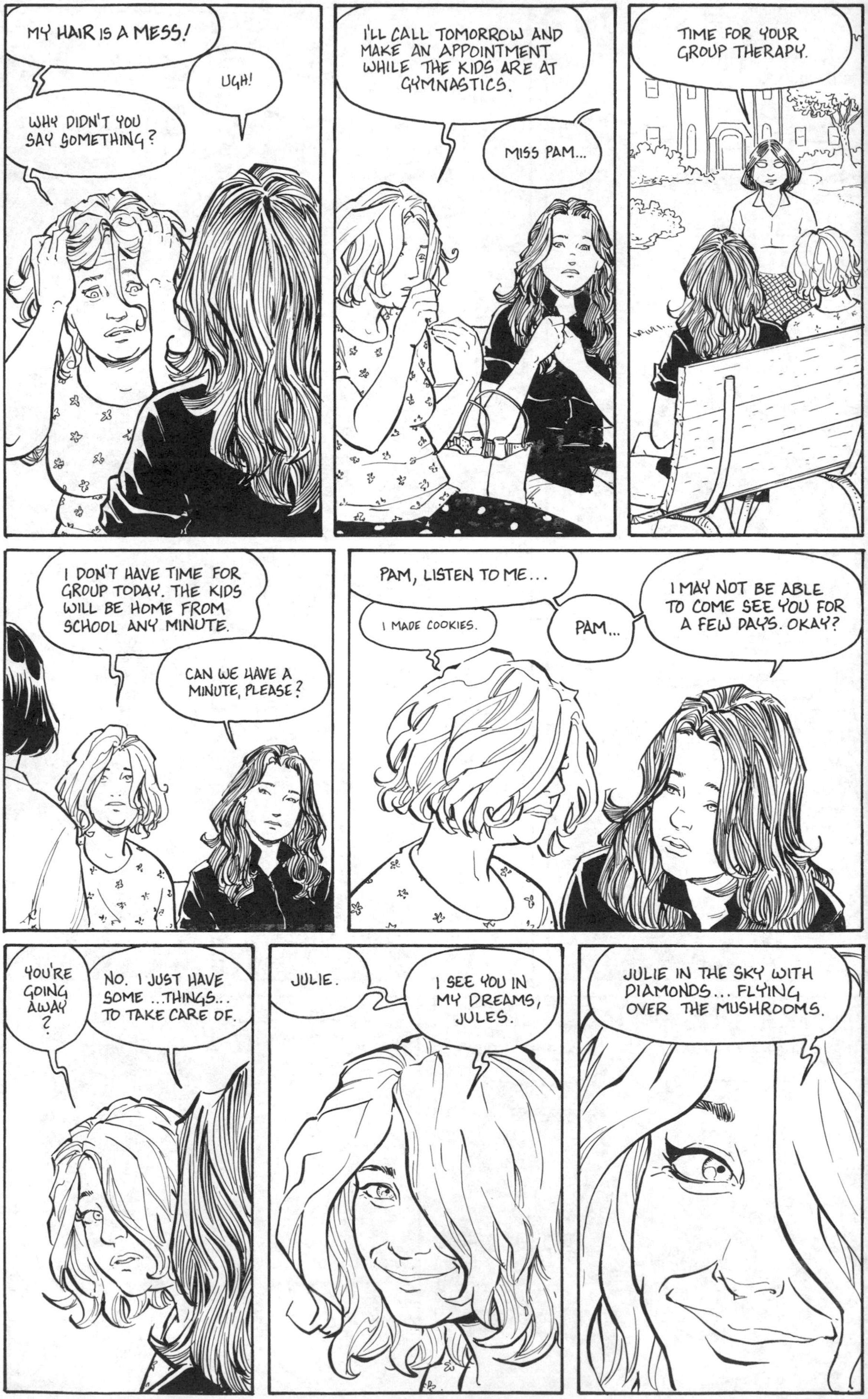
MY HAIR IS A MESS!
WHY DIDN'T YOU SAY SOMETHING?
UGH!
I'LL CALL TOMORROW AND MAKE AN APPOINTMENT WHILE THE KIDS ARE AT GYMNASTICS.
MISS PAM...
TIME FOR YOUR GROUP THERAPY.
I DON'T HAVE TIME FOR GROUP TODAY. THE KIDS WILL BE HOME FROM SCHOOL ANY MINUTE.
CAN WE HAVE A MINUTE, PLEASE?
PAM, LISTEN TO ME...
I MADE COOKIES.
PAM...
I MAY NOT BE ABLE TO COME SEE YOU FOR A FEW DAYS. OKAY?
YOU'RE GOING AWAY?
NO. I JUST HAVE SOME ...THINGS... TO TAKE CARE OF.
JULIE.
I SEE YOU IN MY DREAMS, JULES.
JULIE IN THE SKY WITH DIAMONDS... FLYING OVER THE MUSHROOMS.

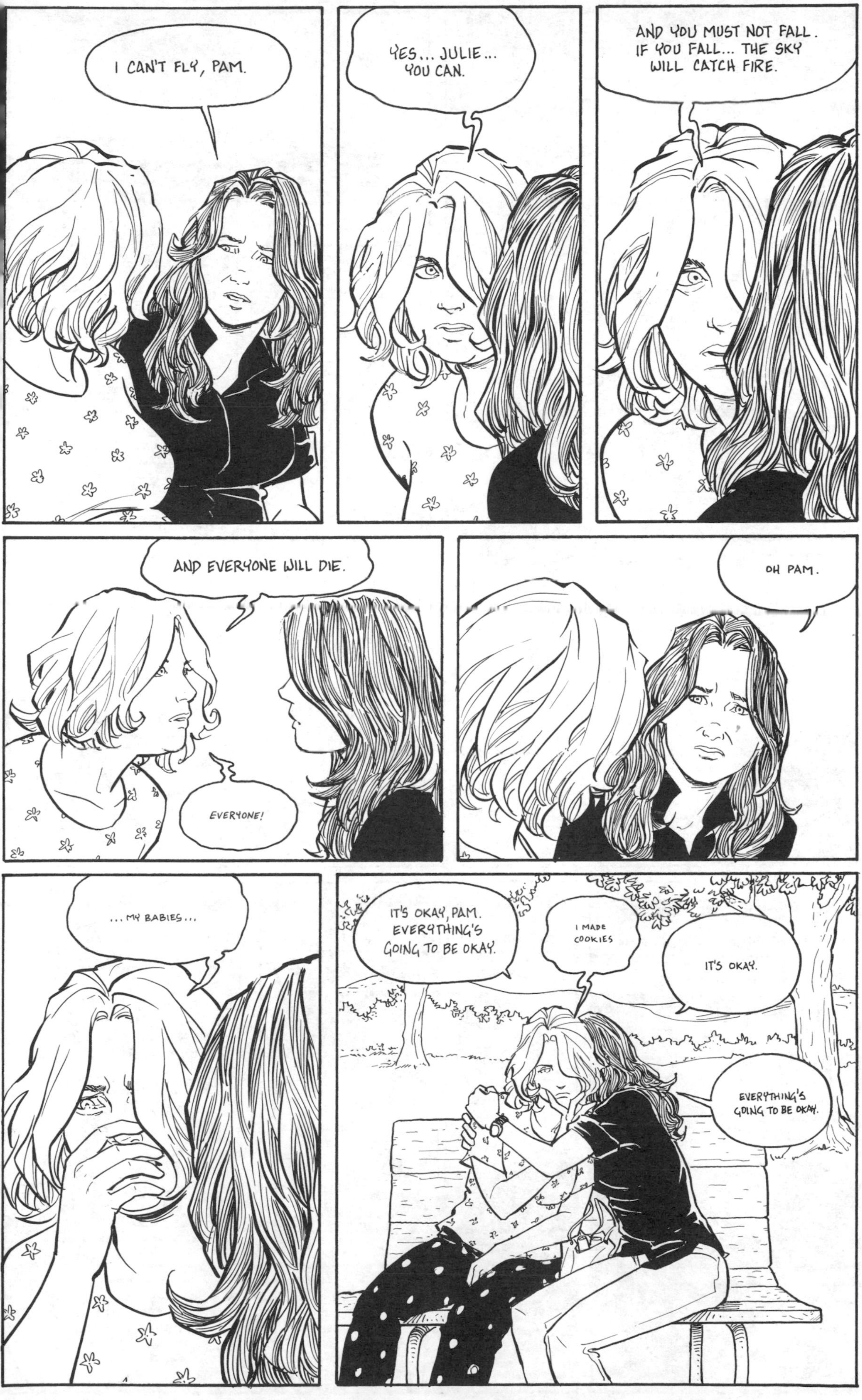
I CAN'T FLY, PAM.
YES... JULIE... YOU CAN.
AND YOU MUST NOT FALL. IF YOU FALL... THE SKY WILL CATCH FIRE.
AND EVERYONE WILL DIE.
EVERYONE!
OH PAM.
...MY BABIES...
IT'S OKAY, PAM. EVERYTHING'S GOING TO BE OKAY.
I MADE COOKIES
IT'S OKAY.
EVERYTHING'S GOING TO BE OKAY.

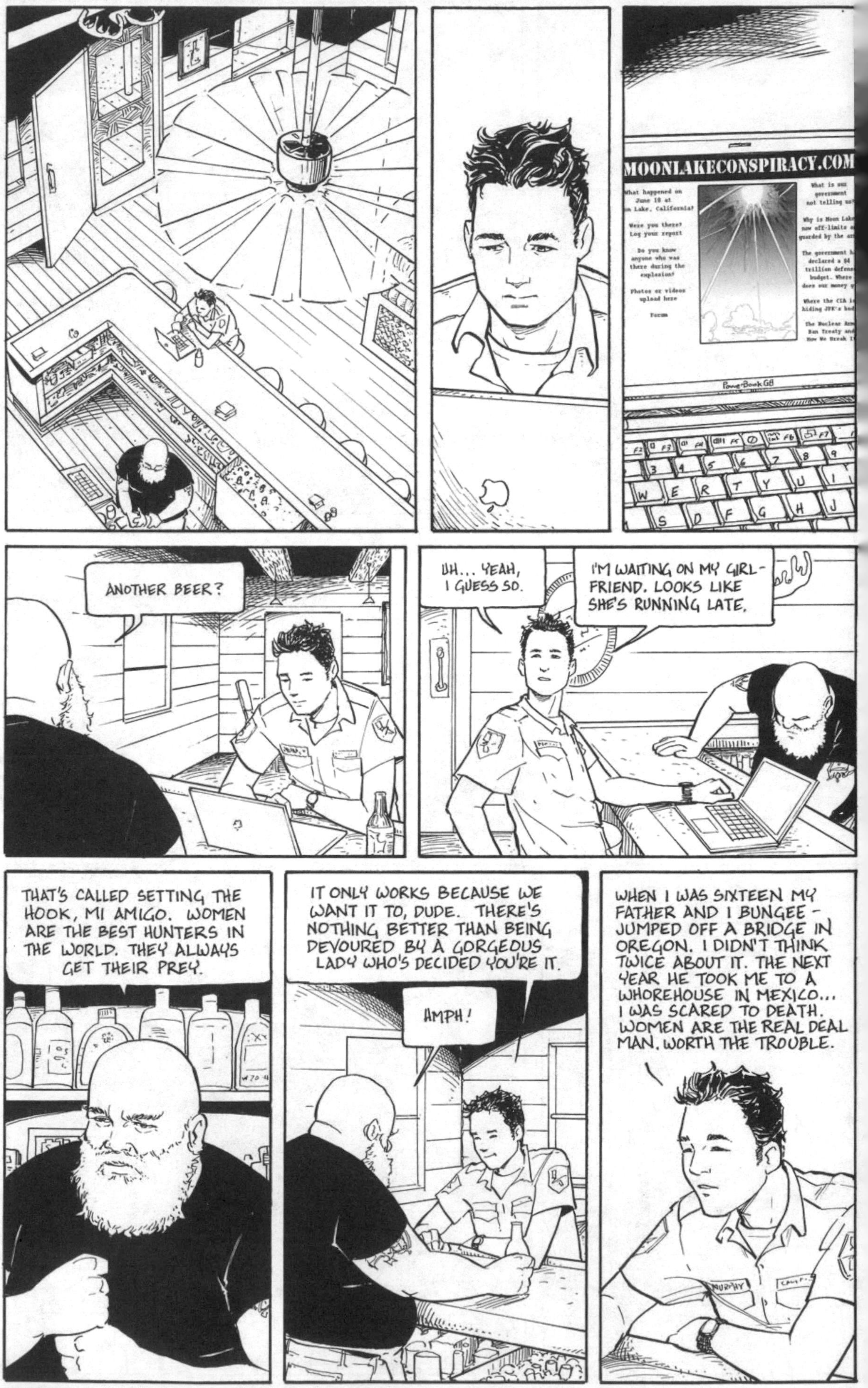

MOONLAKECONSPIRACY.COM
What happened on June 18 at
n Lake, California?
Were you there? Log your report
Do you know anyone who was there during the explosion?
Photos or videos upload here
Forum
What is our government not telling us?
PowerBook G3
ANOTHER BEER?
UH... YEAH, I GUESS SO.
I'M WAITING ON MY GIRLFRIEND. LOOKS LIKE SHE'S RUNNING LATE.
THAT'S CALLED SETTING THE HOOK, MI AMIGO. WOMEN ARE THE BEST HUNTERS IN THE WORLD. THEY ALWAYS GET THEIR PREY.
IT ONLY WORKS BECAUSE WE WANT IT TO, DUDE. THERE'S NOTHING BETTER THAN BEING DEVOURED BY A GORGEOUS LADY WHO'S DECIDED YOU'RE IT.
HMPH!
WHEN I WAS SIXTEEN MY FATHER AND I BUNGEE-JUMPED OFF A BRIDGE IN OREGON. I DIDN'T THINK TWICE ABOUT IT. THE NEXT YEAR HE TOOK ME TO A WHOREHOUSE IN MEXICO... I WAS SCARED TO DEATH. WOMEN ARE THE REAL DEAL MAN. WORTH THE TROUBLE.

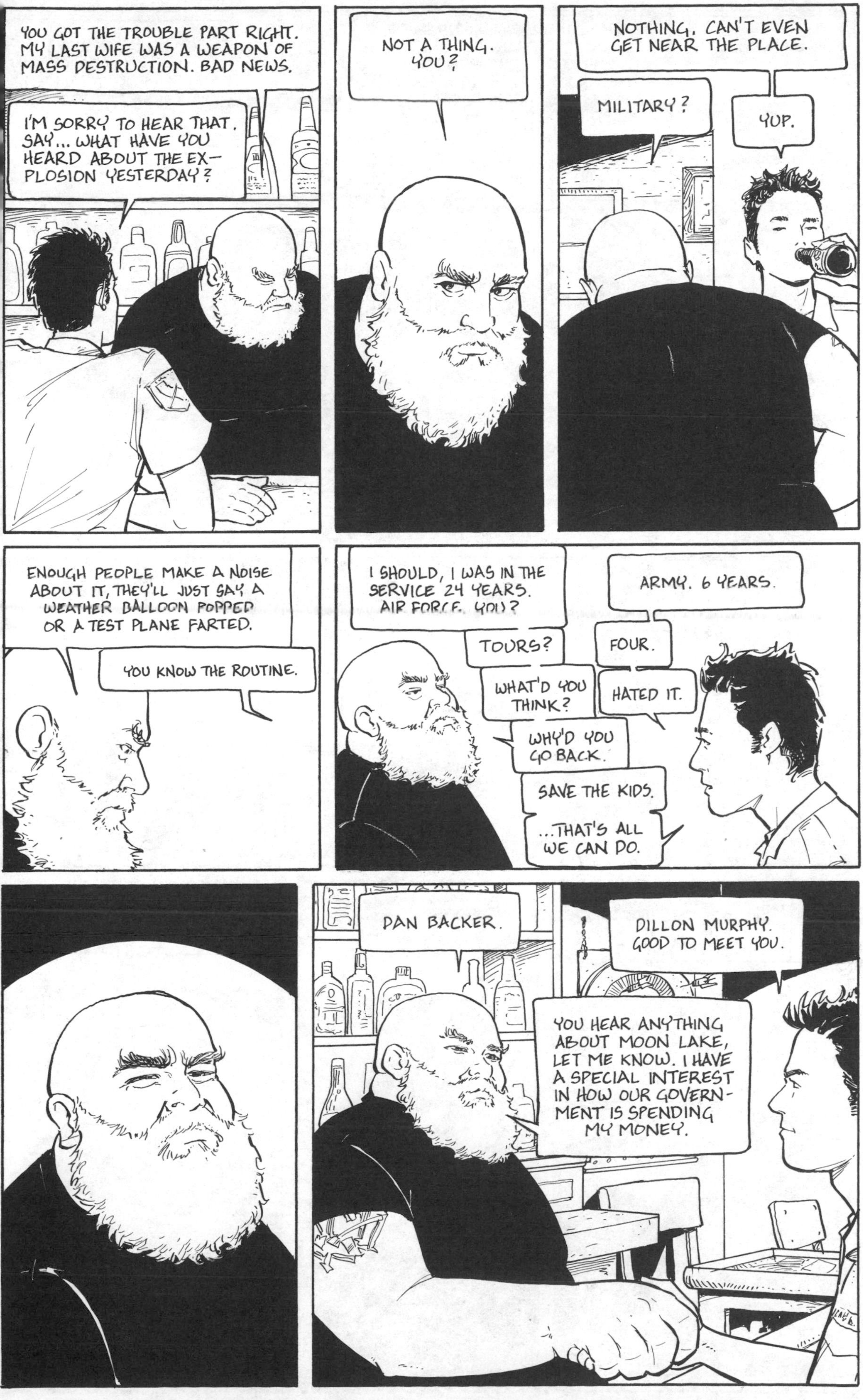
YOU GOT THE TROUBLE PART RIGHT. MY LAST WIFE WAS A WEAPON OF MASS DESTRUCTION. BAD NEWS.
I'M SORRY TO HEAR THAT. SAY... WHAT HAVE YOU HEARD ABOUT THE EX-PLOSION YESTERDAY?
NOT A THING. YOU?
NOTHING. CAN'T EVEN GET NEAR THE PLACE.
MILITARY?
YUP.
ENOUGH PEOPLE MAKE A NOISE ABOUT IT, THEY'LL JUST SAY A WEATHER BALLOON POPPED OR A TEST PLANE FARTED.
YOU KNOW THE ROUTINE.
I SHOULD, I WAS IN THE SERVICE 24 YEARS. AIR FORCE. YOU?
ARMY. 6 YEARS.
TOURS?
FOUR.
WHAT'D YOU THINK?
HATED IT.
WHY'D YOU GO BACK.
SAVE THE KIDS.
...THAT'S ALL WE CAN DO.
DAN BACKER.
DILLON MURPHY. GOOD TO MEET YOU.
YOU HEAR ANYTHING ABOUT MOON LAKE, LET ME KNOW. I HAVE A SPECIAL INTEREST IN HOW OUR GOVERNMENT IS SPENDING MY MONEY.

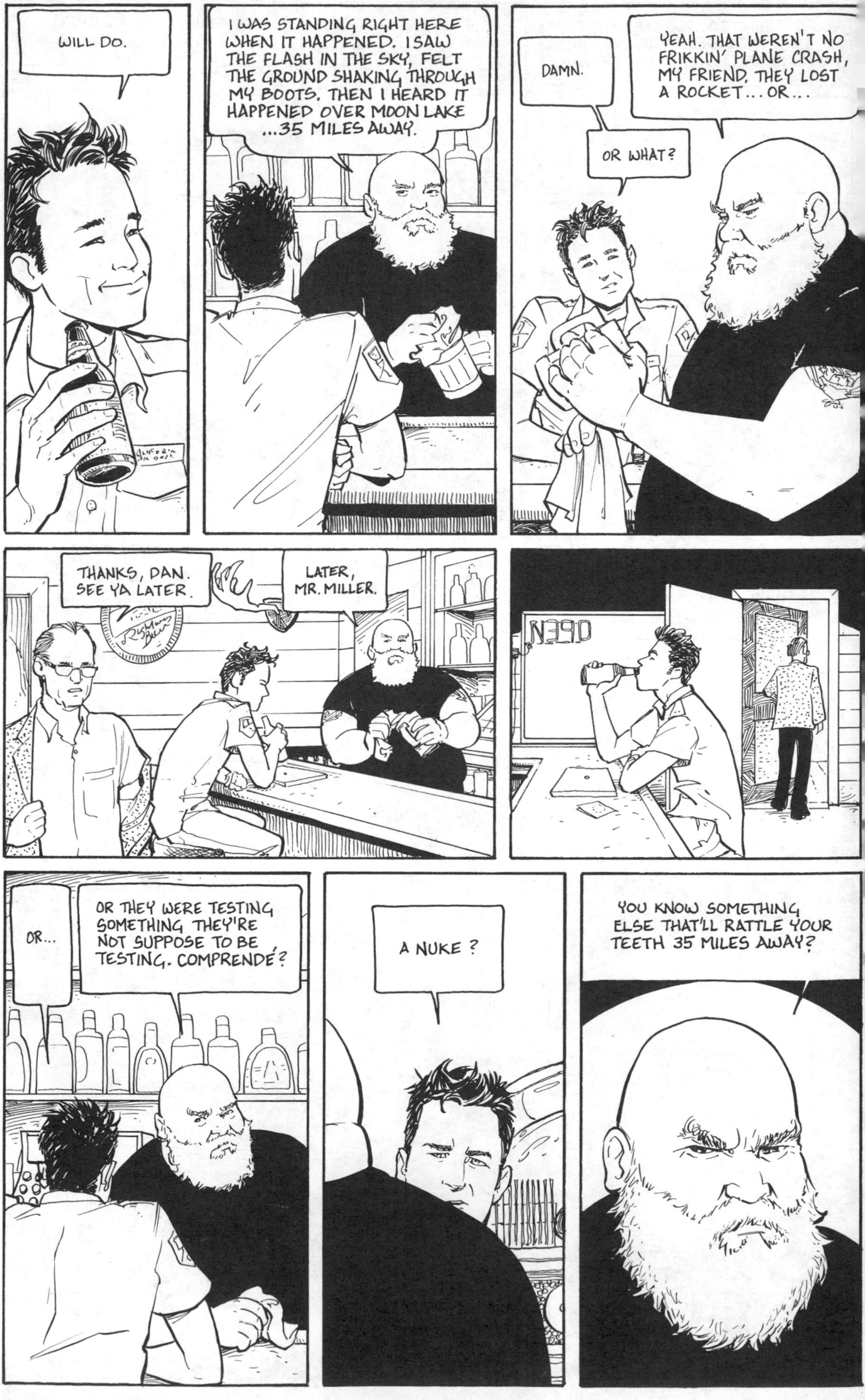
WILL DO.
I WAS STANDING RIGHT HERE WHEN IT HAPPENED. I SAW THE FLASH IN THE SKY, FELT THE GROUND SHAKING THROUGH MY BOOTS. THEN I HEARD IT HAPPENED OVER MOON LAKE ...35 MILES AWAY.
DAMN.
YEAH. THAT WEREN'T NO FRIKKIN' PLANE CRASH, MY FRIEND. THEY LOST A ROCKET... OR...
OR WHAT?
THANKS, DAN. SEE YA LATER.
LATER, MR. MILLER.
OPEN
OR...
OR THEY WERE TESTING SOMETHING THEY'RE NOT SUPPOSE TO BE TESTING. COMPRENDÉ?
A NUKE?
YOU KNOW SOMETHING ELSE THAT'LL RATTLE YOUR TEETH 35 MILES AWAY?

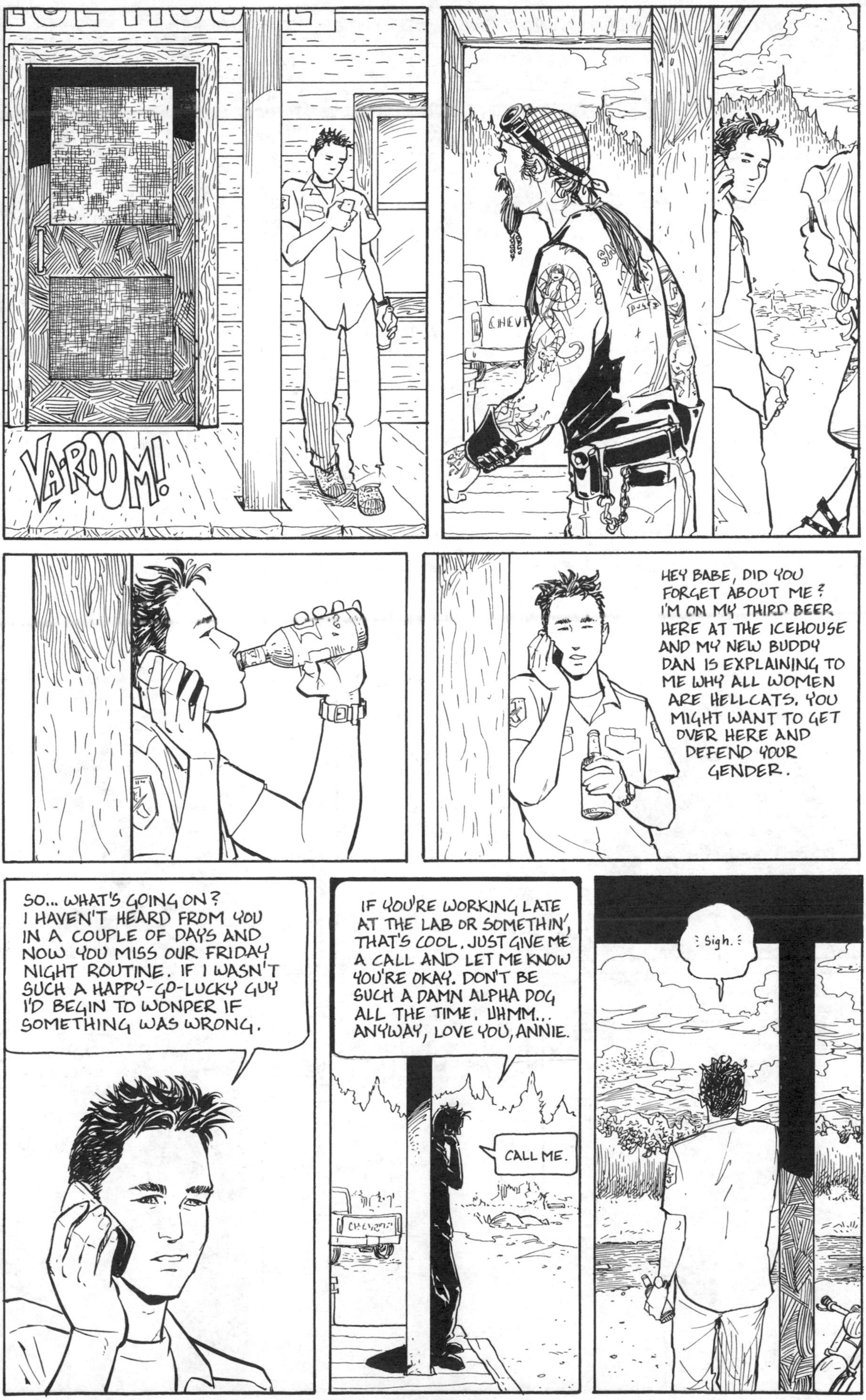
VA-ROOM!
HEY BABE, DID YOU FORGET ABOUT ME? I'M ON MY THIRD BEER HERE AT THE ICEHOUSE AND MY NEW BUDDY DAN IS EXPLAINING TO ME WHY ALL WOMEN ARE HELLCATS. YOU MIGHT WANT TO GET OVER HERE AND DEFEND YOUR GENDER.
SO... WHAT'S GOING ON? I HAVEN'T HEARD FROM YOU IN A COUPLE OF DAYS AND NOW YOU MISS OUR FRIDAY NIGHT ROUTINE. IF I WASN'T SUCH A HAPPY-GO-LUCKY GUY I'D BEGIN TO WONDER IF SOMETHING WAS WRONG.
IF YOU'RE WORKING LATE AT THE LAB OR SOMETHIN', THAT'S COOL. JUST GIVE ME A CALL AND LET ME KNOW YOU'RE OKAY. DON'T BE SUCH A DAMN ALPHA DOG ALL THE TIME. UHMM... ANYWAY, LOVE YOU, ANNIE.
CALL ME.
Sigh.

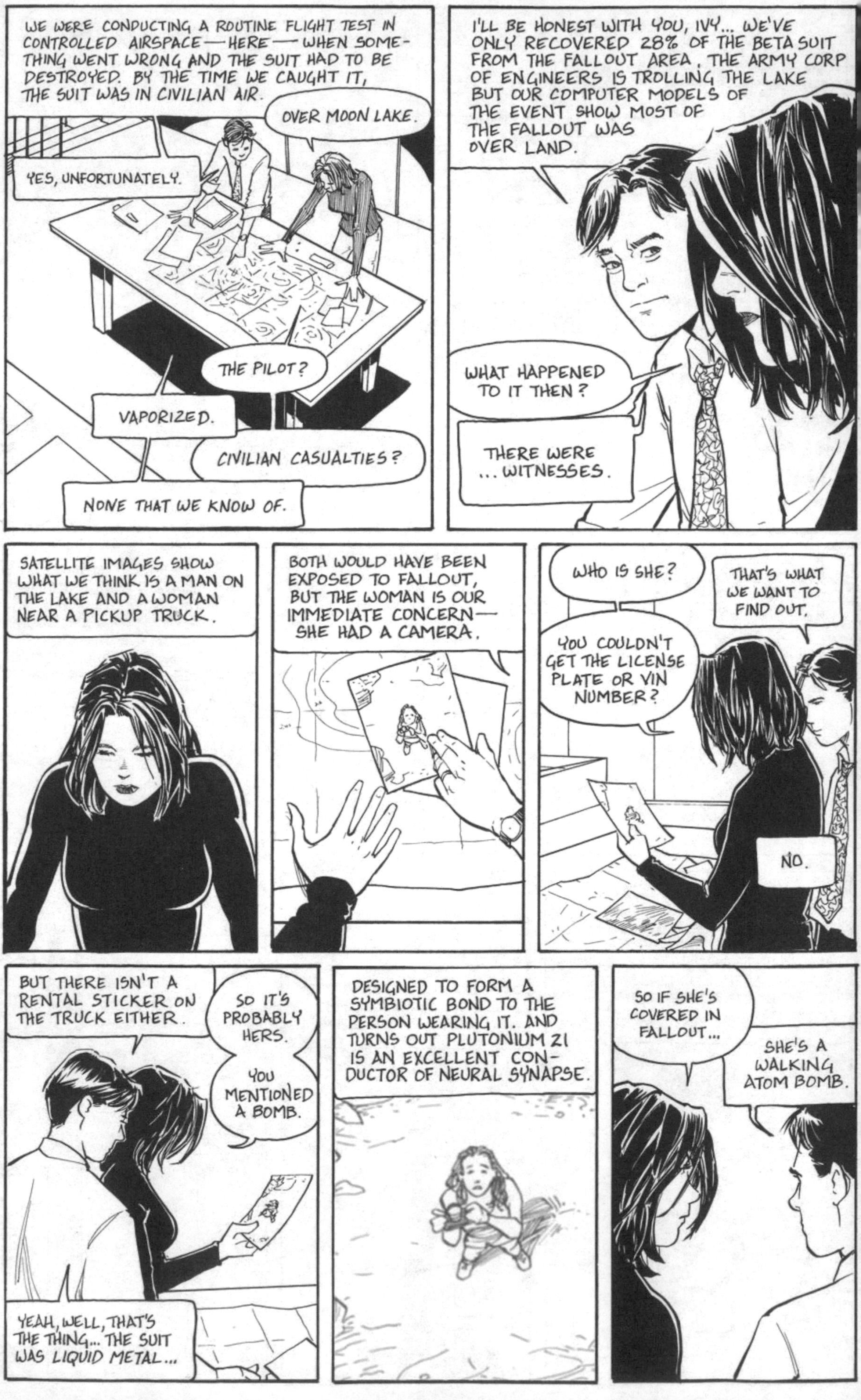
WE WERE CONDUCTING A ROUTINE FLIGHT TEST IN CONTROLLED AIRSPACE—HERE—WHEN SOMETHING WENT WRONG AND THE SUIT HAD TO BE DESTROYED. BY THE TIME WE CAUGHT IT, THE SUIT WAS IN CIVILIAN AIR.
OVER MOON LAKE.
YES, UNFORTUNATELY.
THE PILOT?
VAPORIZED.
CIVILIAN CASUALTIES?
NONE THAT WE KNOW OF.
I'LL BE HONEST WITH YOU, IVY... WE'VE ONLY RECOVERED 28% OF THE BETA SUIT FROM THE FALLOUT AREA, THE ARMY CORP OF ENGINEERS IS TROLLING THE LAKE BUT OUR COMPUTER MODELS OF THE EVENT SHOW MOST OF THE FALLOUT WAS OVER LAND.
WHAT HAPPENED TO IT THEN?
THERE WERE ...WITNESSES.
SATELLITE IMAGES SHOW WHAT WE THINK IS A MAN ON THE LAKE AND A WOMAN NEAR A PICKUP TRUCK.
BOTH WOULD HAVE BEEN EXPOSED TO FALLOUT, BUT THE WOMAN IS OUR IMMEDIATE CONCERN—SHE HAD A CAMERA.
WHO IS SHE?
THAT'S WHAT WE WANT TO FIND OUT.
YOU COULDN'T GET THE LICENSE PLATE OR VIN NUMBER?
NO.
BUT THERE ISN'T A RENTAL STICKER ON THE TRUCK EITHER.
SO IT'S PROBABLY HERS.
YOU MENTIONED A BOMB.
YEAH, WELL, THAT'S THE THING... THE SUIT WAS LIQUID METAL...
DESIGNED TO FORM A SYMBIOTIC BOND TO THE PERSON WEARING IT. AND TURNS OUT PLUTONIUM 21 IS AN EXCELLENT CONDUCTOR OF NEURAL SYNAPSE.
SO IF SHE'S COVERED IN FALLOUT...
SHE'S A WALKING ATOM BOMB.

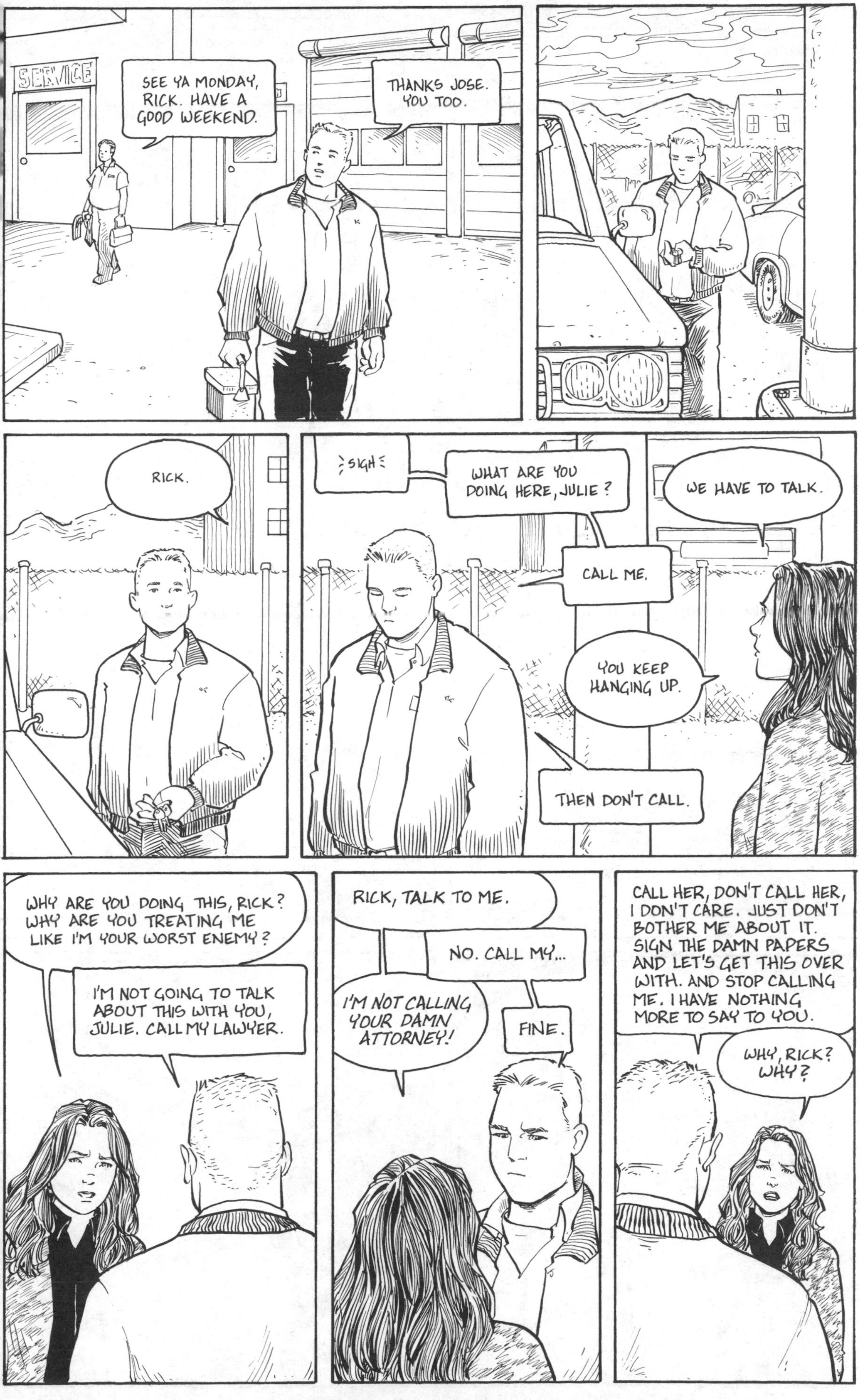
SERVICE
SEE YA MONDAY, RICK. HAVE A GOOD WEEKEND.
THANKS JOSE. YOU TOO.
RICK.
SIGH
WHAT ARE YOU DOING HERE, JULIE?
WE HAVE TO TALK.
CALL ME.
YOU KEEP HANGING UP.
THEN DON'T CALL.
WHY ARE YOU DOING THIS, RICK? WHY ARE YOU TREATING ME LIKE I'M YOUR WORST ENEMY?
I'M NOT GOING TO TALK ABOUT THIS WITH YOU, JULIE. CALL MY LAWYER.
RICK, TALK TO ME.
NO. CALL MY...
I'M NOT CALLING YOUR DAMN ATTORNEY!
FINE.
CALL HER, DON'T CALL HER, I DON'T CARE. JUST DON'T BOTHER ME ABOUT IT. SIGN THE DAMN PAPERS AND LET'S GET THIS OVER WITH. AND STOP CALLING ME. I HAVE NOTHING MORE TO SAY TO YOU.
WHY, RICK? WHY?

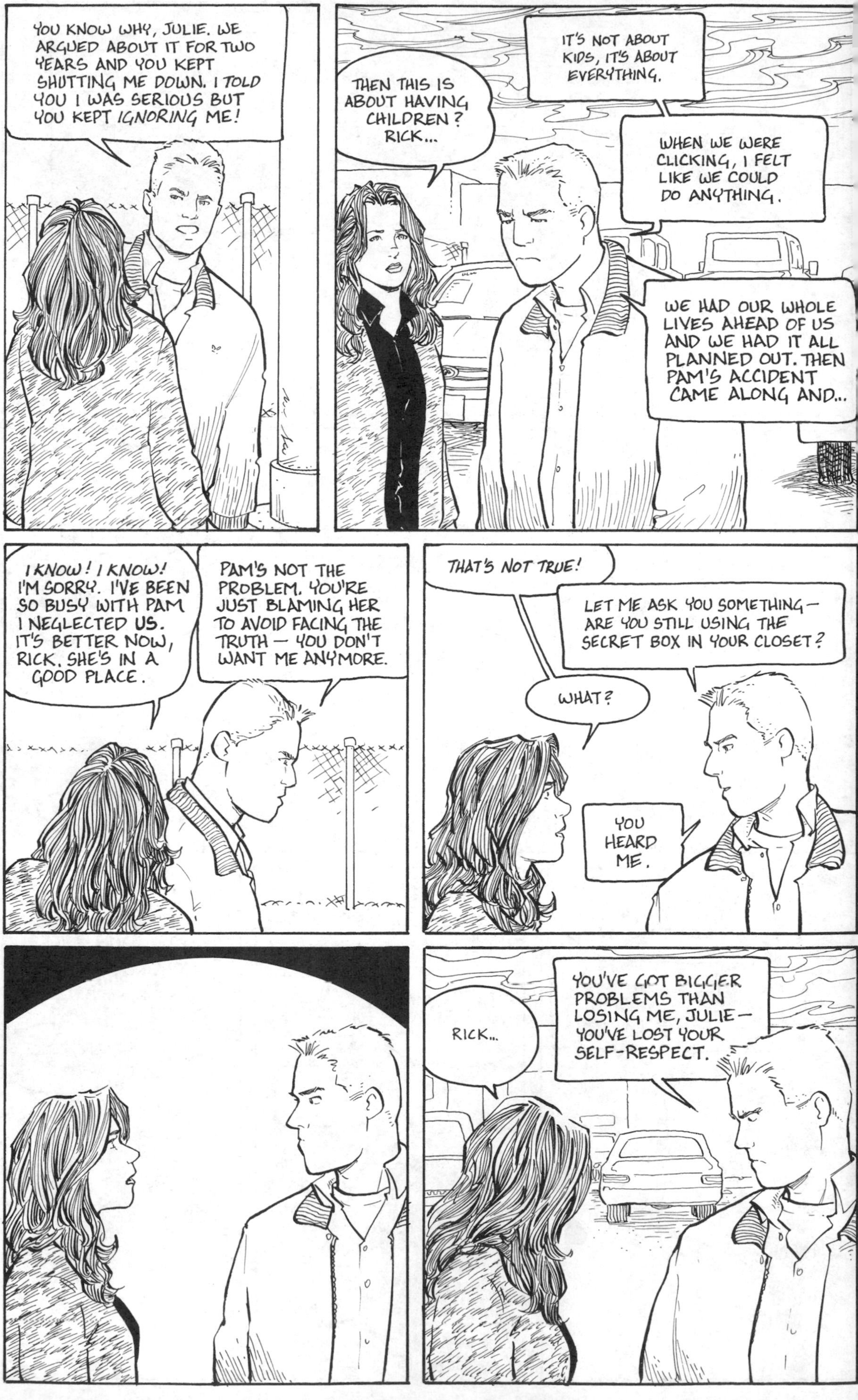
YOU KNOW WHY, JULIE. WE ARGUED ABOUT IT FOR TWO YEARS AND YOU KEPT SHUTTING ME DOWN. I TOLD YOU I WAS SERIOUS BUT YOU KEPT IGNORING ME!
THEN THIS IS ABOUT HAVING CHILDREN? RICK...
IT'S NOT ABOUT KIDS, IT'S ABOUT EVERYTHING.
WHEN WE WERE CLICKING, I FELT LIKE WE COULD DO ANYTHING.
WE HAD OUR WHOLE LIVES AHEAD OF US AND WE HAD IT ALL PLANNED OUT. THEN PAM'S ACCIDENT CAME ALONG AND...
I KNOW! I KNOW! I'M SORRY. I'VE BEEN SO BUSY WITH PAM I NEGLECTED US. IT'S BETTER NOW, RICK. SHE'S IN A GOOD PLACE.
PAM'S NOT THE PROBLEM. YOU'RE JUST BLAMING HER TO AVOID FACING THE TRUTH — YOU DON'T WANT ME ANYMORE.
THAT'S NOT TRUE!
LET ME ASK YOU SOMETHING — ARE YOU STILL USING THE SECRET BOX IN YOUR CLOSET?
WHAT?
YOU HEARD ME.
RICK...
YOU'VE GOT BIGGER PROBLEMS THAN LOSING ME, JULIE — YOU'VE LOST YOUR SELF-RESPECT.

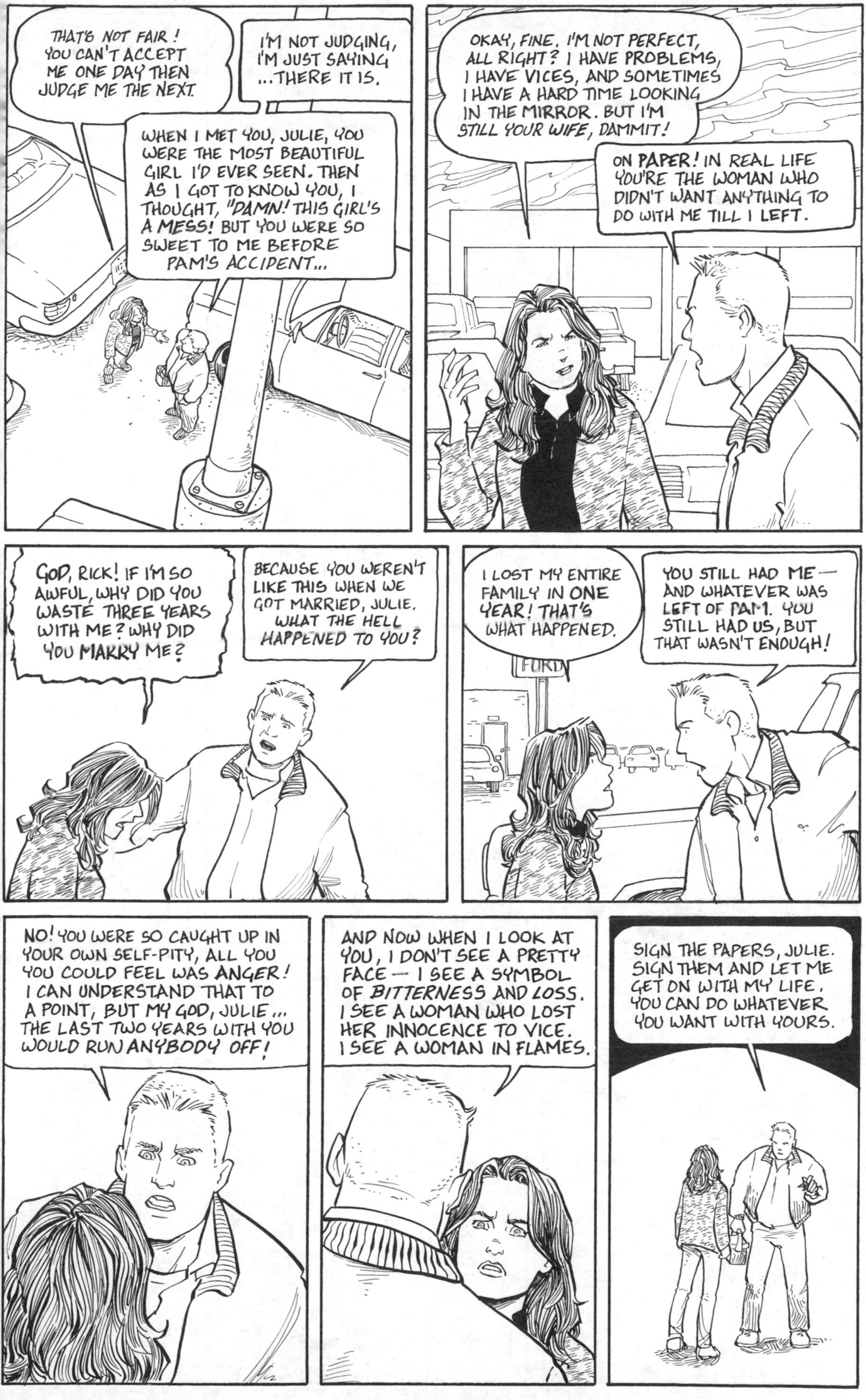
THAT'S NOT FAIR! YOU CAN'T ACCEPT ME ONE DAY THEN JUDGE ME THE NEXT.
I'M NOT JUDGING, I'M JUST SAYING ...THERE IT IS.
WHEN I MET YOU, JULIE, YOU WERE THE MOST BEAUTIFUL GIRL I'D EVER SEEN. THEN AS I GOT TO KNOW YOU, I THOUGHT, "DAMN! THIS GIRL'S A MESS! BUT YOU WERE SO SWEET TO ME BEFORE PAM'S ACCIDENT...
OKAY, FINE. I'M NOT PERFECT, ALL RIGHT? I HAVE PROBLEMS, I HAVE VICES, AND SOMETIMES I HAVE A HARD TIME LOOKING IN THE MIRROR. BUT I'M STILL YOUR WIFE, DAMMIT!
ON PAPER! IN REAL LIFE YOU'RE THE WOMAN WHO DIDN'T WANT ANYTHING TO DO WITH ME TILL I LEFT.
GOD, RICK! IF I'M SO AWFUL, WHY DID YOU WASTE THREE YEARS WITH ME? WHY DID YOU MARRY ME?
BECAUSE YOU WEREN'T LIKE THIS WHEN WE GOT MARRIED, JULIE. WHAT THE HELL HAPPENED TO YOU?
I LOST MY ENTIRE FAMILY IN ONE YEAR! THAT'S WHAT HAPPENED.
FORD
YOU STILL HAD ME — AND WHATEVER WAS LEFT OF PAM. YOU STILL HAD US, BUT THAT WASN'T ENOUGH!
NO! YOU WERE SO CAUGHT UP IN YOUR OWN SELF-PITY, ALL YOU YOU COULD FEEL WAS ANGER! I CAN UNDERSTAND THAT TO A POINT, BUT MY GOD, JULIE... THE LAST TWO YEARS WITH YOU WOULD RUN ANYBODY OFF!
AND NOW WHEN I LOOK AT YOU, I DON'T SEE A PRETTY FACE — I SEE A SYMBOL OF BITTERNESS AND LOSS. I SEE A WOMAN WHO LOST HER INNOCENCE TO VICE. I SEE A WOMAN IN FLAMES.
SIGN THE PAPERS, JULIE. SIGN THEM AND LET ME GET ON WITH MY LIFE. YOU CAN DO WHATEVER YOU WANT WITH YOURS.

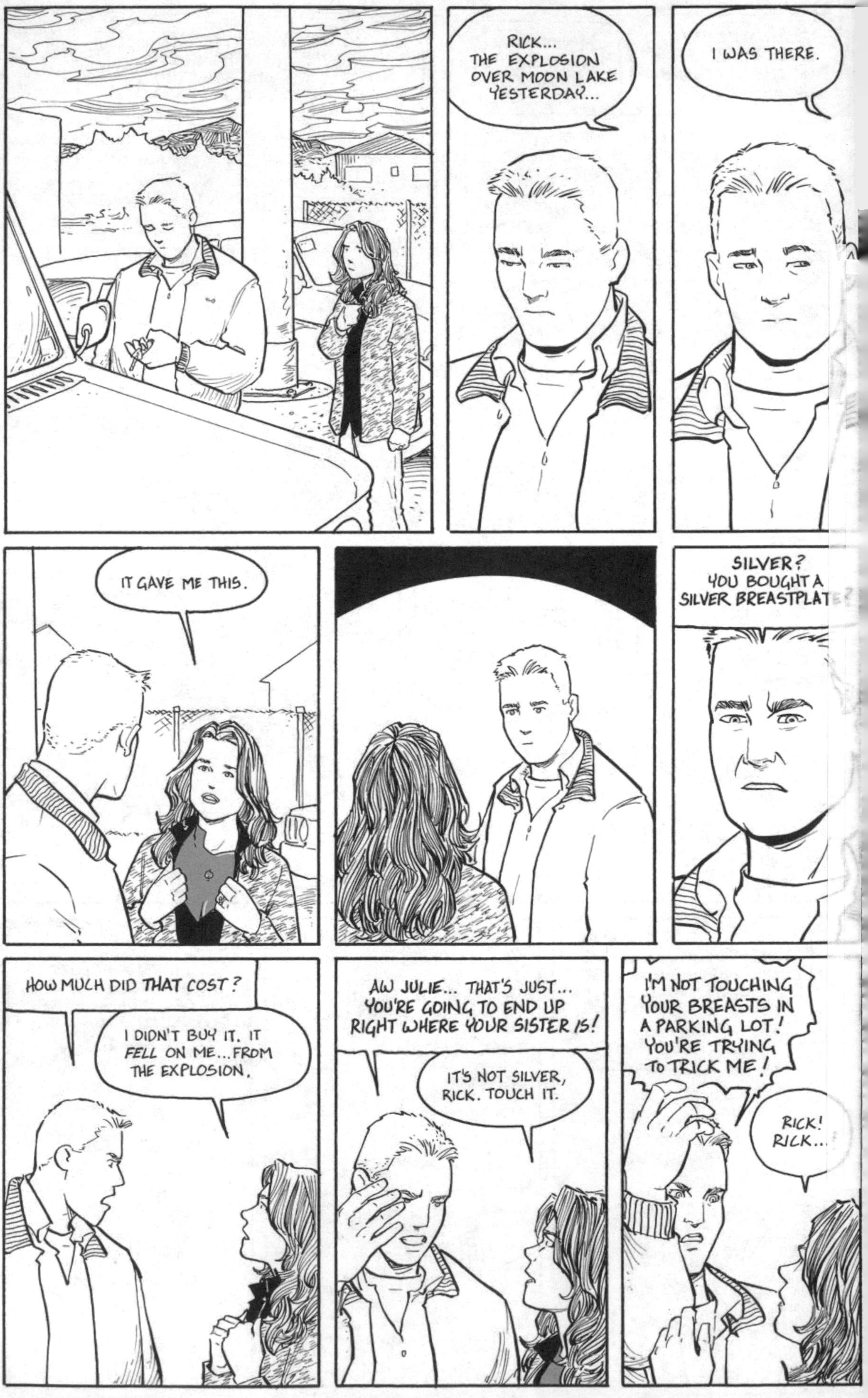
RICK... THE EXPLOSION OVER MOON LAKE YESTERDAY...
I WAS THERE.
IT GAVE ME THIS.
SILVER? YOU BOUGHT A SILVER BREASTPLAT
HOW MUCH DID THAT COST?
I DIDN'T BUY IT. IT FELL ON ME...FROM THE EXPLOSION.
AW JULIE... THAT'S JUST... YOU'RE GOING TO END UP RIGHT WHERE YOUR SISTER IS!
IT'S NOT SILVER, RICK. TOUCH IT.
I'M NOT TOUCHING YOUR BREASTS IN A PARKING LOT! YOU'RE TRYING TO TRICK ME!
RICK! RICK...

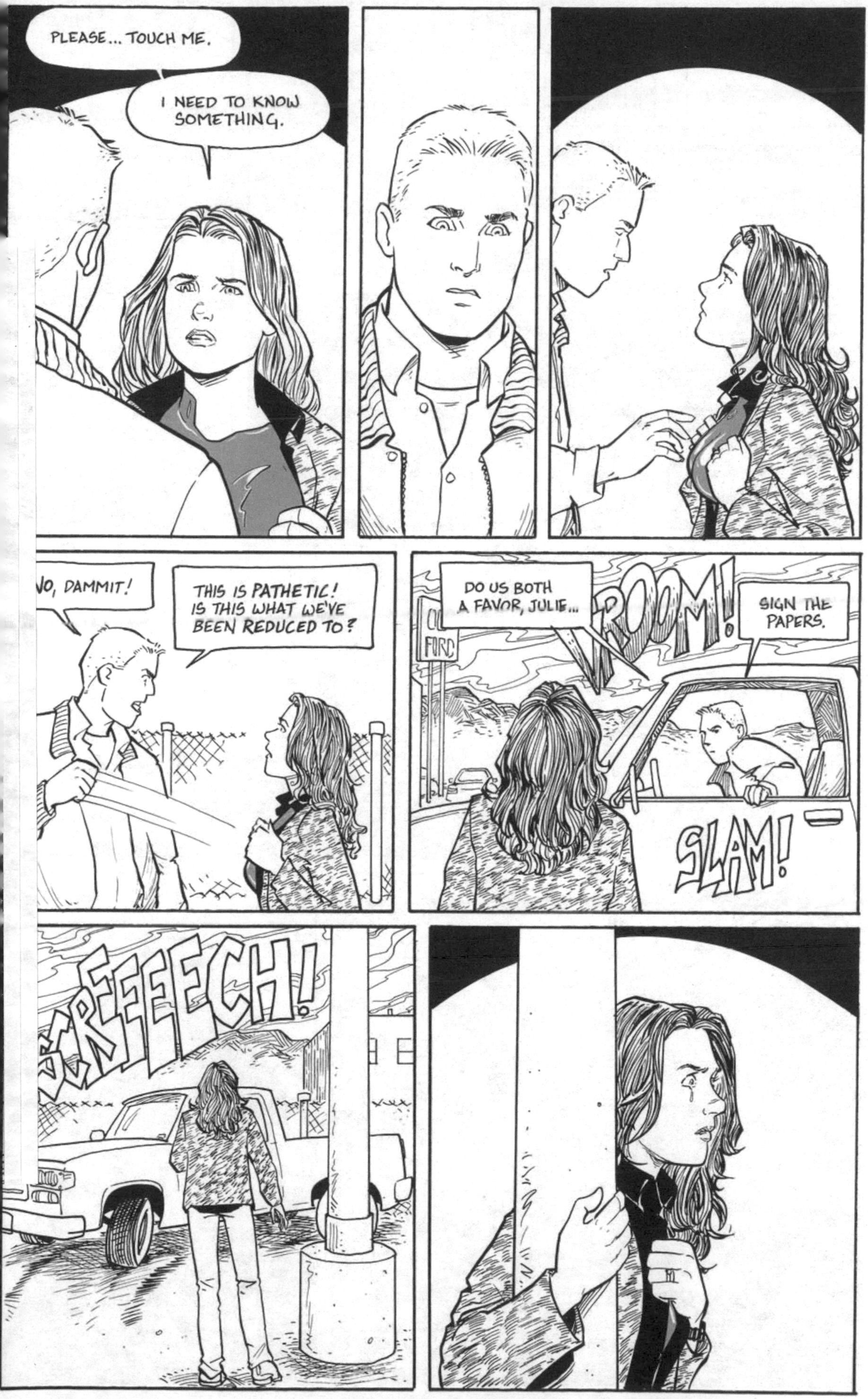
PLEASE... TOUCH ME.
I NEED TO KNOW SOMETHING.
NO, DAMMIT!
THIS IS PATHETIC! IS THIS WHAT WE'VE BEEN REDUCED TO?
DO US BOTH A FAVOR, JULIE...
VROOM!
SIGN THE PAPERS.
SLAM!
SCREEEECH!

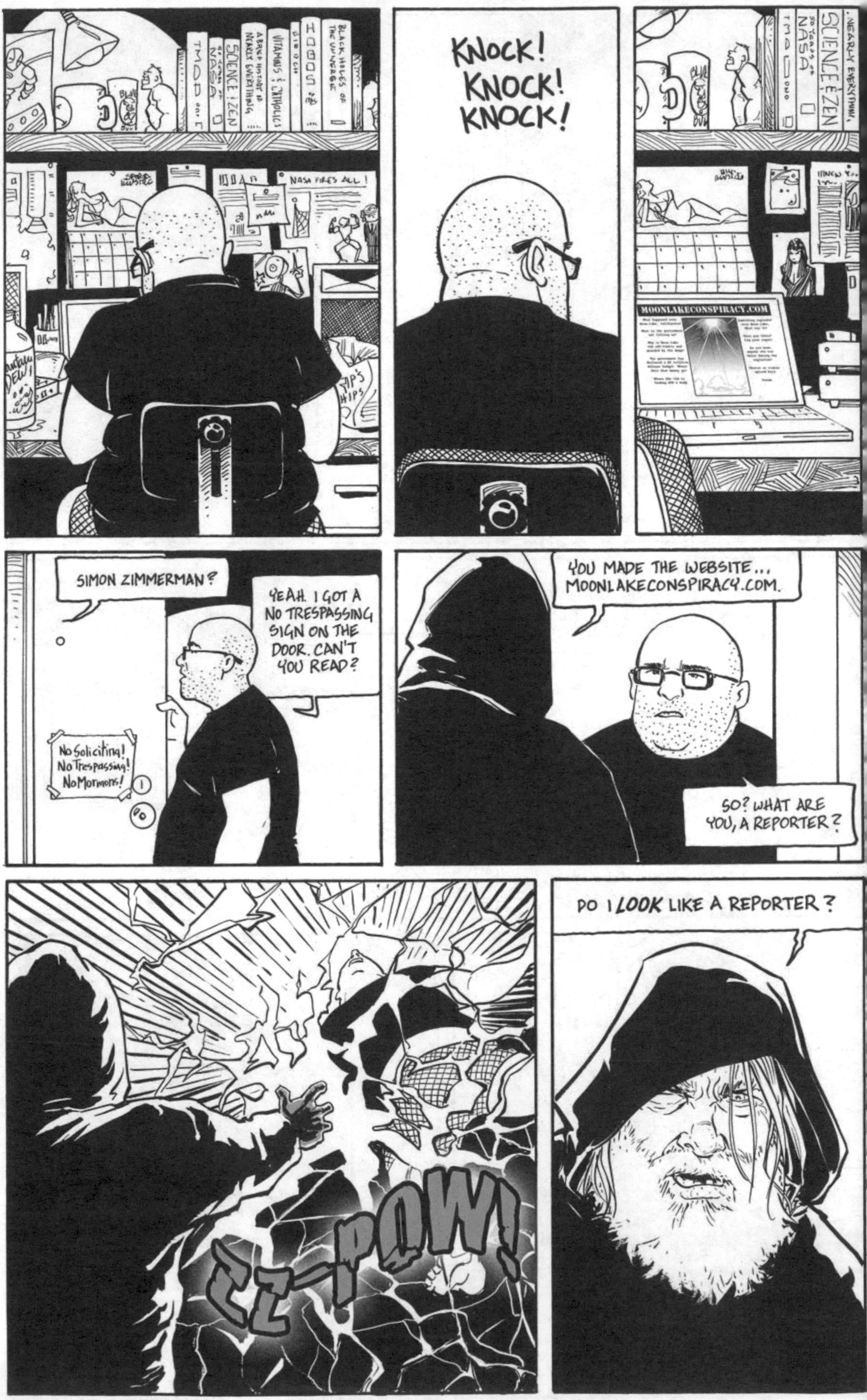
KNOCK! KNOCK! KNOCK!
MOONLAKECONSPIRACY.COM
SIMON ZIMMERMAN?
YEAH. I GOT A NO TRESPASSING SIGN ON THE DOOR. CAN'T YOU READ?
No Soliciting! No Trespassing! No Mormons!
YOU MADE THE WEBSITE... MOONLAKECONSPIRACY.COM.
SO? WHAT ARE YOU, A REPORTER?
ZZ-POW!
DO I LOOK LIKE A REPORTER?

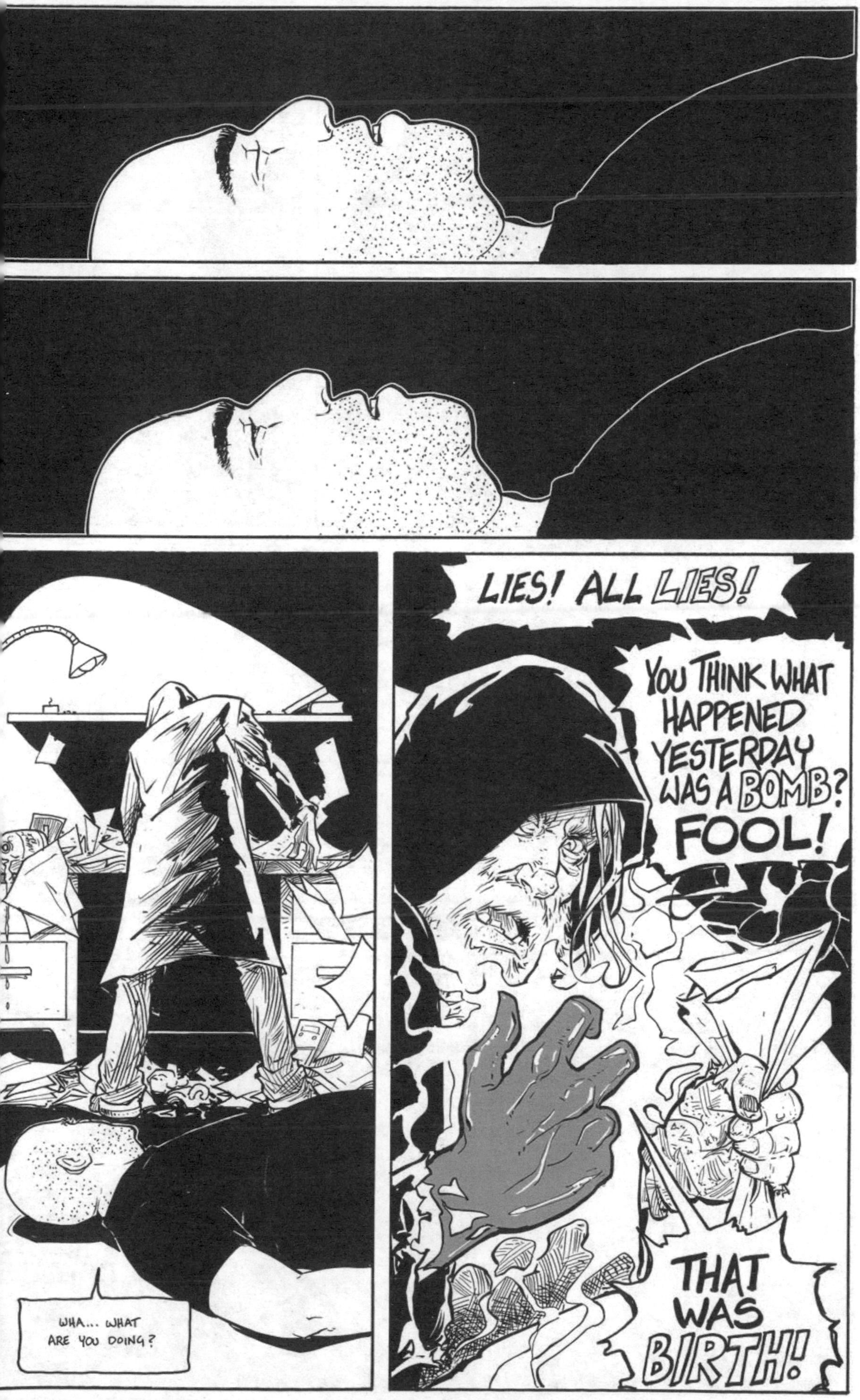
WHA... WHAT ARE YOU DOING?
LIES! ALL LIES!
YOU THINK WHAT HAPPENED YESTERDAY WAS A BOMB? FOOL!
THAT WAS BIRTH!

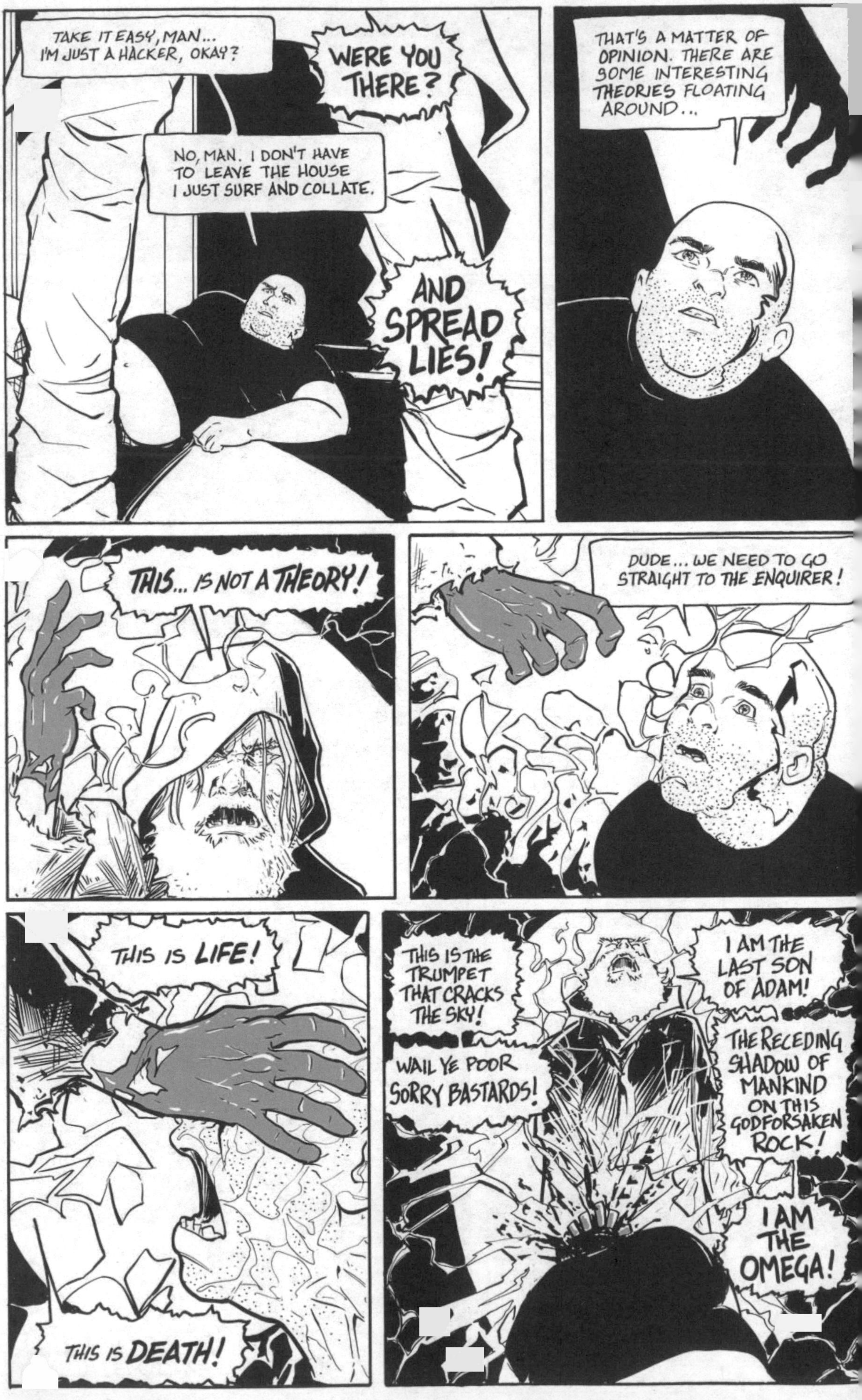
TAKE IT EASY, MAN... I'M JUST A HACKER, OKAY?
WERE YOU THERE?
NO, MAN. I DON'T HAVE TO LEAVE THE HOUSE I JUST SURF AND COLLATE.
AND SPREAD LIES!
THAT'S A MATTER OF OPINION. THERE ARE SOME INTERESTING THEORIES FLOATING AROUND...
THIS... IS NOT A THEORY!
DUDE... WE NEED TO GO STRAIGHT TO THE ENQUIRER!
THIS IS LIFE!
THIS IS DEATH!
THIS IS THE TRUMPET THAT CRACKS THE SKY!
WAIL YE POOR SORRY BASTARDS!
I AM THE LAST SON OF ADAM!
THE RECEDING SHADOW OF MANKIND ON THIS GODFORSAKEN ROCK!
I AM THE OMEGA!

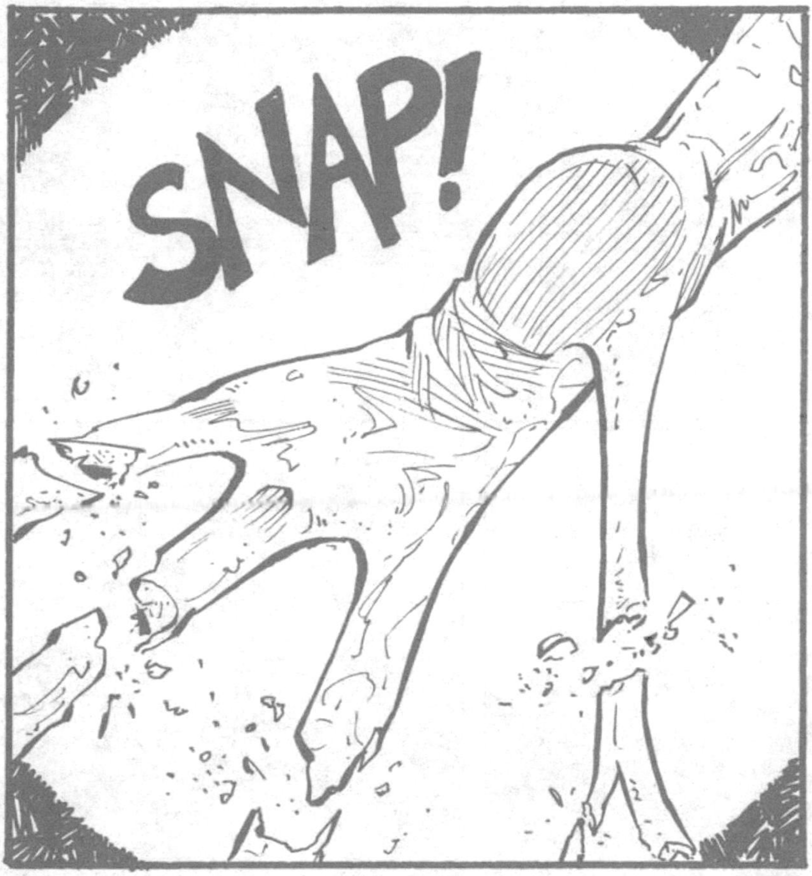
SNAP!

A human being is a part of a whole, called by us —universe—, a part limited in time and space. He experiences himself, his thoughts and feelings as something separated from the rest... a kind of optical delusion of his consciousness. This delusion is a kind of prison for us, restricting us to our personal desires and to affection for a few persons nearest to us. Our task must be to free ourselves from this prison by widening our circle of compassion to embrace all living creatures and the whole of nature in its beauty.

—Albert Einstein

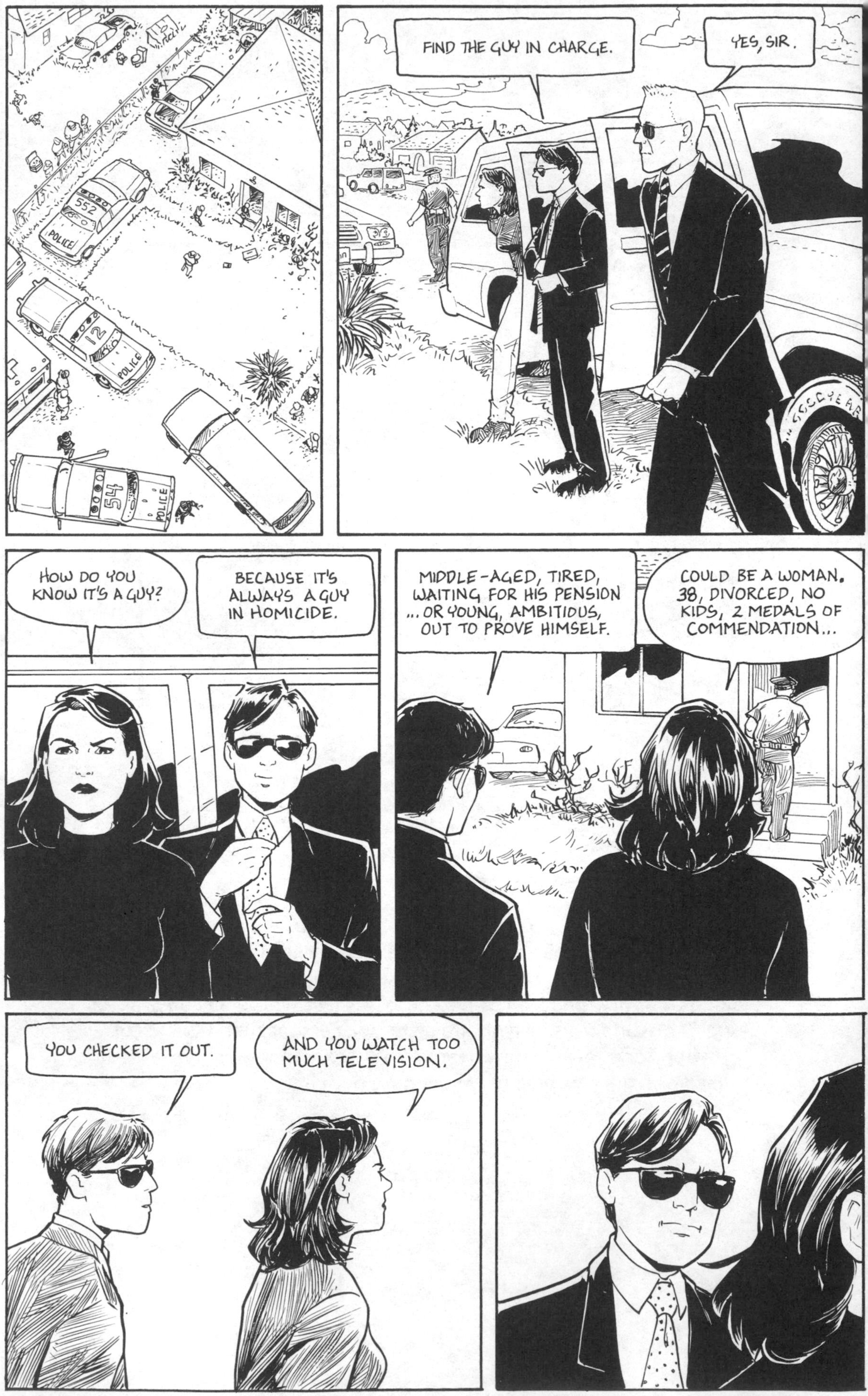

FIND THE GUY IN CHARGE.
YES, SIR.
HOW DO YOU KNOW IT'S A GUY?
BECAUSE IT'S ALWAYS A GUY IN HOMICIDE.
MIDDLE-AGED, TIRED, WAITING FOR HIS PENSION ...OR YOUNG, AMBITIOUS, OUT TO PROVE HIMSELF.
COULD BE A WOMAN. 38, DIVORCED, NO KIDS, 2 MEDALS OF COMMENDATION...
YOU CHECKED IT OUT.
AND YOU WATCH TOO MUCH TELEVISION.

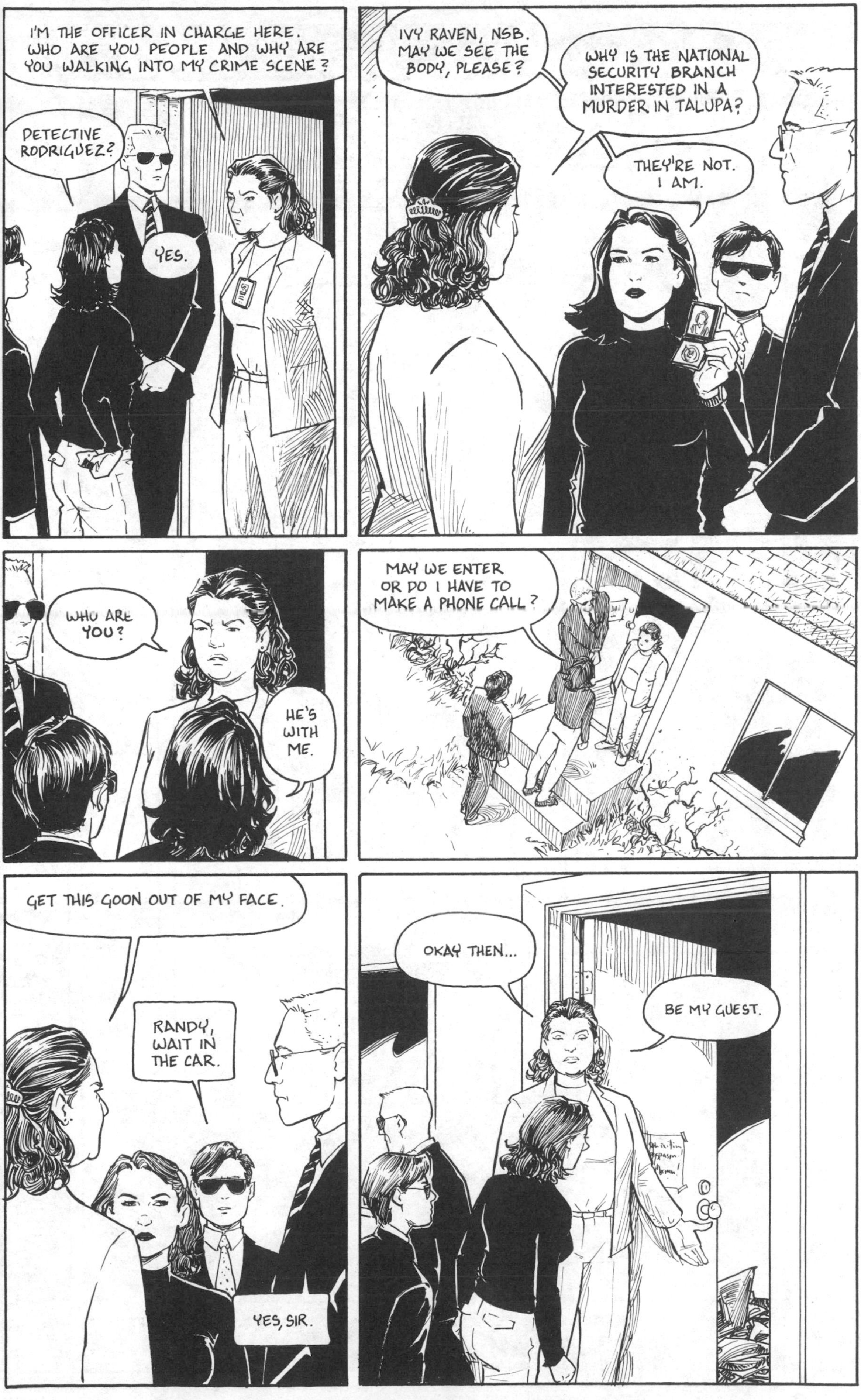
I'M THE OFFICER IN CHARGE HERE. WHO ARE YOU PEOPLE AND WHY ARE YOU WALKING INTO MY CRIME SCENE?
DETECTIVE RODRIGUEZ?
YES.
IVY RAVEN, NSB. MAY WE SEE THE BODY, PLEASE?
WHY IS THE NATIONAL SECURITY BRANCH INTERESTED IN A MURDER IN TALUPA?
THEY'RE NOT. I AM.
WHO ARE YOU?
HE'S WITH ME.
MAY WE ENTER OR DO I HAVE TO MAKE A PHONE CALL?
GET THIS GOON OUT OF MY FACE.
RANDY, WAIT IN THE CAR.
YES, SIR.
OKAY THEN...
BE MY GUEST.

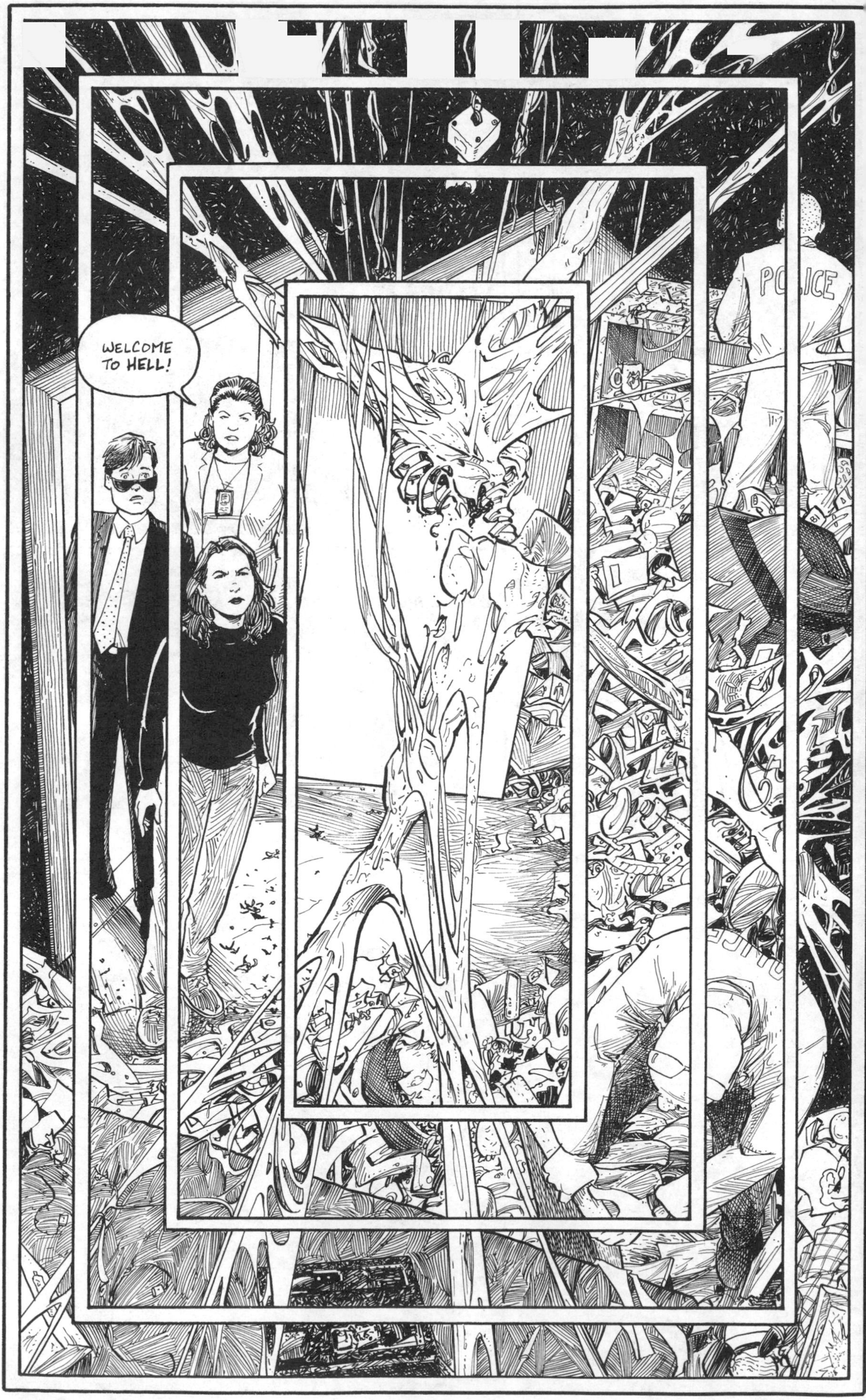
WELCOME TO HELL!
POLICE

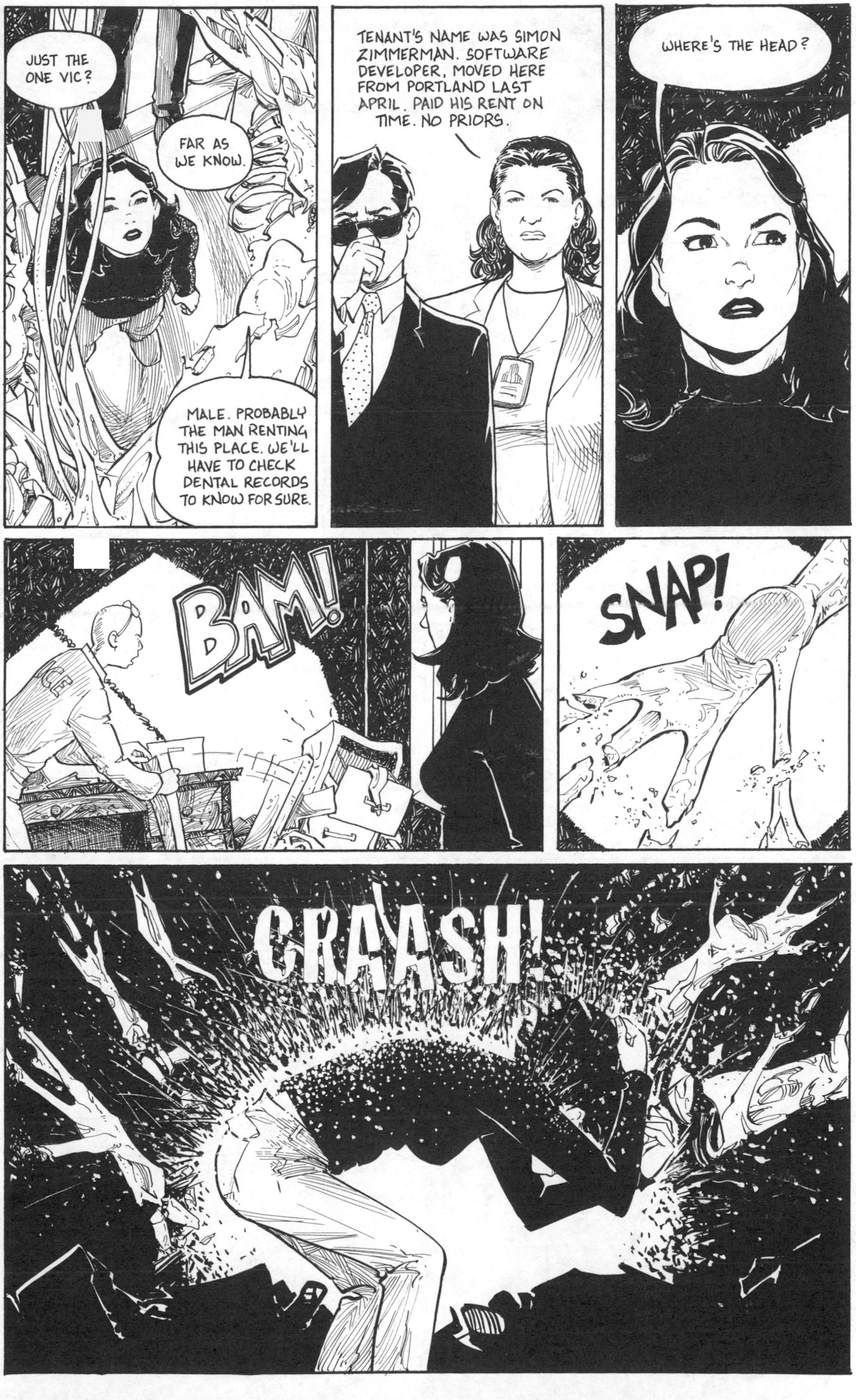
JUST THE ONE VIC?
FAR AS WE KNOW.
MALE. PROBABLY THE MAN RENTING THIS PLACE. WE'LL HAVE TO CHECK DENTAL RECORDS TO KNOW FOR SURE.
TENANT'S NAME WAS SIMON ZIMMERMAN. SOFTWARE DEVELOPER, MOVED HERE FROM PORTLAND LAST APRIL. PAID HIS RENT ON TIME. NO PRIORS.
WHERE'S THE HEAD?
BAM!
SNAP!
CRAASH!

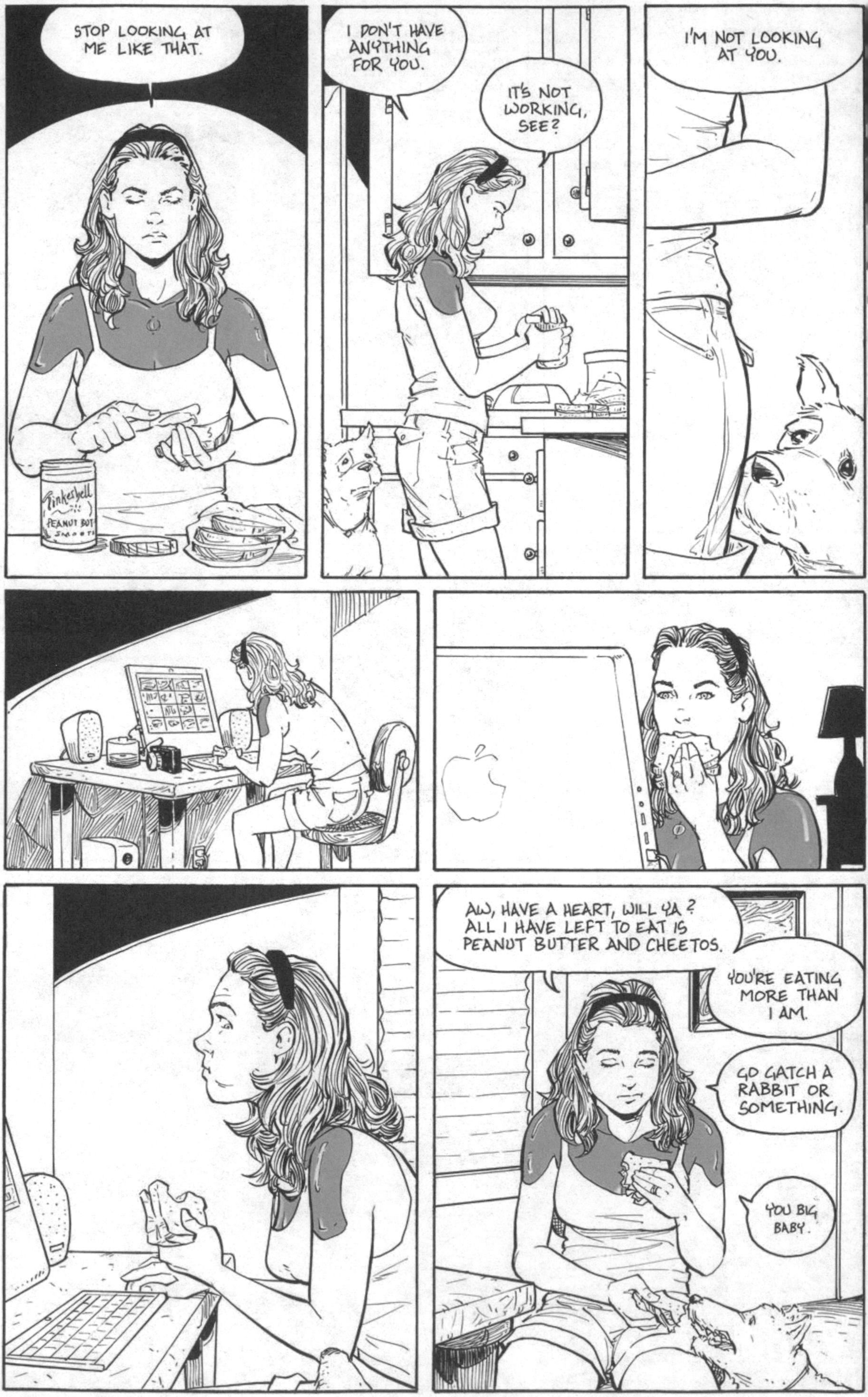
STOP LOOKING AT ME LIKE THAT.
I DON'T HAVE ANYTHING FOR YOU.
IT'S NOT WORKING, SEE?
I'M NOT LOOKING AT YOU.
AW, HAVE A HEART, WILL YA? ALL I HAVE LEFT TO EAT IS PEANUT BUTTER AND CHEETOS.
YOU'RE EATING MORE THAN I AM.
GO CATCH A RABBIT OR SOMETHING.
YOU BIG BABY.

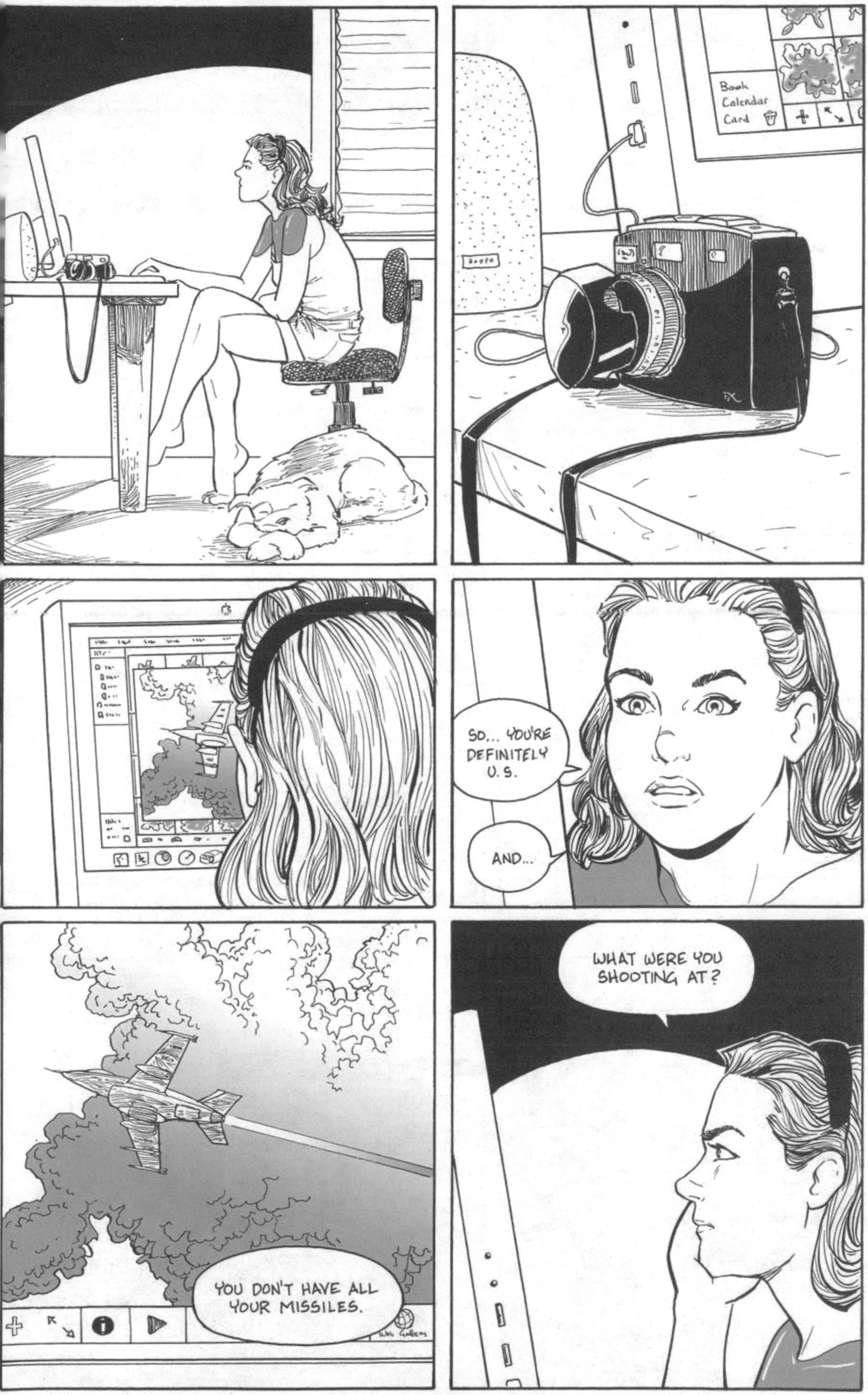
Book
Calendar
Card
SO... YOU'RE DEFINITELY U.S.
AND...
YOU DON'T HAVE ALL YOUR MISSILES.
WHAT WERE YOU SHOOTING AT?

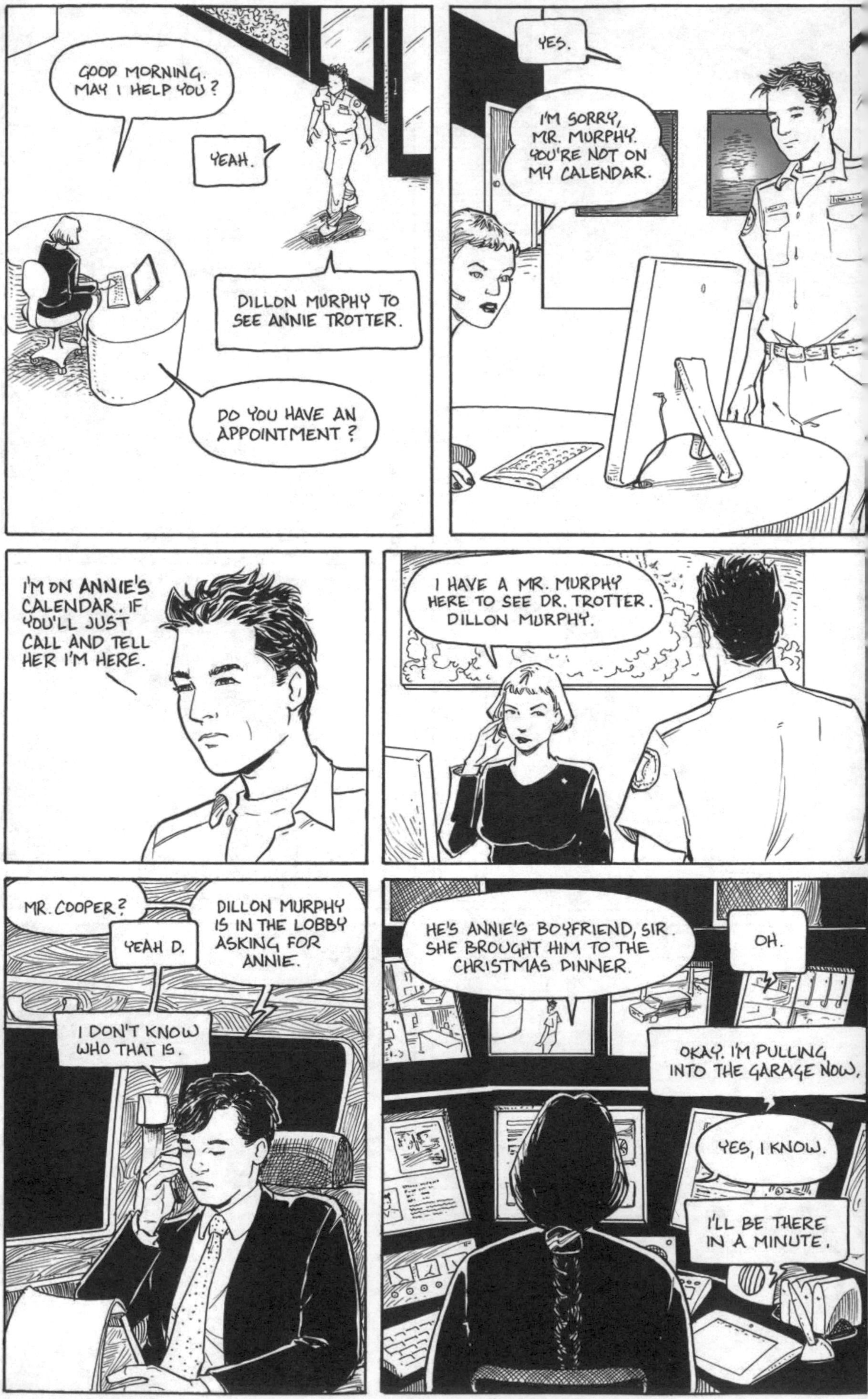
GOOD MORNING. MAY I HELP YOU?
YEAH.
DILLON MURPHY TO SEE ANNIE TROTTER.
DO YOU HAVE AN APPOINTMENT?
YES.
I'M SORRY, MR. MURPHY. YOU'RE NOT ON MY CALENDAR.
I'M ON ANNIE'S CALENDAR. IF YOU'LL JUST CALL AND TELL HER I'M HERE.
I HAVE A MR. MURPHY HERE TO SEE DR. TROTTER. DILLON MURPHY.
MR. COOPER?
YEAH D.
DILLON MURPHY IS IN THE LOBBY ASKING FOR ANNIE.
I DON'T KNOW WHO THAT IS.
HE'S ANNIE'S BOYFRIEND, SIR. SHE BROUGHT HIM TO THE CHRISTMAS DINNER.
OH.
OKAY. I'M PULLING INTO THE GARAGE NOW.
YES, I KNOW.
I'LL BE THERE IN A MINUTE.

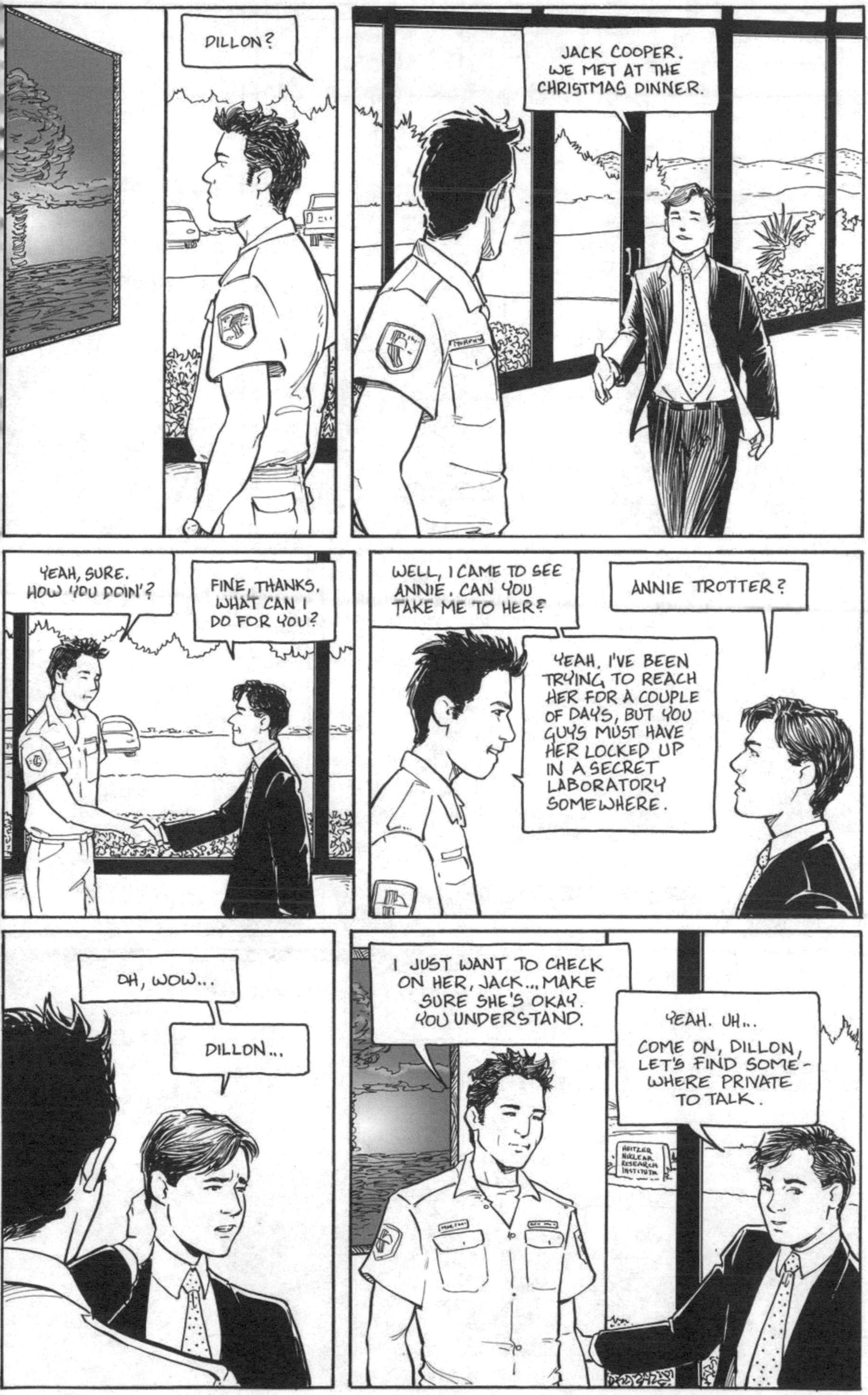
DILLON?
JACK COOPER. WE MET AT THE CHRISTMAS DINNER.
YEAH, SURE. HOW YOU DOIN'?
FINE, THANKS. WHAT CAN I DO FOR YOU?
WELL, I CAME TO SEE ANNIE. CAN YOU TAKE ME TO HER?
ANNIE TROTTER?
YEAH. I'VE BEEN TRYING TO REACH HER FOR A COUPLE OF DAYS, BUT YOU GUYS MUST HAVE HER LOCKED UP IN A SECRET LABORATORY SOMEWHERE.
OH, WOW...
DILLON...
I JUST WANT TO CHECK ON HER, JACK... MAKE SURE SHE'S OKAY. YOU UNDERSTAND.
YEAH. UH..
COME ON, DILLON, LET'S FIND SOME-WHERE PRIVATE TO TALK.

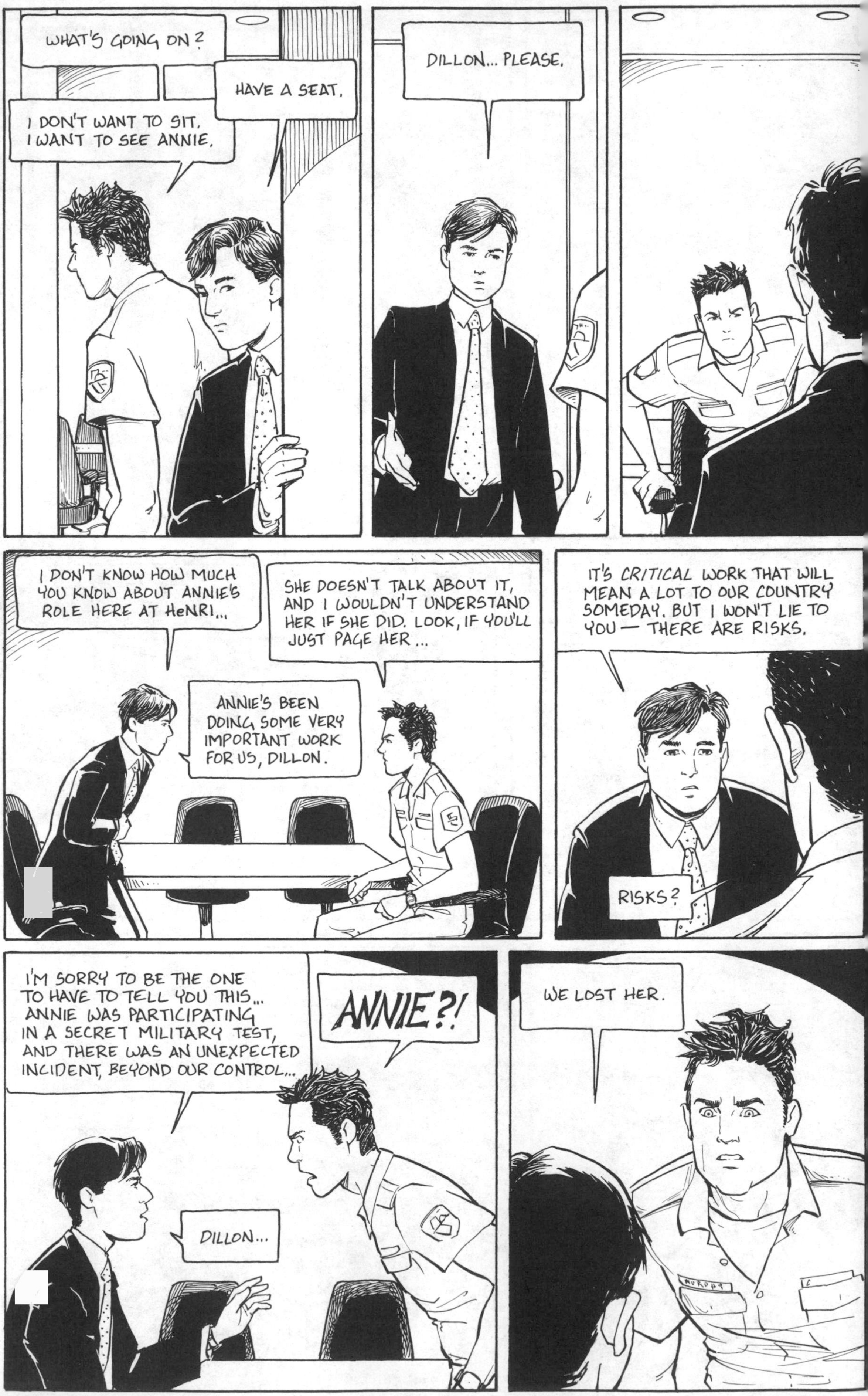
WHAT'S GOING ON?
HAVE A SEAT.
I DON'T WANT TO SIT. I WANT TO SEE ANNIE.
DILLON... PLEASE.
I DON'T KNOW HOW MUCH YOU KNOW ABOUT ANNIE'S ROLE HERE AT HeNRI...
SHE DOESN'T TALK ABOUT IT, AND I WOULDN'T UNDERSTAND HER IF SHE DID. LOOK, IF YOU'LL JUST PAGE HER...
ANNIE'S BEEN DOING SOME VERY IMPORTANT WORK FOR US, DILLON.
IT'S *CRITICAL* WORK THAT WILL MEAN A LOT TO OUR COUNTRY SOMEDAY. BUT I WON'T LIE TO YOU — THERE ARE RISKS.
RISKS?
I'M SORRY TO BE THE ONE TO HAVE TO TELL YOU THIS... ANNIE WAS PARTICIPATING IN A SECRET MILITARY TEST, AND THERE WAS AN UNEXPECTED INCIDENT, BEYOND OUR CONTROL...
ANNIE?!
DILLON...
WE LOST HER.

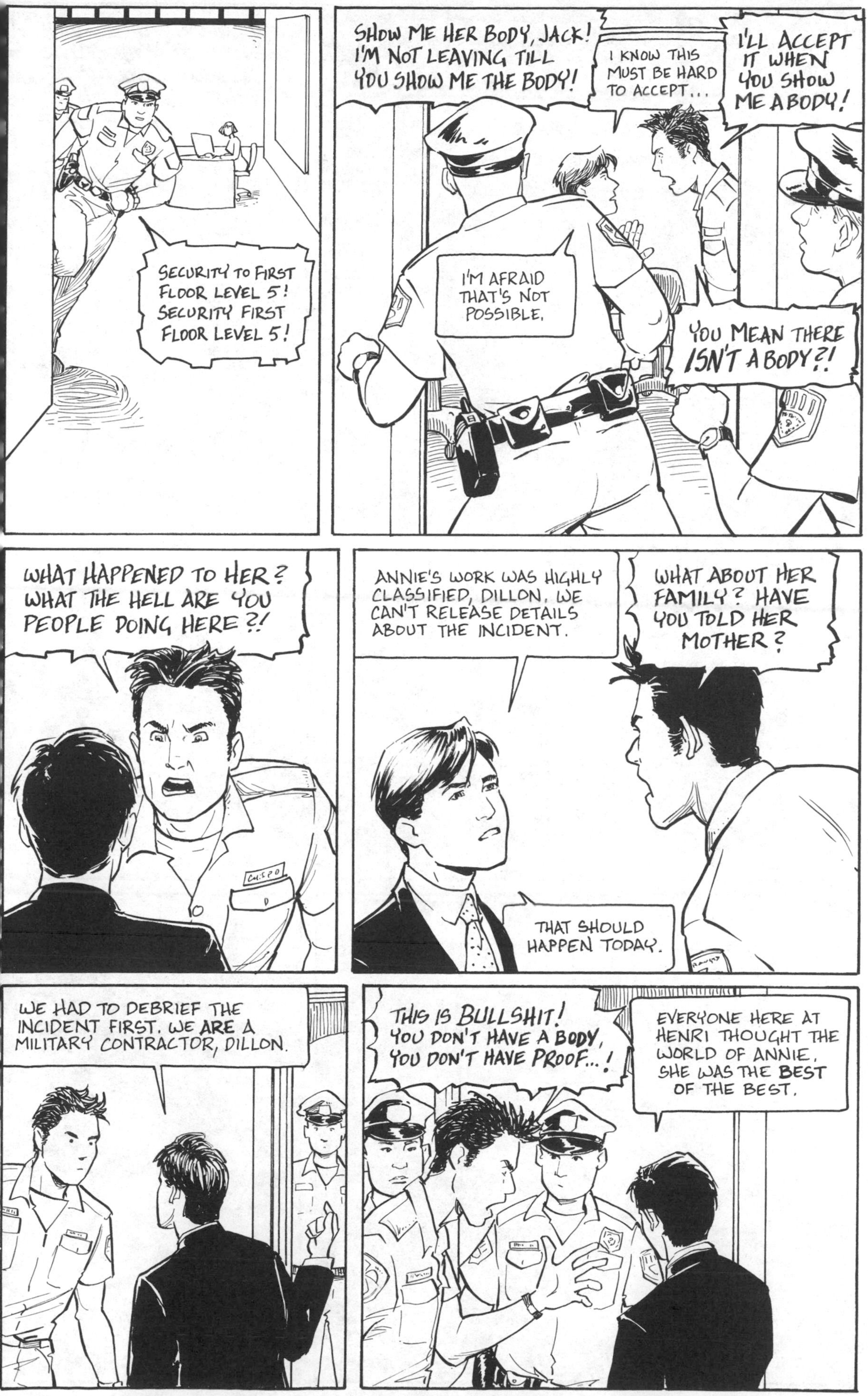
SECURITY TO FIRST FLOOR LEVEL 5! SECURITY FIRST FLOOR LEVEL 5!
SHOW ME HER BODY, JACK! I'M NOT LEAVING TILL YOU SHOW ME THE BODY!
I KNOW THIS MUST BE HARD TO ACCEPT...
I'LL ACCEPT IT WHEN YOU SHOW ME A BODY!
I'M AFRAID THAT'S NOT POSSIBLE.
YOU MEAN THERE ISN'T A BODY?!
WHAT HAPPENED TO HER? WHAT THE HELL ARE YOU PEOPLE DOING HERE?!
ANNIE'S WORK WAS HIGHLY CLASSIFIED, DILLON. WE CAN'T RELEASE DETAILS ABOUT THE INCIDENT.
WHAT ABOUT HER FAMILY? HAVE YOU TOLD HER MOTHER?
THAT SHOULD HAPPEN TODAY.
WE HAD TO DEBRIEF THE INCIDENT FIRST. WE ARE A MILITARY CONTRACTOR, DILLON.
THIS IS BULLSHIT! YOU DON'T HAVE A BODY, YOU DON'T HAVE PROOF...!
EVERYONE HERE AT HENRI THOUGHT THE WORLD OF ANNIE. SHE WAS THE BEST OF THE BEST.

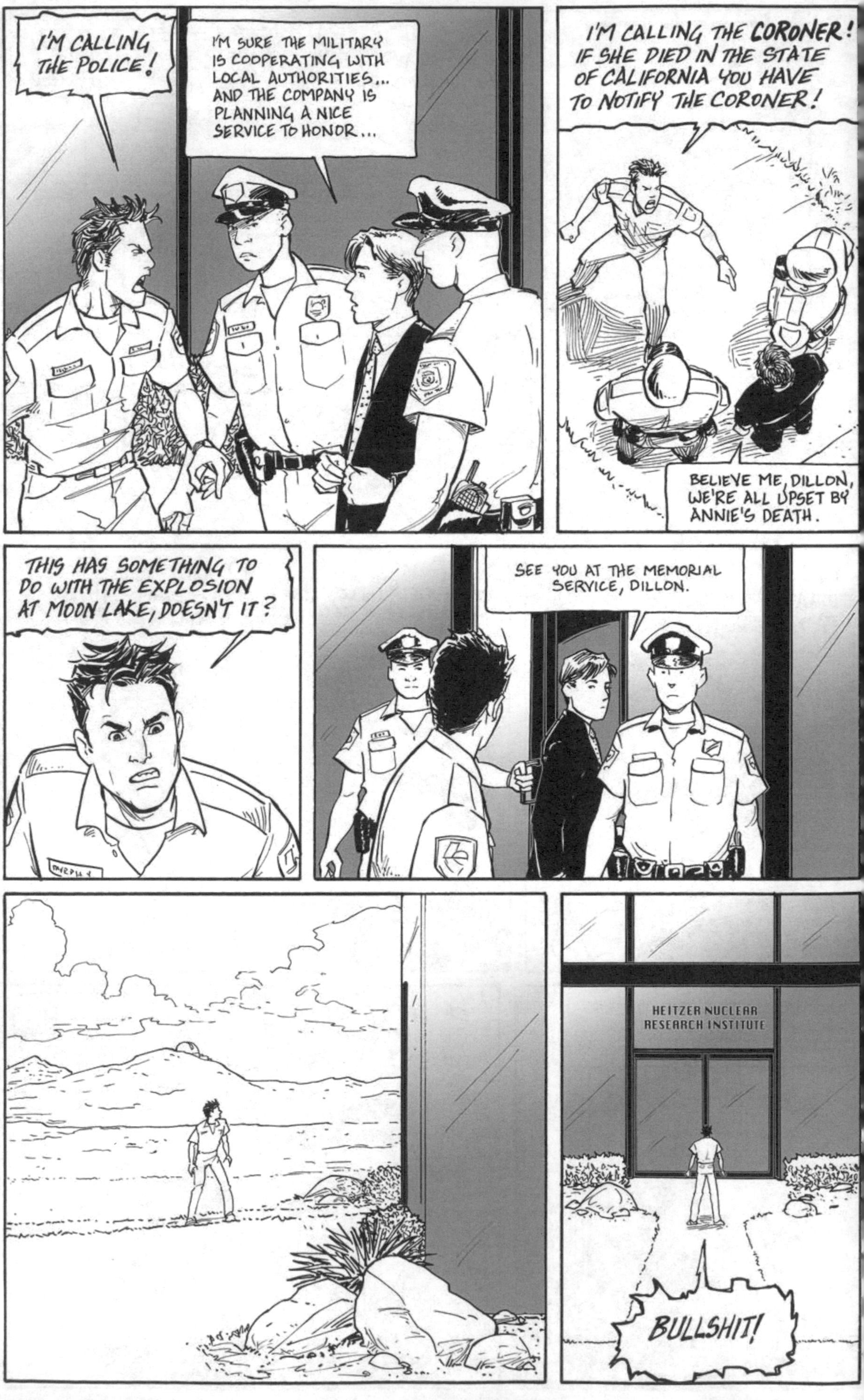

I'M CALLING THE POLICE!
I'M SURE THE MILITARY IS COOPERATING WITH LOCAL AUTHORITIES... AND THE COMPANY IS PLANNING A NICE SERVICE TO HONOR...
I'M CALLING THE CORONER! IF SHE DIED IN THE STATE OF CALIFORNIA YOU HAVE TO NOTIFY THE CORONER!
BELIEVE ME, DILLON, WE'RE ALL UPSET BY ANNIE'S DEATH.
THIS HAS SOMETHING TO DO WITH THE EXPLOSION AT MOON LAKE, DOESN'T IT?
SEE YOU AT THE MEMORIAL SERVICE, DILLON.
HEITZER NUCLEAR RESEARCH INSTITUTE
BULLSHIT!

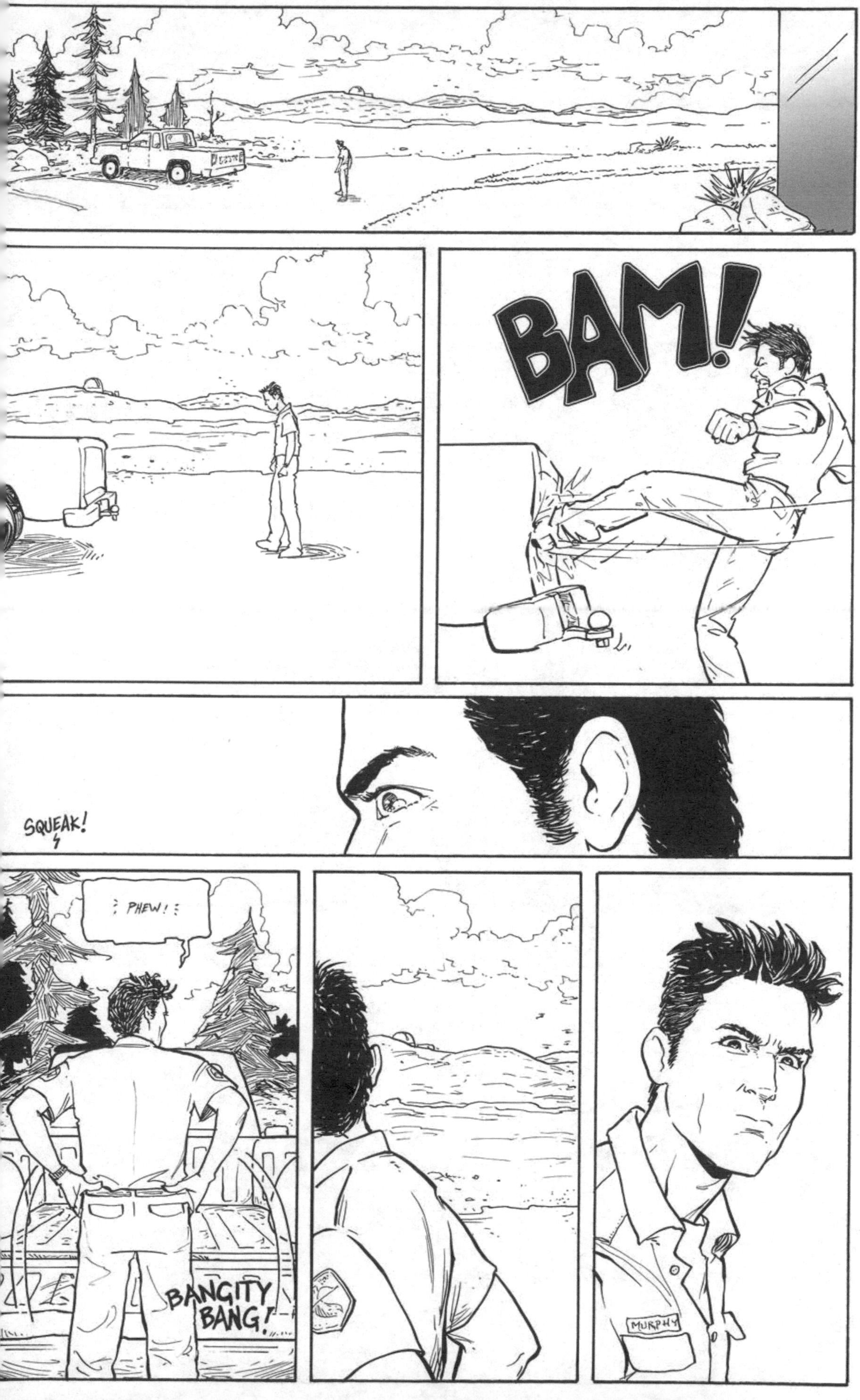
BAM!
SQUEAK!
PHEW!
BANGITY BANG!
MURPHY

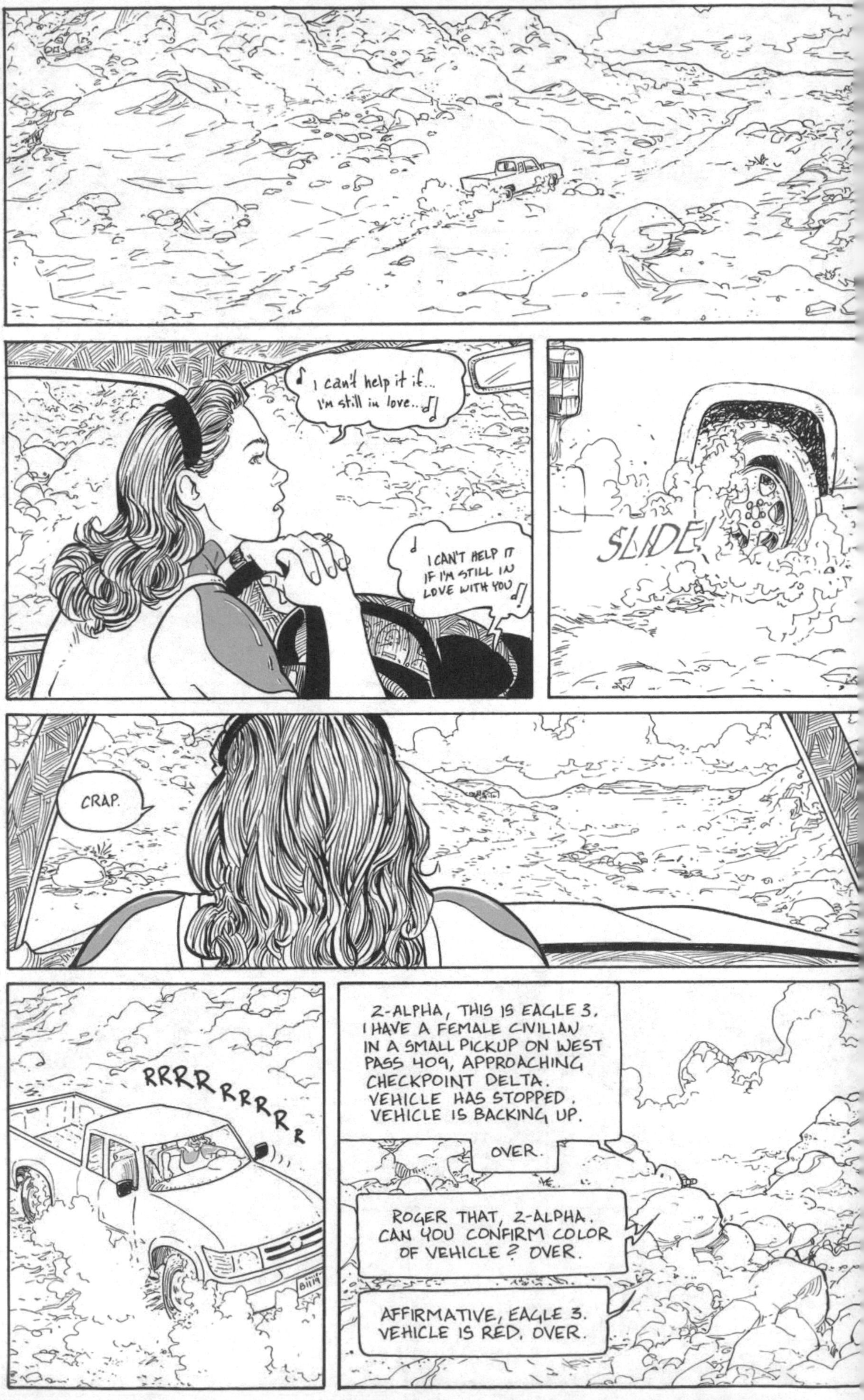
I can't help it if... I'm still in love...
I CAN'T HELP IT IF I'M STILL IN LOVE WITH YOU
SLIDE!
CRAP.
RRRRRRRRR
2-ALPHA, THIS IS EAGLE 3. I HAVE A FEMALE CIVILIAN IN A SMALL PICKUP ON WEST PASS 409, APPROACHING CHECKPOINT DELTA. VEHICLE HAS STOPPED. VEHICLE IS BACKING UP.
OVER.
ROGER THAT, 2-ALPHA. CAN YOU CONFIRM COLOR OF VEHICLE? OVER.
AFFIRMATIVE, EAGLE 3. VEHICLE IS RED. OVER.

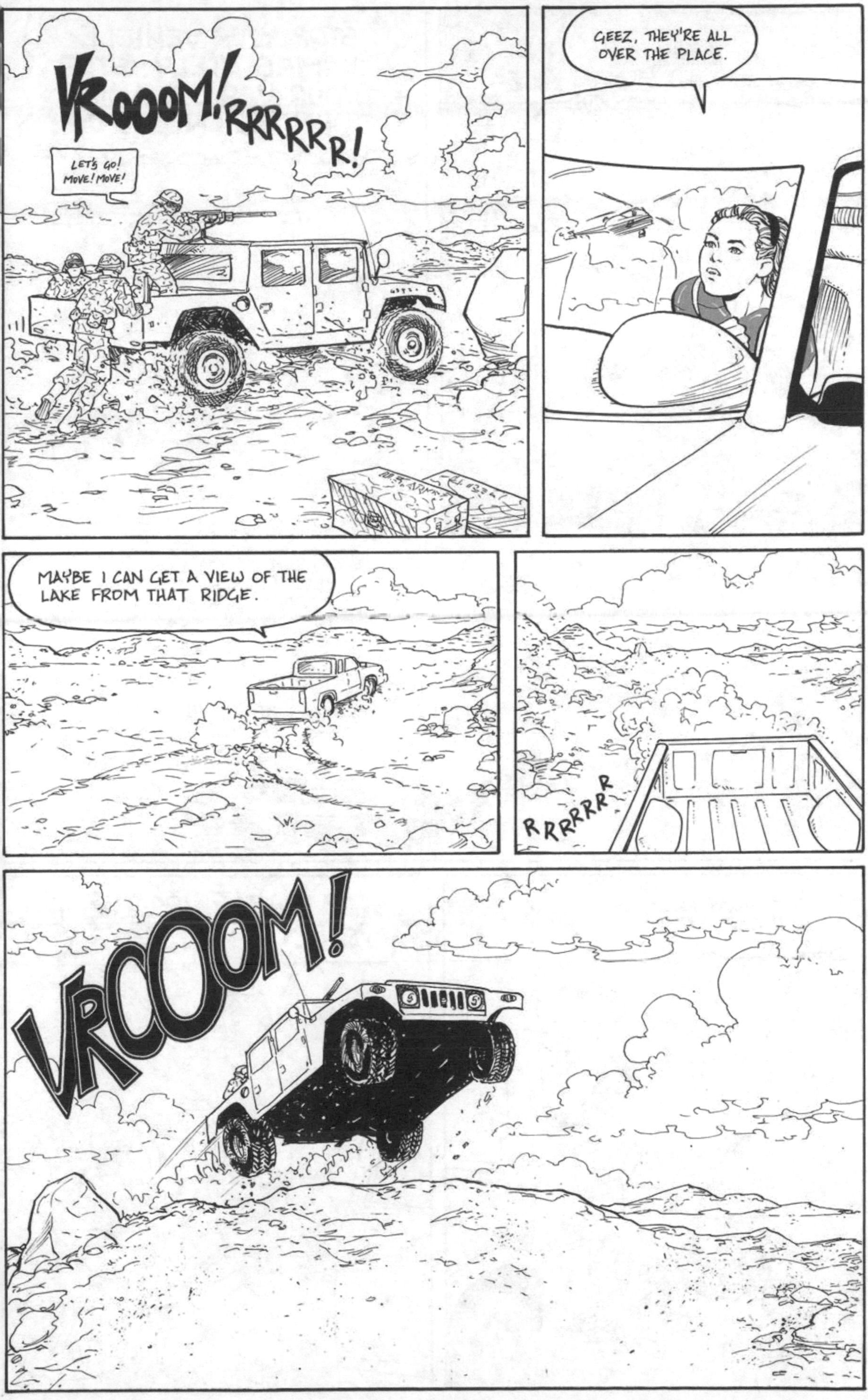
VROOOM! RRRRRRR!
LET'S GO! MOVE! MOVE!
GEEZ, THEY'RE ALL OVER THE PLACE.
MAYBE I CAN GET A VIEW OF THE LAKE FROM THAT RIDGE.
RRRRRRR
VRCOOOM!

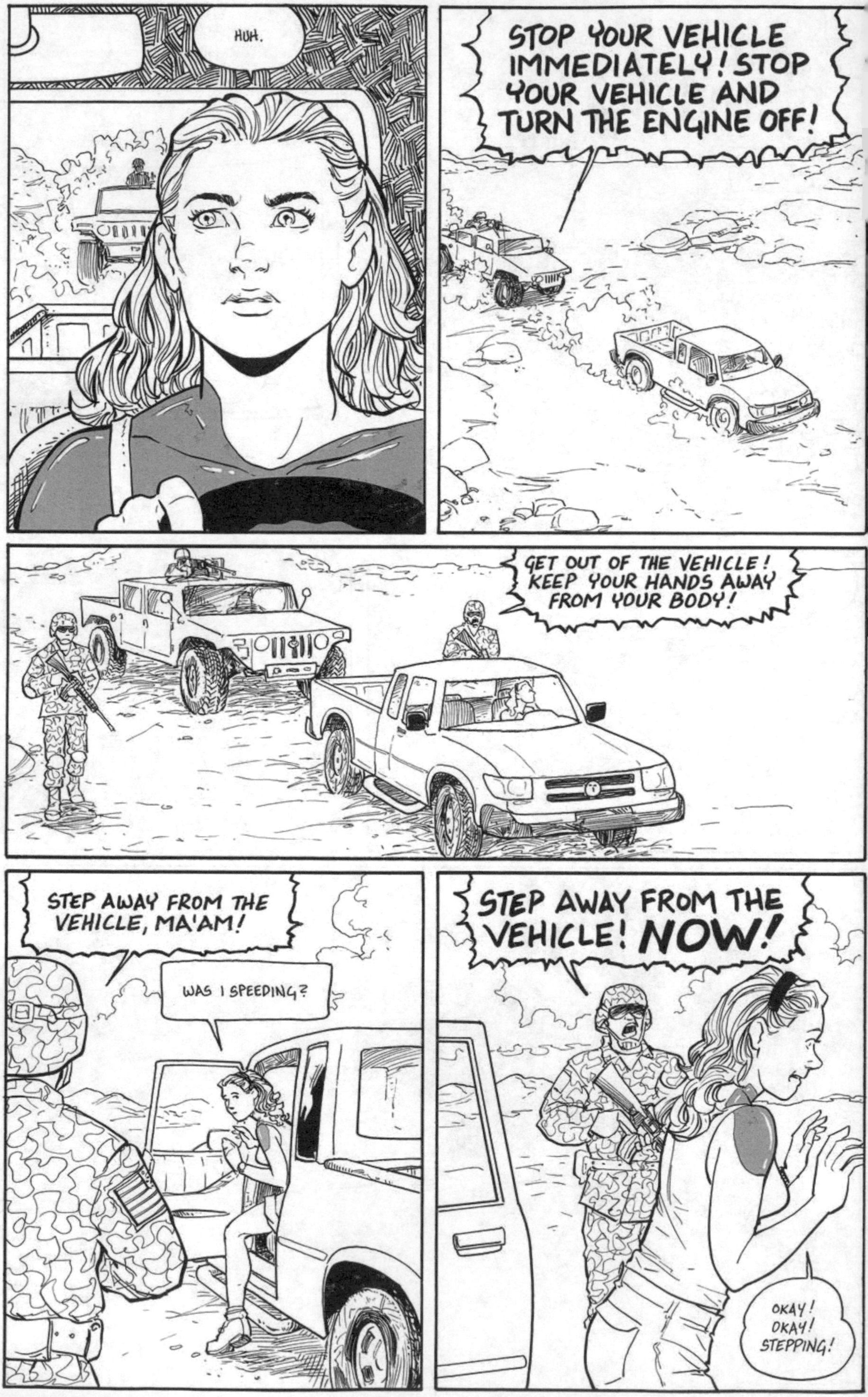
HUH.
STOP YOUR VEHICLE IMMEDIATELY! STOP YOUR VEHICLE AND TURN THE ENGINE OFF!
GET OUT OF THE VEHICLE! KEEP YOUR HANDS AWAY FROM YOUR BODY!
STEP AWAY FROM THE VEHICLE, MA'AM!
WAS I SPEEDING?
STEP AWAY FROM THE VEHICLE! NOW!
OKAY! OKAY! STEPPING!

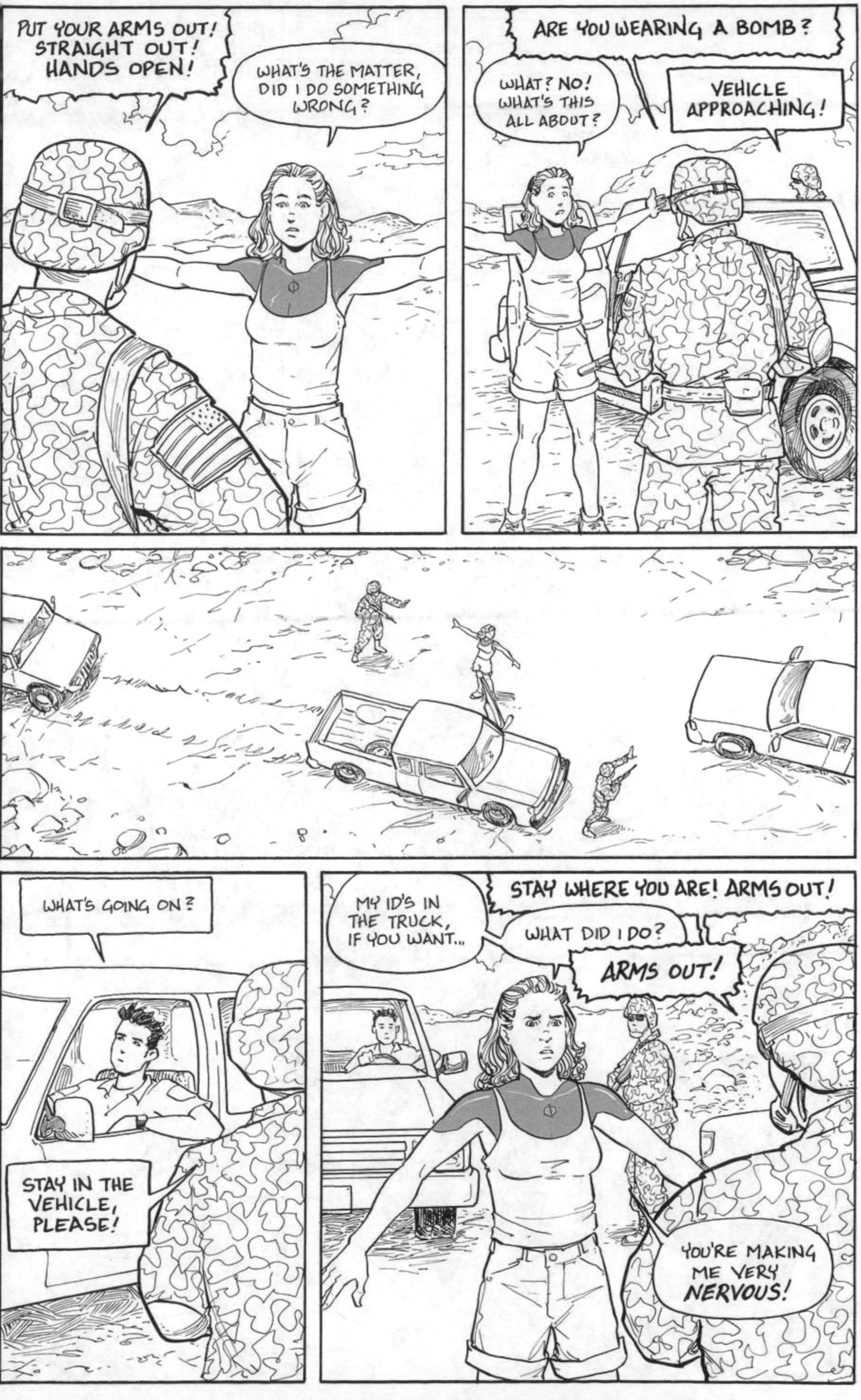
PUT YOUR ARMS OUT! STRAIGHT OUT! HANDS OPEN!
WHAT'S THE MATTER, DID I DO SOMETHING WRONG?
ARE YOU WEARING A BOMB?
WHAT? NO! WHAT'S THIS ALL ABOUT?
VEHICLE APPROACHING!
WHAT'S GOING ON?
STAY IN THE VEHICLE, PLEASE!
MY ID'S IN THE TRUCK, IF YOU WANT...
STAY WHERE YOU ARE! ARMS OUT!
WHAT DID I DO?
ARMS OUT!
YOU'RE MAKING ME VERY NERVOUS!

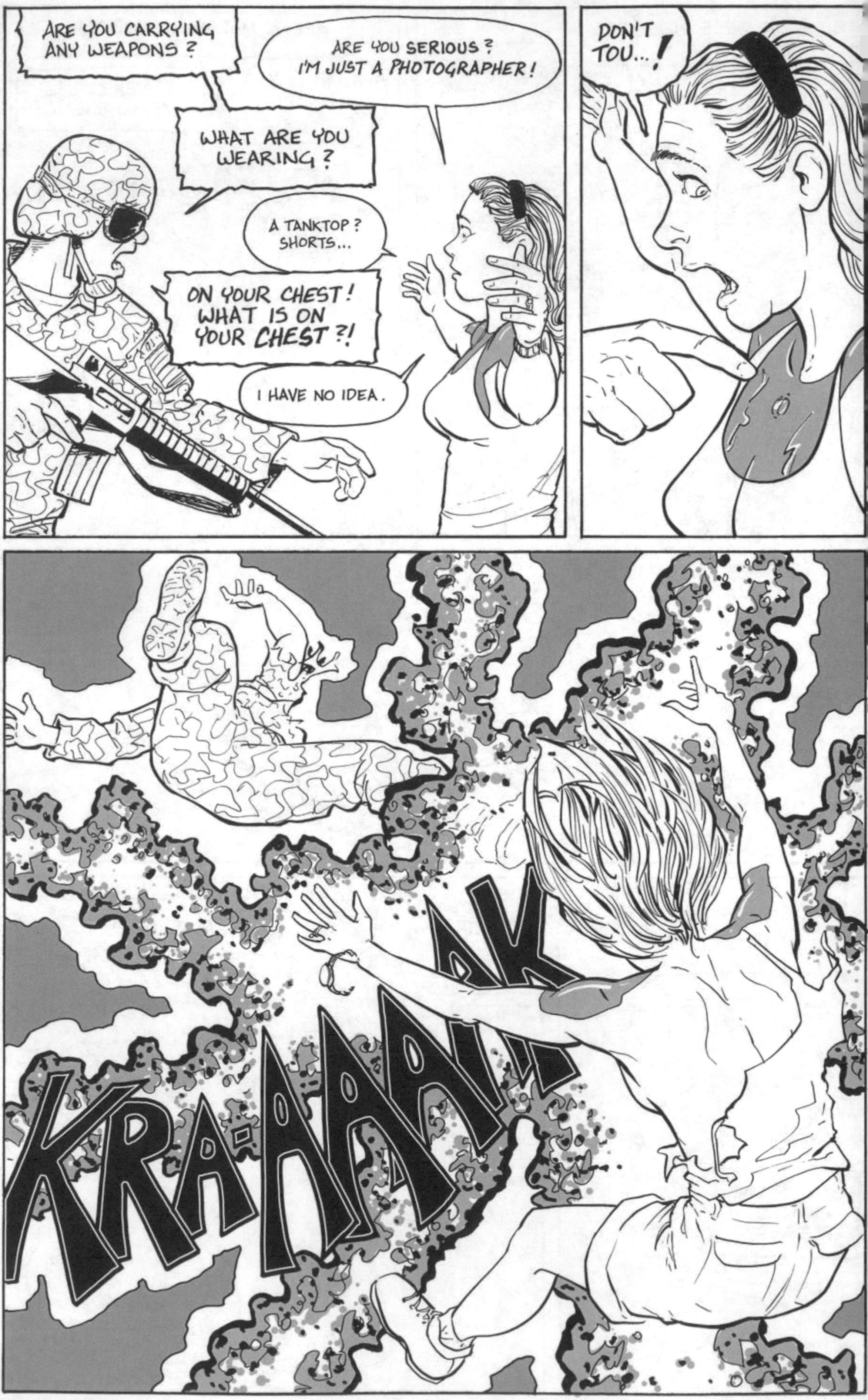
ARE YOU CARRYING ANY WEAPONS ?
ARE YOU SERIOUS ? I'M JUST A PHOTOGRAPHER !
WHAT ARE YOU WEARING ?
A TANKTOP ? SHORTS...
ON YOUR CHEST ! WHAT IS ON YOUR CHEST ?!
I HAVE NO IDEA .
DON'T TOU... !
KRA-AAAAAAK

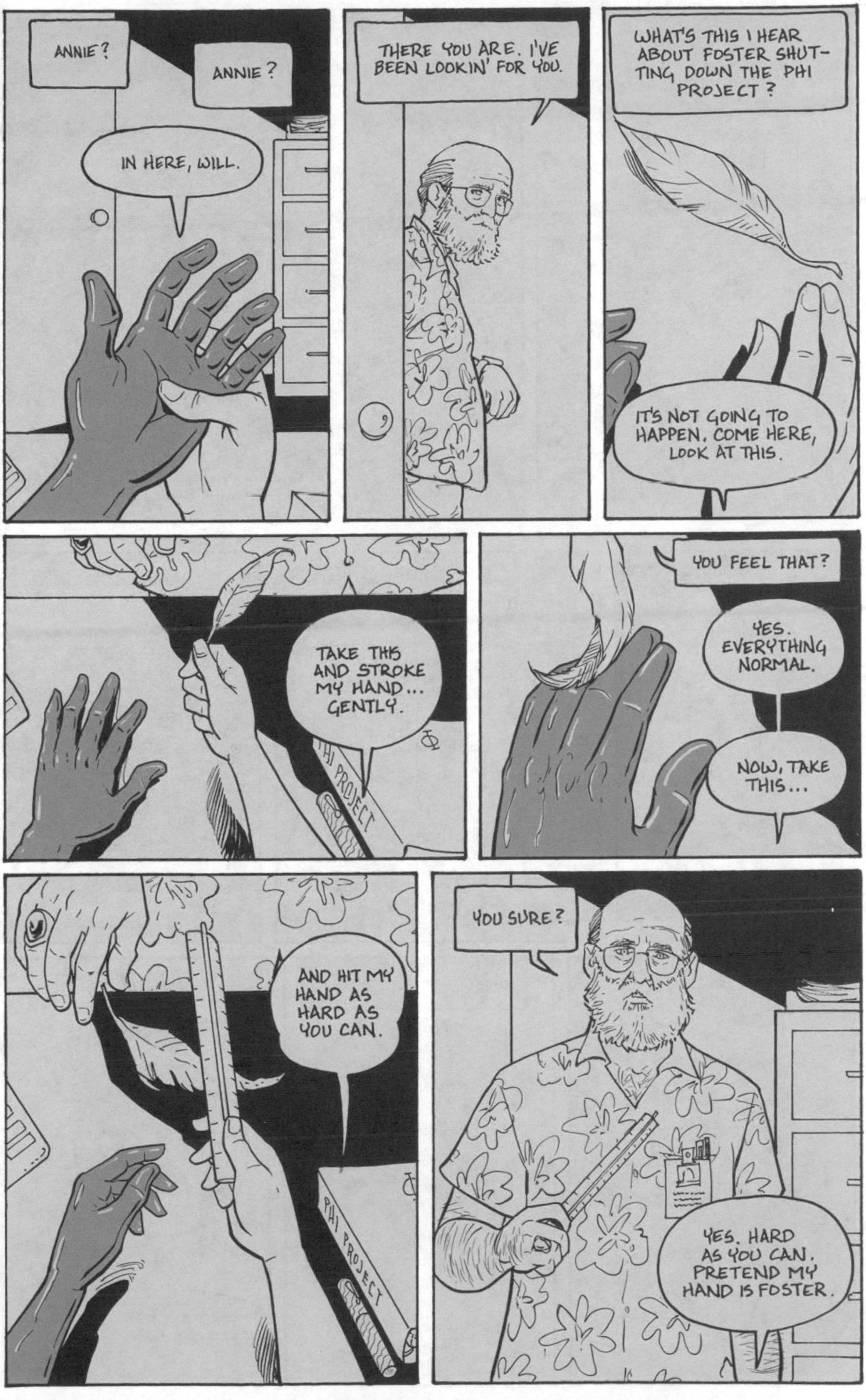
ANNIE?
ANNIE?
IN HERE, WILL.
THERE YOU ARE. I'VE BEEN LOOKIN' FOR YOU.
WHAT'S THIS I HEAR ABOUT FOSTER SHUT-TING DOWN THE PHI PROJECT?
IT'S NOT GOING TO HAPPEN. COME HERE, LOOK AT THIS.
TAKE THIS AND STROKE MY HAND... GENTLY.
PHI PROJECT
YOU FEEL THAT?
YES. EVERYTHING NORMAL.
NOW, TAKE THIS...
AND HIT MY HAND AS HARD AS YOU CAN.
PHI PROJECT
YOU SURE?
YES. HARD AS YOU CAN. PRETEND MY HAND IS FOSTER.

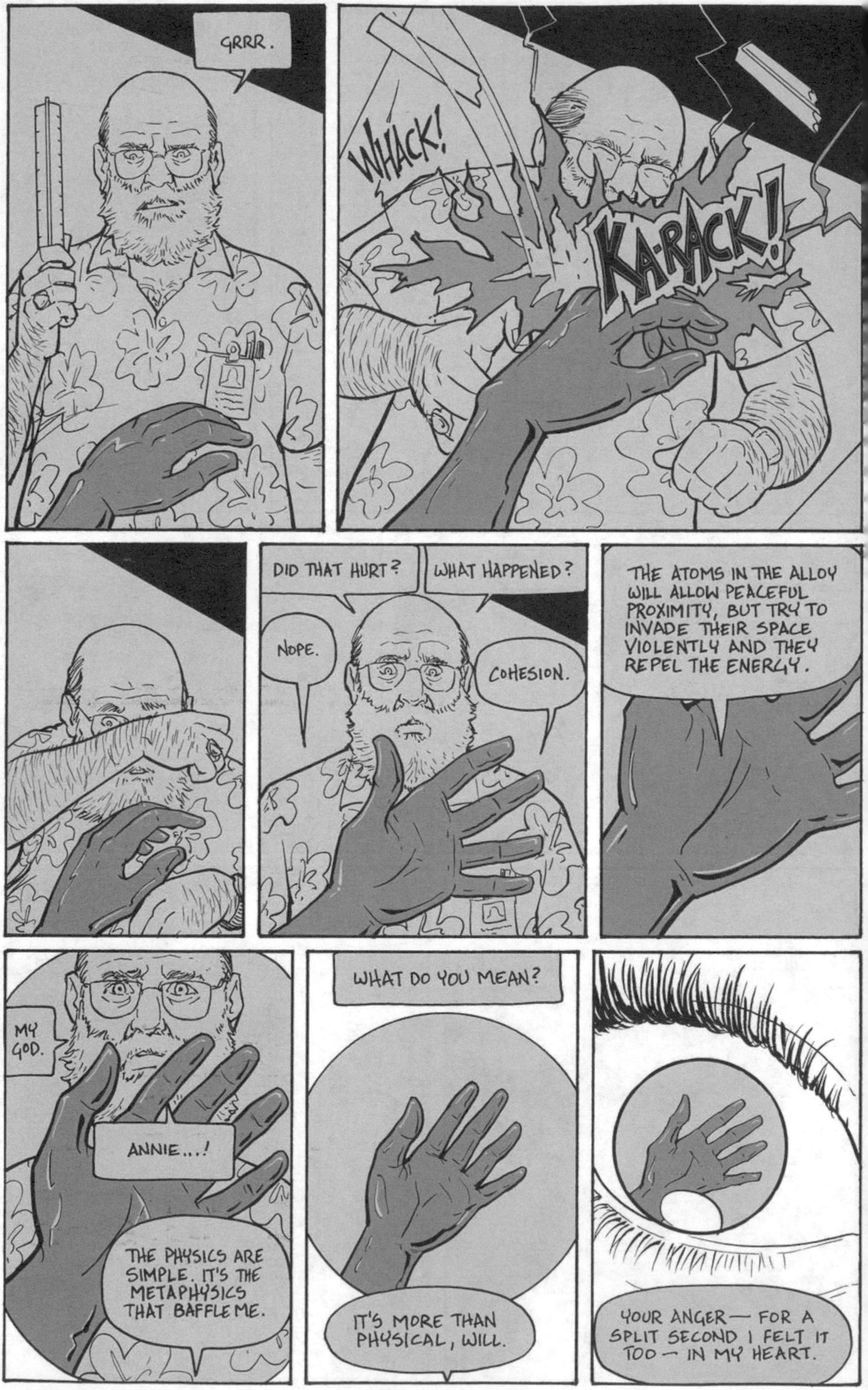
GRRR.
WHACK!
KA-RACK!
DID THAT HURT?
NOPE.
WHAT HAPPENED?
COHESION.
THE ATOMS IN THE ALLOY WILL ALLOW PEACEFUL PROXIMITY, BUT TRY TO INVADE THEIR SPACE VIOLENTLY AND THEY REPEL THE ENERGY.
MY GOD.
ANNIE...!
THE PHYSICS ARE SIMPLE. IT'S THE METAPHYSICS THAT BAFFLE ME.
WHAT DO YOU MEAN?
IT'S MORE THAN PHYSICAL, WILL.
YOUR ANGER— FOR A SPLIT SECOND I FELT IT TOO — IN MY HEART.

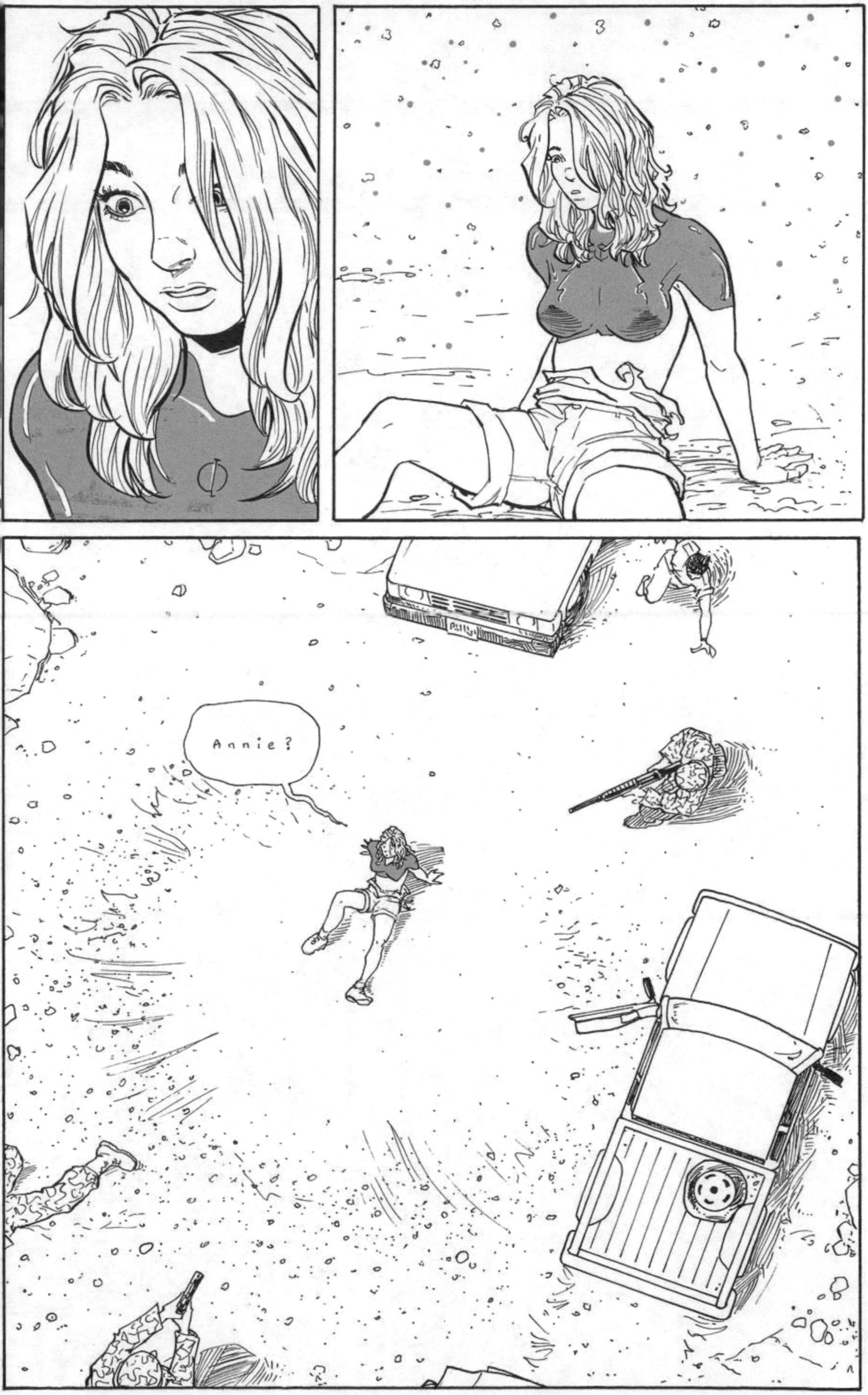
Annie?

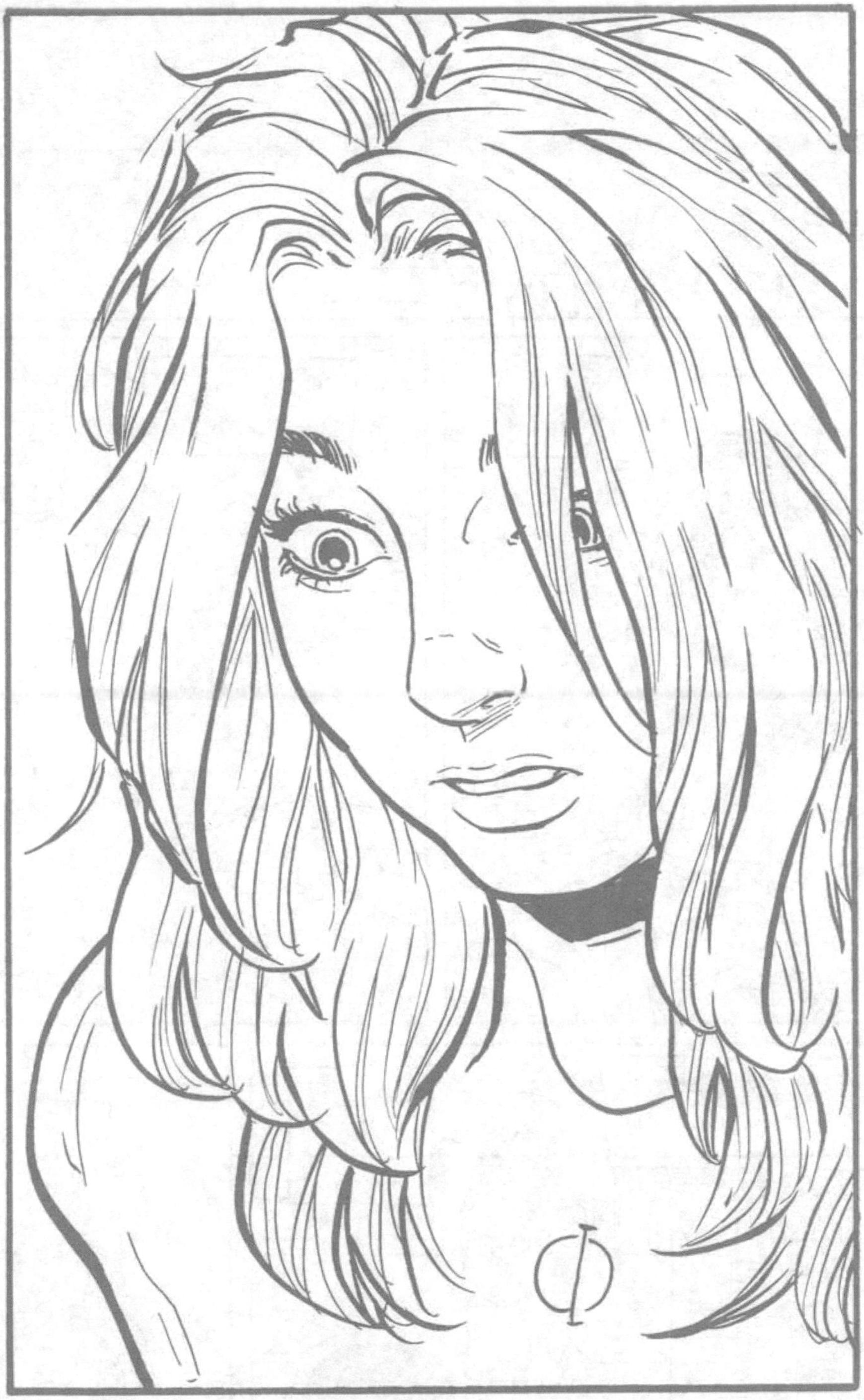

Now he has departed from this strange world a little ahead of me. That means nothing. People like us, who believe in physics, know that the distinction between past, present, and future is only a stubbornly persistent illusion.

—Albert Einstein

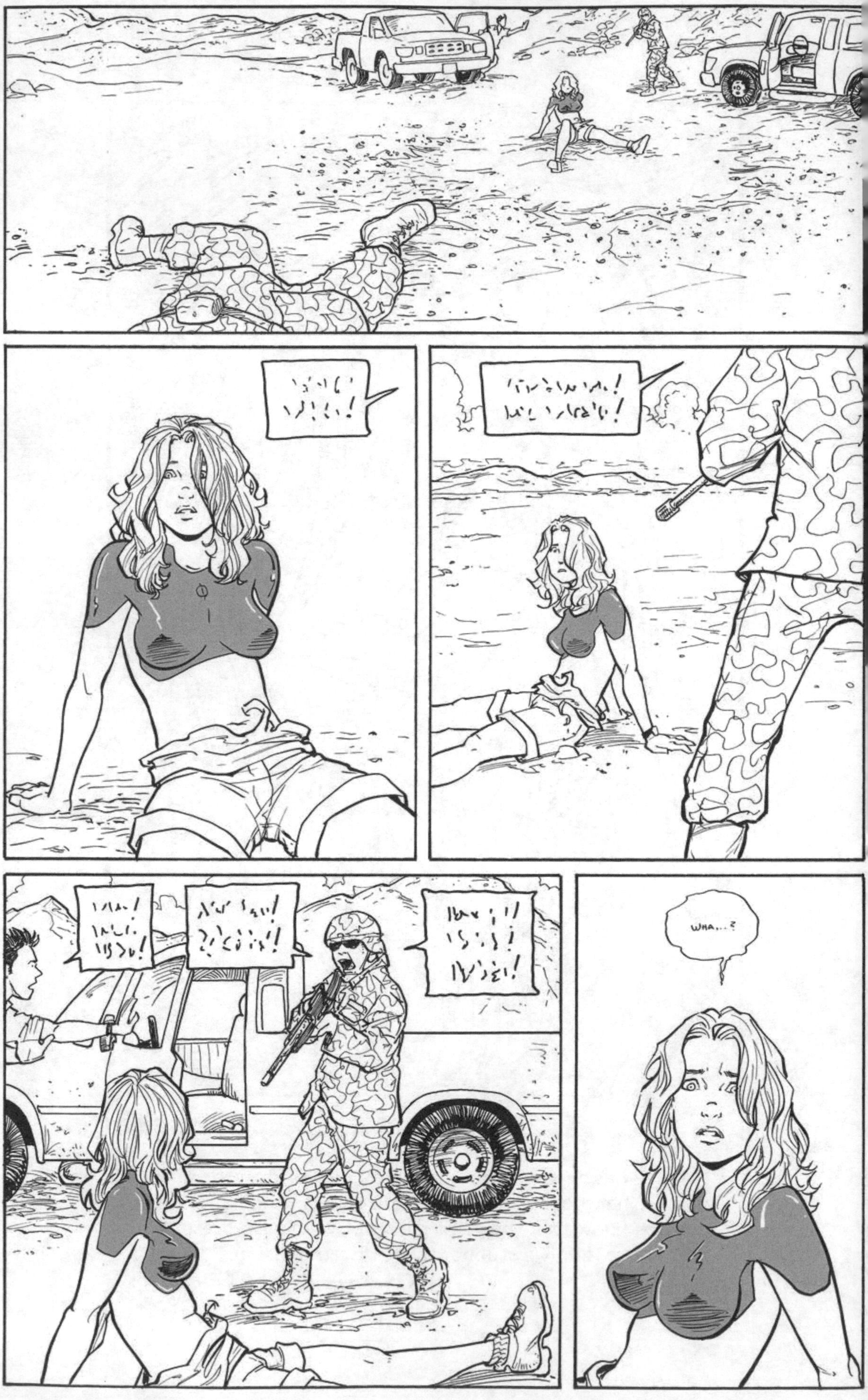
WHA...?

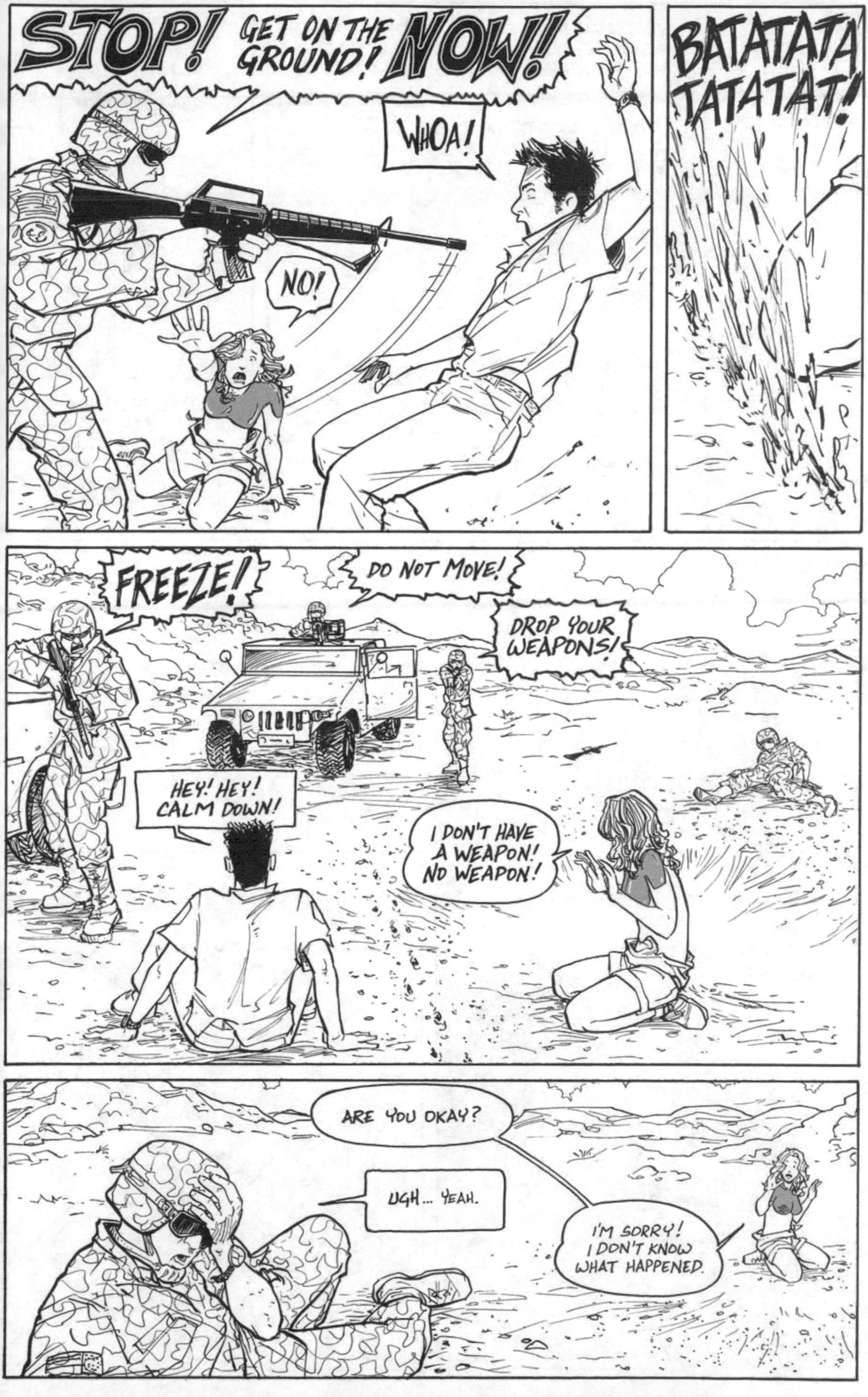
STOP! GET ON THE GROUND! NOW!!
WHOA!
NO!
BATATATA TATATAT!
FREEZE!
DO NOT MOVE!
DROP YOUR WEAPONS!
HEY! HEY! CALM DOWN!
I DON'T HAVE A WEAPON! NO WEAPON!
ARE YOU OKAY?
UGH... YEAH.
I'M SORRY! I DON'T KNOW WHAT HAPPENED.

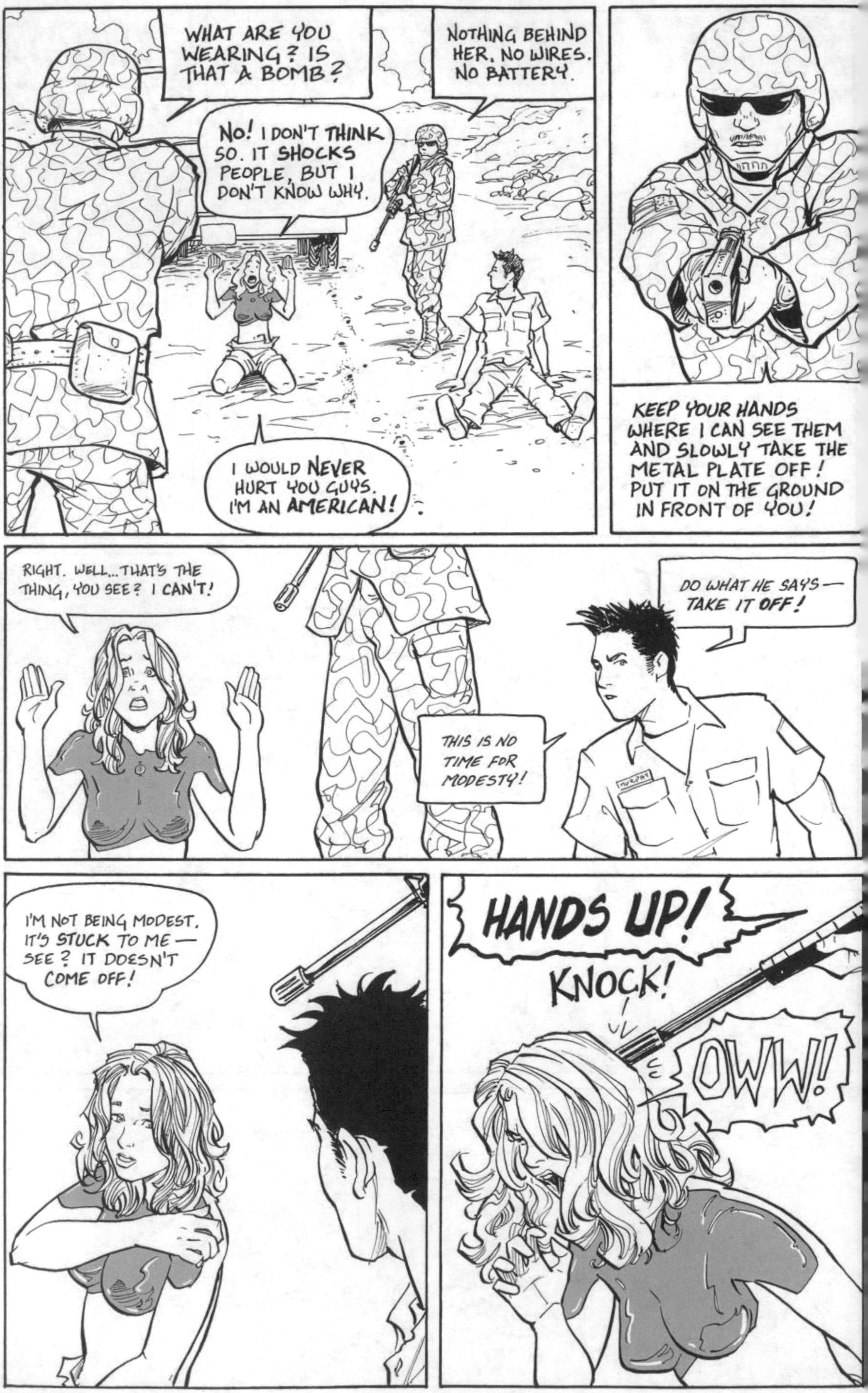
WHAT ARE YOU WEARING? IS THAT A BOMB?
NOTHING BEHIND HER. NO WIRES. NO BATTERY.
NO! I DON'T THINK SO. IT SHOCKS PEOPLE, BUT I DON'T KNOW WHY.
I WOULD NEVER HURT YOU GUYS. I'M AN AMERICAN!
KEEP YOUR HANDS WHERE I CAN SEE THEM AND SLOWLY TAKE THE METAL PLATE OFF! PUT IT ON THE GROUND IN FRONT OF YOU!
RIGHT. WELL... THAT'S THE THING, YOU SEE? I CAN'T!
DO WHAT HE SAYS— TAKE IT OFF!
THIS IS NO TIME FOR MODESTY!
MURPHY
I'M NOT BEING MODEST. IT'S STUCK TO ME— SEE? IT DOESN'T COME OFF!
HANDS UP!
KNOCK!
OWW!

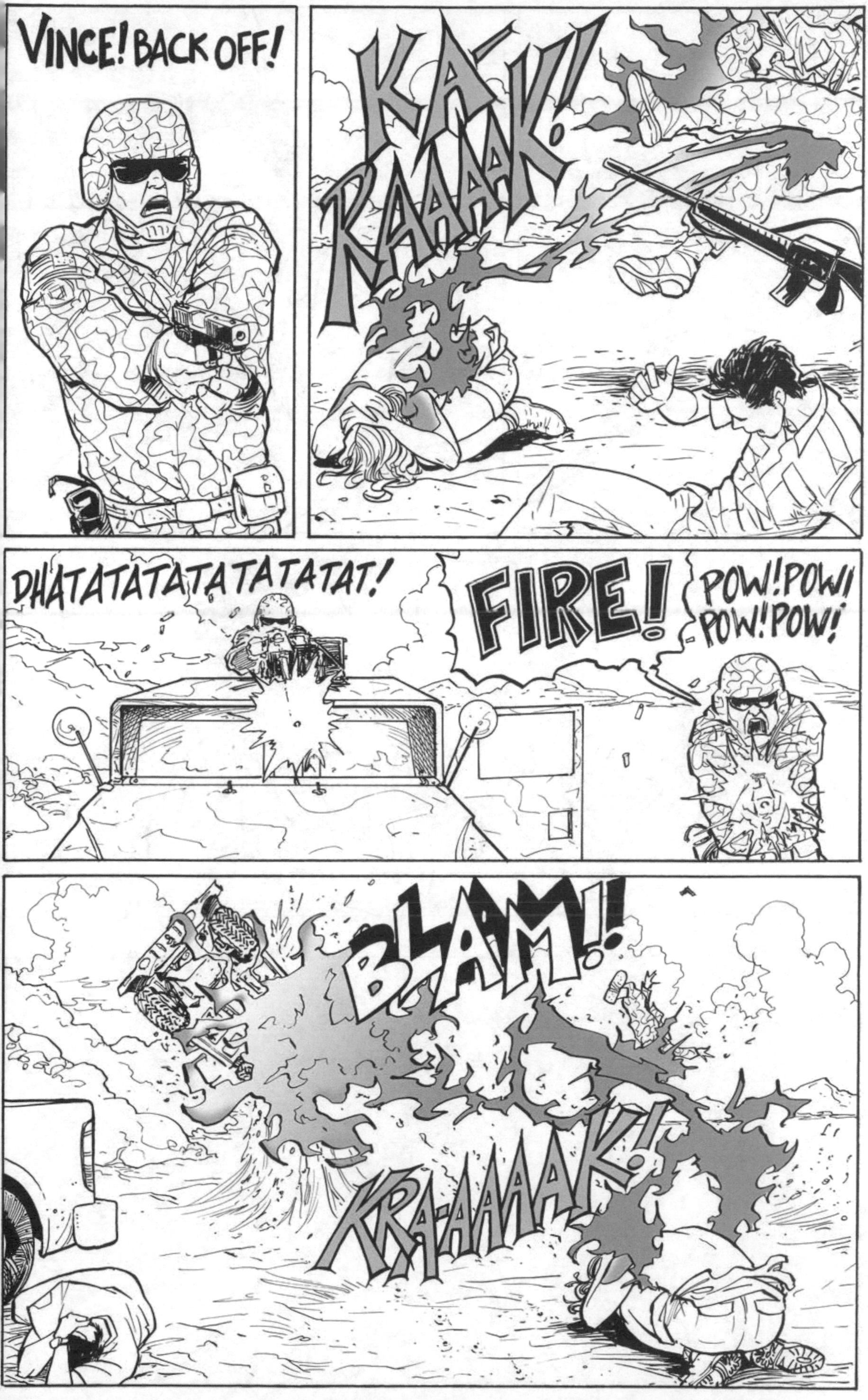
VINCE! BACK OFF!
KA-RAAAAK!
DHATATATATATATATAT!
FIRE!
POW! POW!
POW! POW!
BLAM!!
KRA-AAAAK!

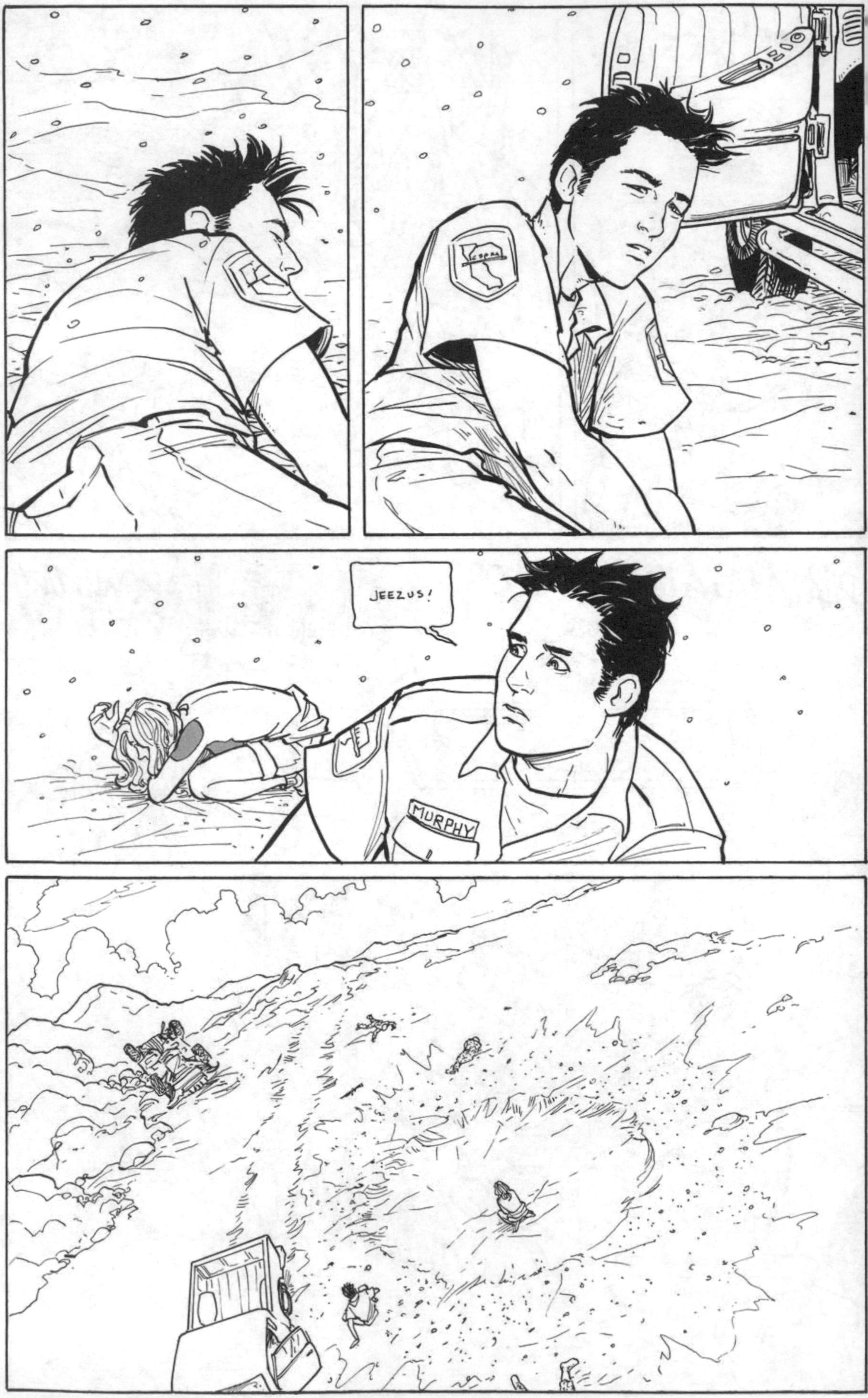
JEEZUS!
MURPHY

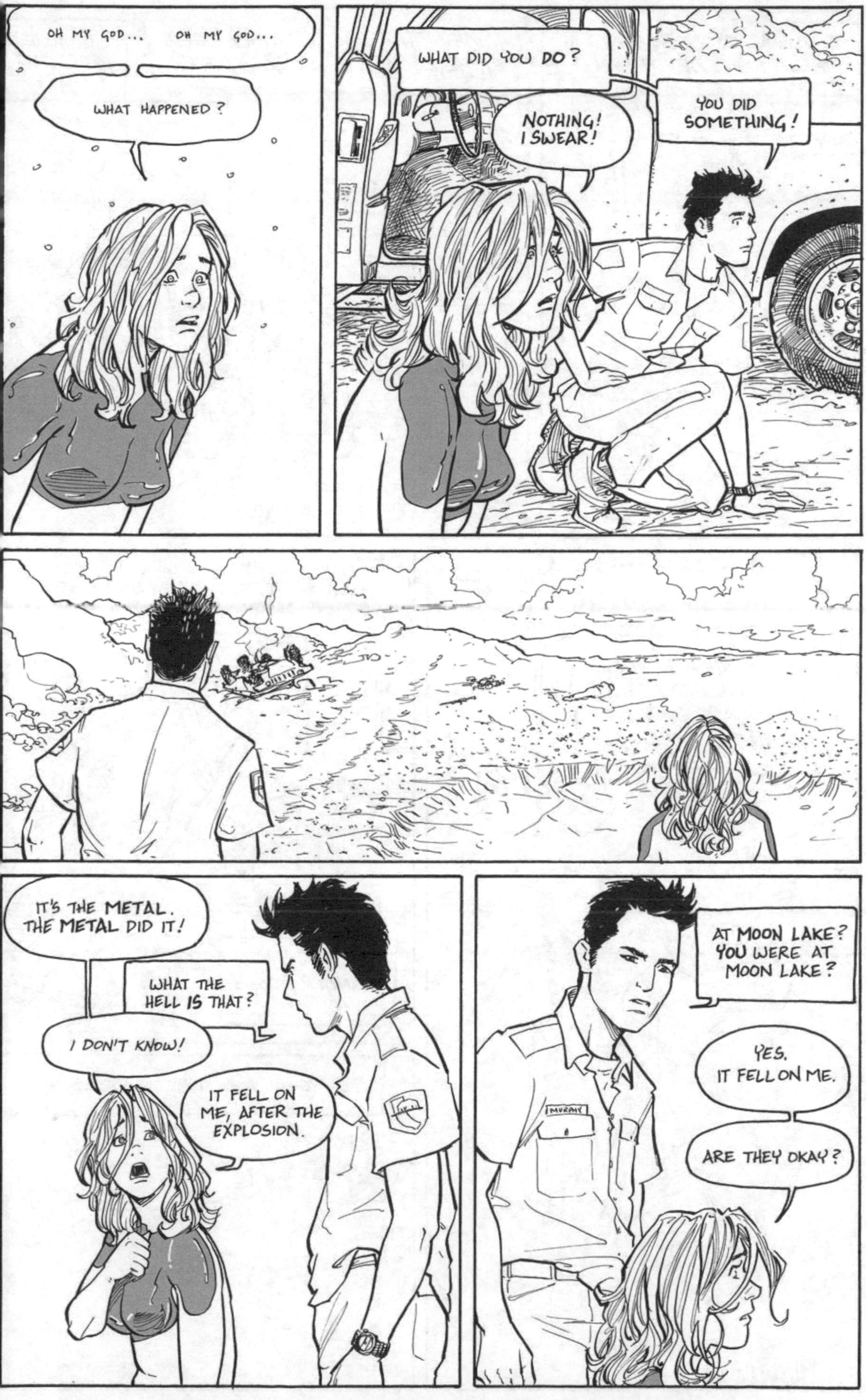
OH MY GOD... OH MY GOD...
WHAT HAPPENED?
WHAT DID YOU DO?
NOTHING! I SWEAR!
YOU DID SOMETHING!
IT'S THE METAL. THE METAL DID IT!
WHAT THE HELL IS THAT?
I DON'T KNOW!
IT FELL ON ME, AFTER THE EXPLOSION.
AT MOON LAKE? YOU WERE AT MOON LAKE?
YES. IT FELL ON ME.
ARE THEY OKAY?

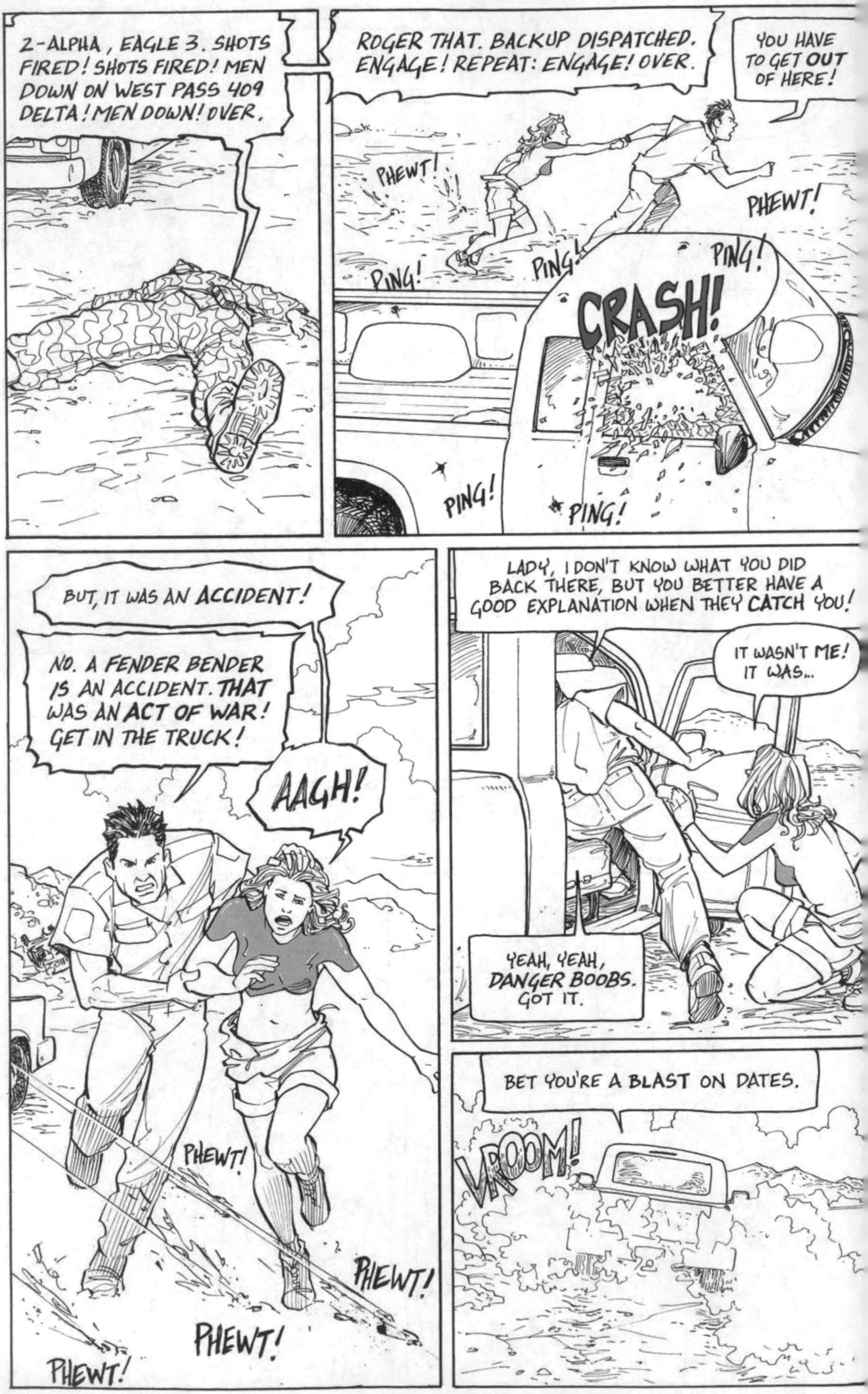
2-ALPHA, EAGLE 3. SHOTS FIRED! SHOTS FIRED! MEN DOWN ON WEST PASS 409 DELTA! MEN DOWN! OVER.
ROGER THAT. BACKUP DISPATCHED. ENGAGE! REPEAT: ENGAGE! OVER.
YOU HAVE TO GET OUT OF HERE!
PHEWT!
PHEWT!
PING!
PING!
PING!
CRASH!
PING!
PING!
BUT, IT WAS AN ACCIDENT!
NO. A FENDER BENDER IS AN ACCIDENT. THAT WAS AN ACT OF WAR! GET IN THE TRUCK!
AAGH!
PHEWT!
PHEWT!
PHEWT!
PHEWT!
LADY, I DON'T KNOW WHAT YOU DID BACK THERE, BUT YOU BETTER HAVE A GOOD EXPLANATION WHEN THEY CATCH YOU!
IT WASN'T ME! IT WAS...
YEAH, YEAH, DANGER BOOBS. GOT IT.
BET YOU'RE A BLAST ON DATES.
VROOM!

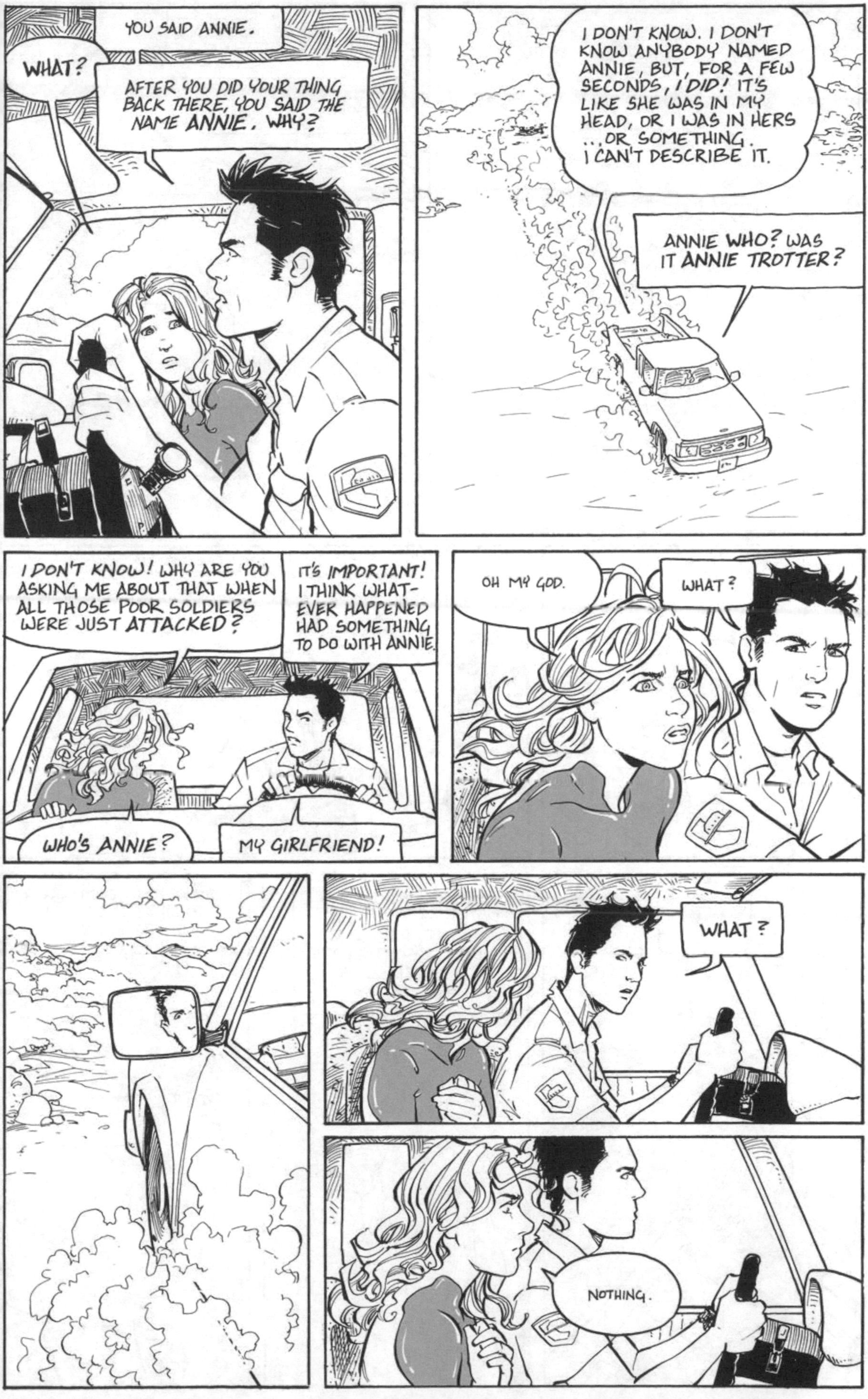
YOU SAID ANNIE.
WHAT?
AFTER YOU DID YOUR THING BACK THERE, YOU SAID THE NAME ANNIE. WHY?
I DON'T KNOW. I DON'T KNOW ANYBODY NAMED ANNIE, BUT, FOR A FEW SECONDS, I DID! IT'S LIKE SHE WAS IN MY HEAD, OR I WAS IN HERS ...OR SOMETHING. I CAN'T DESCRIBE IT.
ANNIE WHO? WAS IT ANNIE TROTTER?
I DON'T KNOW! WHY ARE YOU ASKING ME ABOUT THAT WHEN ALL THOSE POOR SOLDIERS WERE JUST ATTACKED?
IT'S IMPORTANT! I THINK WHATEVER HAPPENED HAD SOMETHING TO DO WITH ANNIE.
WHO'S ANNIE?
MY GIRLFRIEND!
OH MY GOD.
WHAT?
WHAT?
NOTHING.

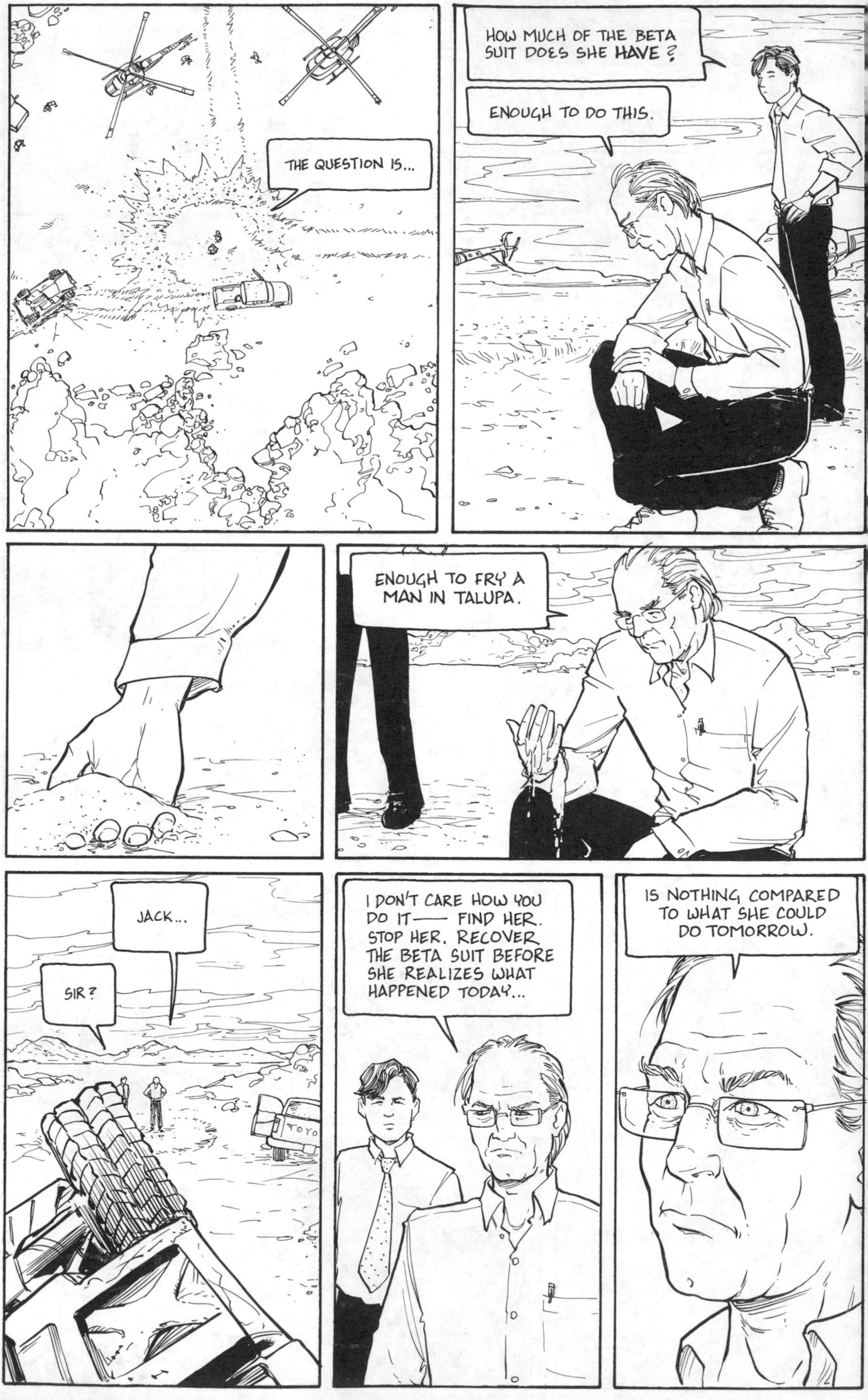
THE QUESTION IS...
HOW MUCH OF THE BETA SUIT DOES SHE **HAVE**?
ENOUGH TO DO THIS.
ENOUGH TO FRY A MAN IN TALUPA.
JACK...
SIR?
I DON'T CARE HOW YOU DO IT— FIND HER. STOP HER. RECOVER THE BETA SUIT BEFORE SHE REALIZES WHAT HAPPENED TODAY...
IS NOTHING COMPARED TO WHAT SHE COULD DO TOMORROW.

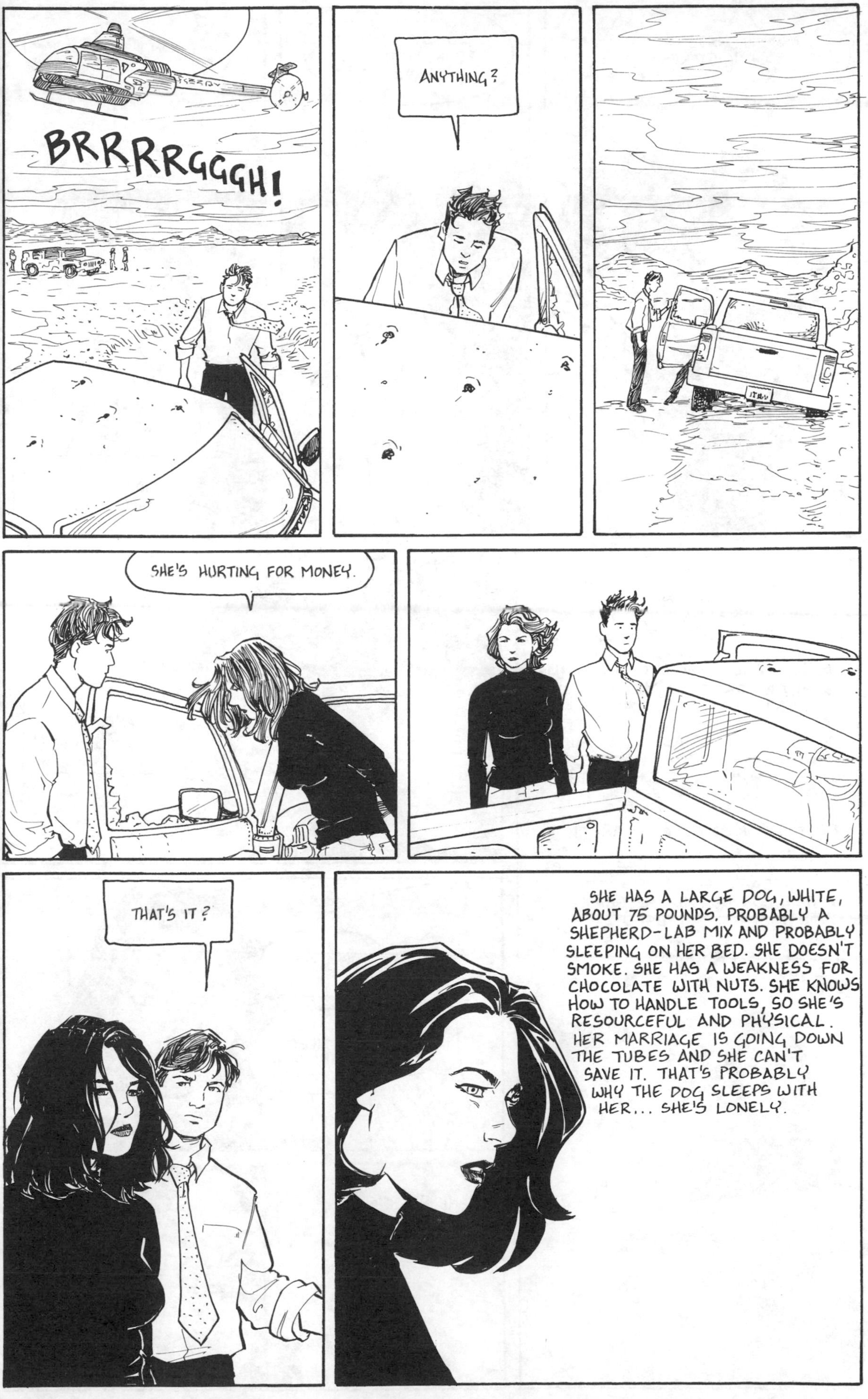
BRRRRGGGH!
ANYTHING?
SHE'S HURTING FOR MONEY.
THAT'S IT?
SHE HAS A LARGE DOG, WHITE, ABOUT 75 POUNDS. PROBABLY A SHEPHERD-LAB MIX AND PROBABLY SLEEPING ON HER BED. SHE DOESN'T SMOKE. SHE HAS A WEAKNESS FOR CHOCOLATE WITH NUTS. SHE KNOWS HOW TO HANDLE TOOLS, SO SHE'S RESOURCEFUL AND PHYSICAL. HER MARRIAGE IS GOING DOWN THE TUBES AND SHE CAN'T SAVE IT. THAT'S PROBABLY WHY THE DOG SLEEPS WITH HER... SHE'S LONELY.

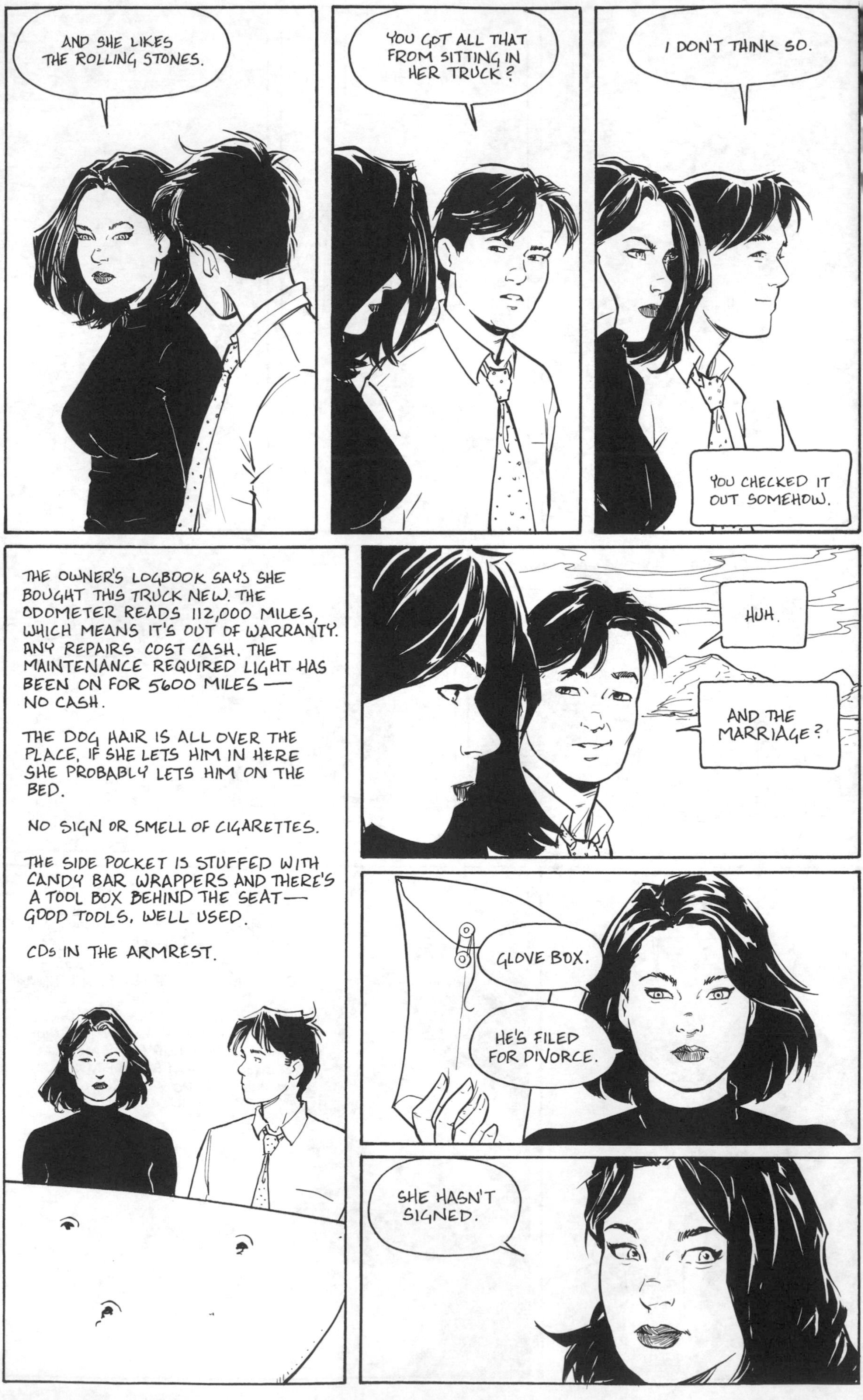
AND SHE LIKES THE ROLLING STONES.
YOU GOT ALL THAT FROM SITTING IN HER TRUCK?
I DON'T THINK SO.
YOU CHECKED IT OUT SOMEHOW.
THE OWNER'S LOGBOOK SAYS SHE BOUGHT THIS TRUCK NEW. THE ODOMETER READS 112,000 MILES, WHICH MEANS IT'S OUT OF WARRANTY. ANY REPAIRS COST CASH. THE MAINTENANCE REQUIRED LIGHT HAS BEEN ON FOR 5600 MILES — NO CASH.
THE DOG HAIR IS ALL OVER THE PLACE. IF SHE LETS HIM IN HERE SHE PROBABLY LETS HIM ON THE BED.
NO SIGN OR SMELL OF CIGARETTES.
THE SIDE POCKET IS STUFFED WITH CANDY BAR WRAPPERS AND THERE'S A TOOL BOX BEHIND THE SEAT — GOOD TOOLS, WELL USED.
CDs IN THE ARMREST.
HUH.
AND THE MARRIAGE?
GLOVE BOX.
HE'S FILED FOR DIVORCE.
SHE HASN'T SIGNED.

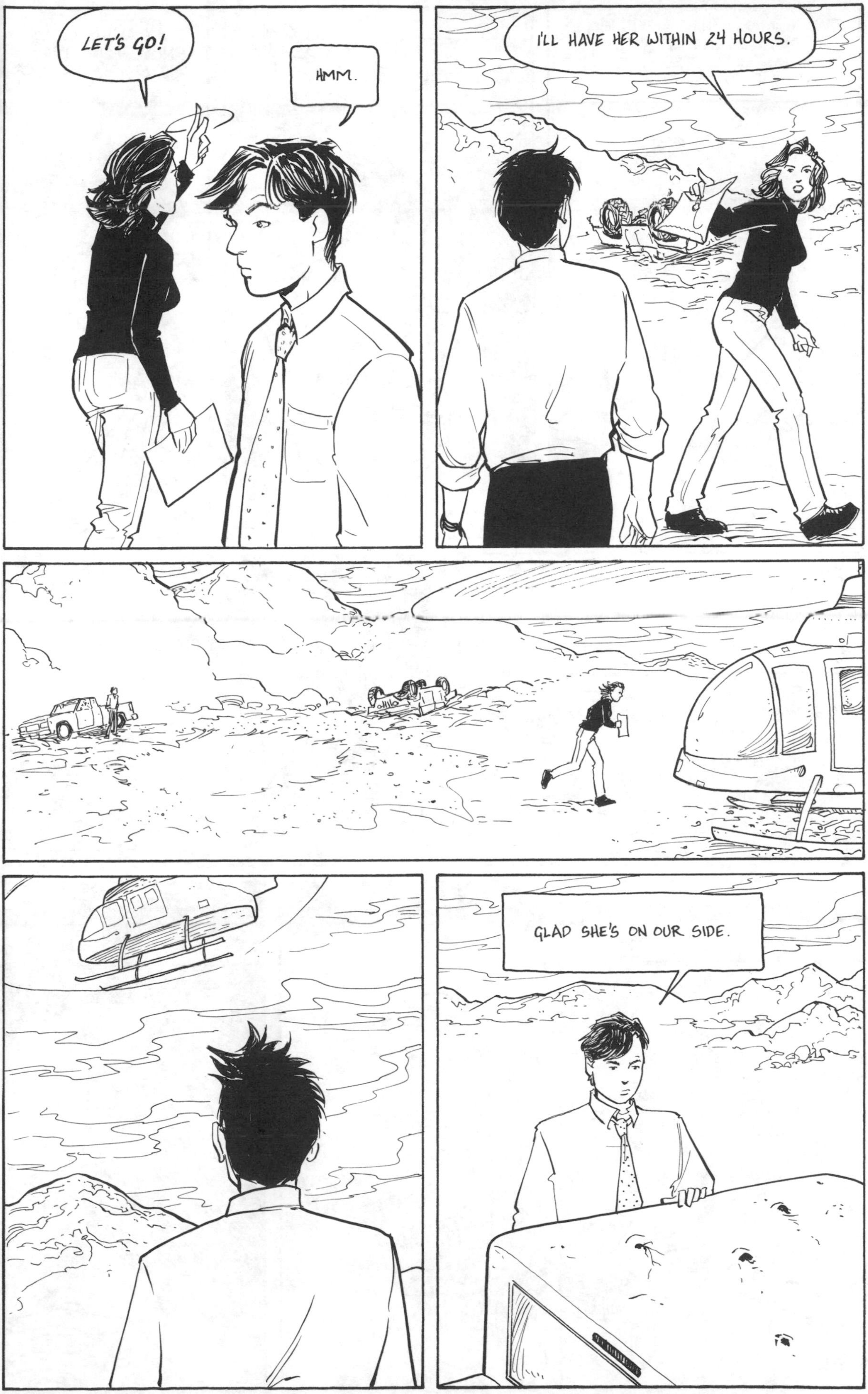
LET'S GO!
HMM.
I'LL HAVE HER WITHIN 24 HOURS.
GLAD SHE'S ON OUR SIDE.

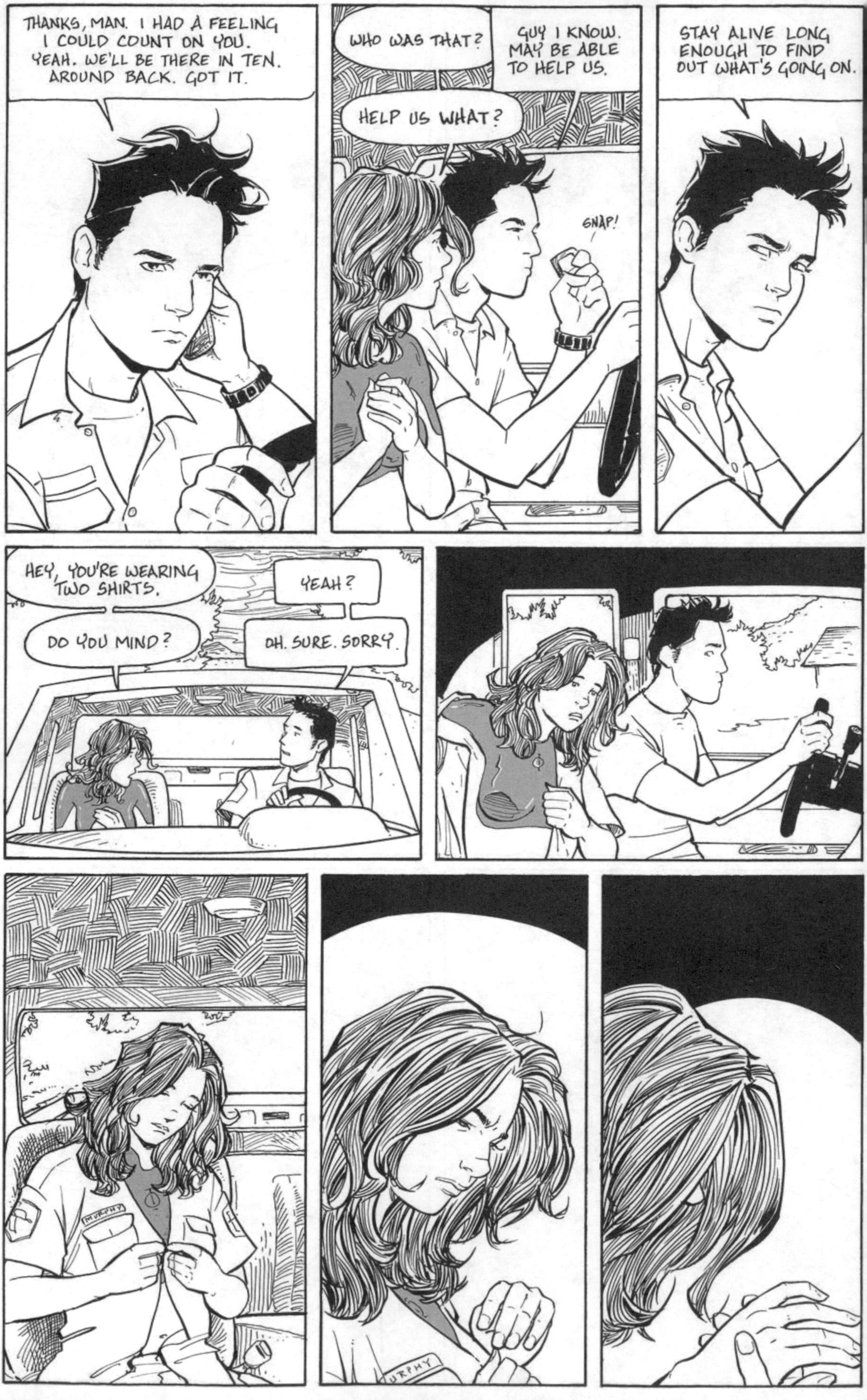

THANKS, MAN. I HAD A FEELING I COULD COUNT ON YOU. YEAH. WE'LL BE THERE IN TEN. AROUND BACK. GOT IT.
WHO WAS THAT?
GUY I KNOW. MAY BE ABLE TO HELP US.
HELP US WHAT?
SNAP!
STAY ALIVE LONG ENOUGH TO FIND OUT WHAT'S GOING ON.
HEY, YOU'RE WEARING TWO SHIRTS.
YEAH?
DO YOU MIND?
OH. SURE. SORRY.
MURPHY
URPHY

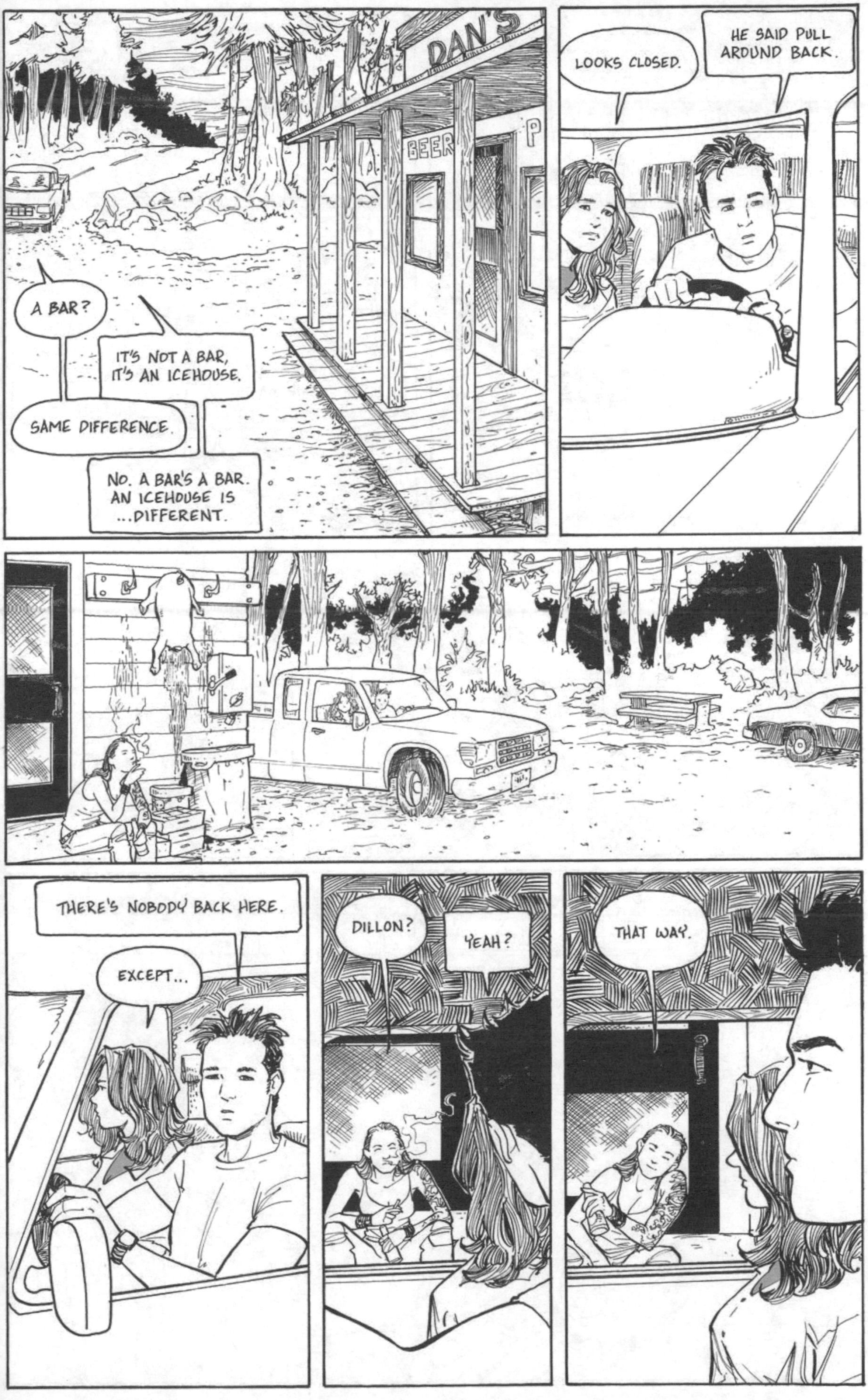

DAN'S
BEER
A BAR?
IT'S NOT A BAR, IT'S AN ICEHOUSE.
SAME DIFFERENCE.
NO. A BAR'S A BAR. AN ICEHOUSE IS ...DIFFERENT.
LOOKS CLOSED.
HE SAID PULL AROUND BACK.
THERE'S NOBODY BACK HERE.
EXCEPT...
DILLON?
YEAH?
THAT WAY.

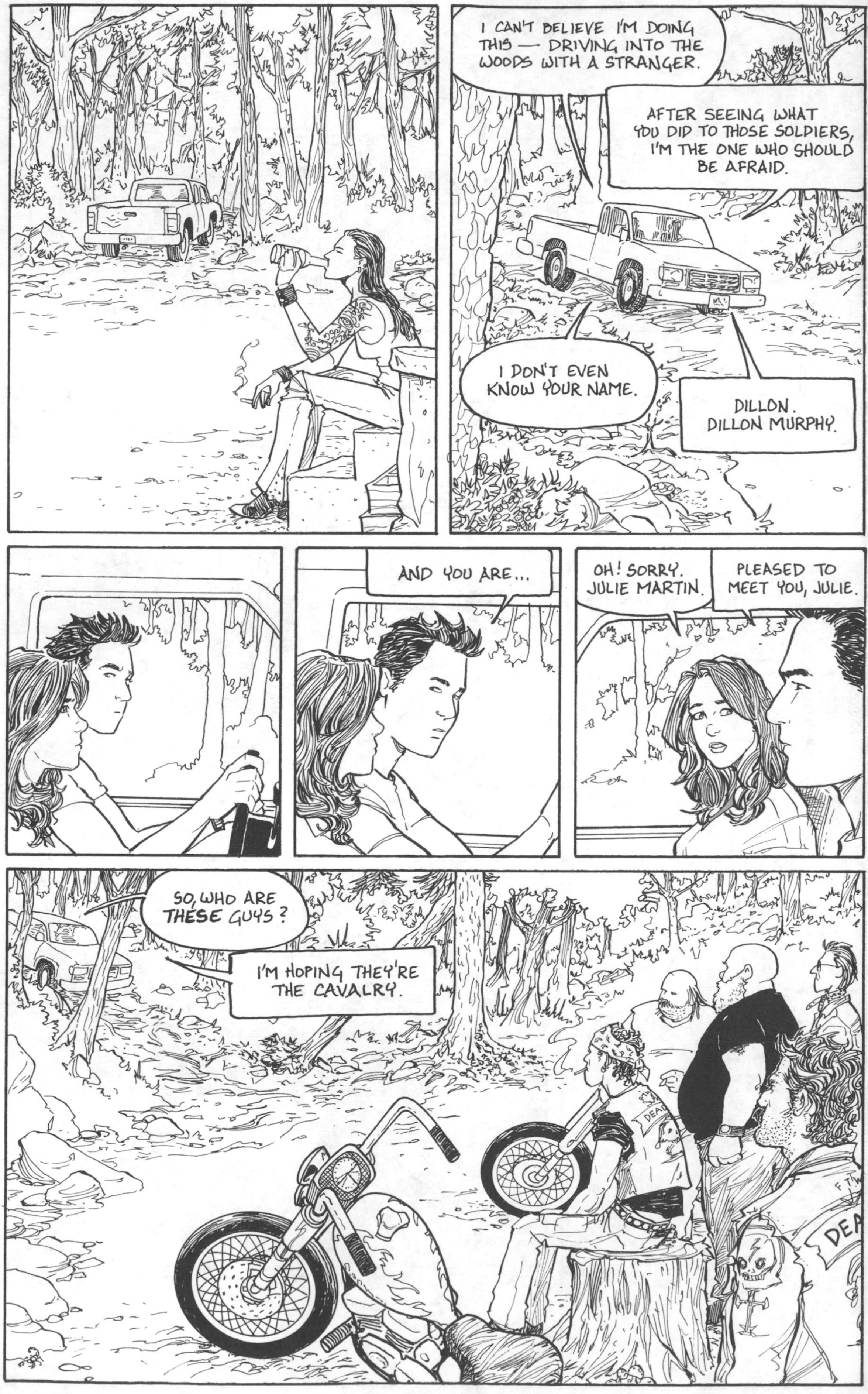
I CAN'T BELIEVE I'M DOING THIS — DRIVING INTO THE WOODS WITH A STRANGER.
AFTER SEEING WHAT YOU DID TO THOSE SOLDIERS, I'M THE ONE WHO SHOULD BE AFRAID.
I DON'T EVEN KNOW YOUR NAME.
DILLON. DILLON MURPHY.
AND YOU ARE...
OH! SORRY. JULIE MARTIN.
PLEASED TO MEET YOU, JULIE.
SO, WHO ARE THESE GUYS?
I'M HOPING THEY'RE THE CAVALRY.

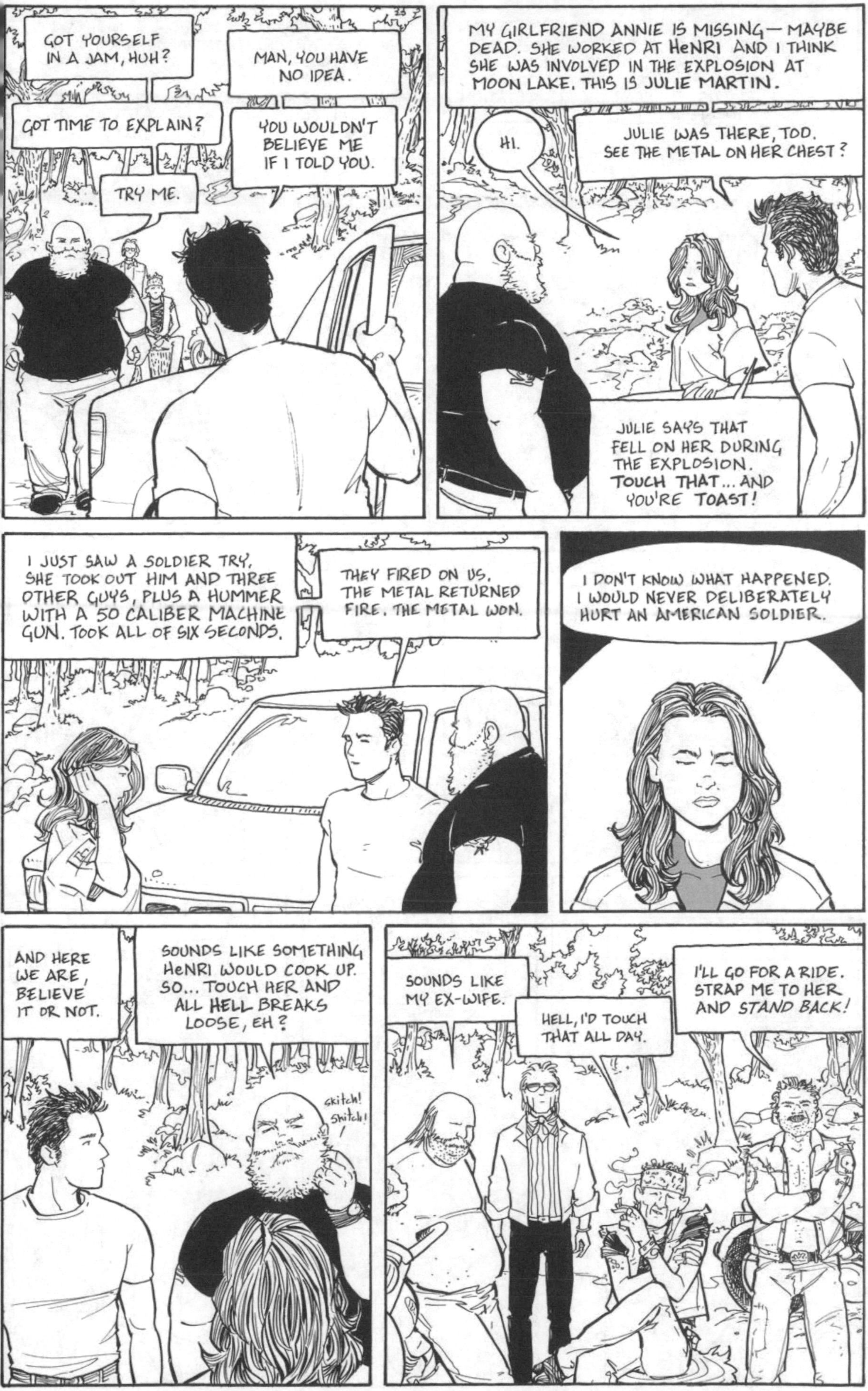
GOT YOURSELF IN A JAM, HUH?
MAN, YOU HAVE NO IDEA.
GOT TIME TO EXPLAIN?
YOU WOULDN'T BELIEVE ME IF I TOLD YOU.
TRY ME.
MY GIRLFRIEND ANNIE IS MISSING— MAYBE DEAD. SHE WORKED AT HeNRI AND I THINK SHE WAS INVOLVED IN THE EXPLOSION AT MOON LAKE. THIS IS JULIE MARTIN.
HI.
JULIE WAS THERE, TOD. SEE THE METAL ON HER CHEST?
JULIE SAYS THAT FELL ON HER DURING THE EXPLOSION. TOUCH THAT... AND YOU'RE TOAST!
I JUST SAW A SOLDIER TRY. SHE TOOK OUT HIM AND THREE OTHER GUYS, PLUS A HUMMER WITH A 50 CALIBER MACHINE GUN. TOOK ALL OF SIX SECONDS.
THEY FIRED ON US. THE METAL RETURNED FIRE. THE METAL WON.
I DON'T KNOW WHAT HAPPENED. I WOULD NEVER DELIBERATELY HURT AN AMERICAN SOLDIER.
AND HERE WE ARE, BELIEVE IT OR NOT.
SOUNDS LIKE SOMETHING HeNRI WOULD COOK UP. SO... TOUCH HER AND ALL HELL BREAKS LOOSE, EH?
Skitch! Skitch!
SOUNDS LIKE MY EX-WIFE.
HELL, I'D TOUCH THAT ALL DAY.
I'LL GO FOR A RIDE. STRAP ME TO HER AND STAND BACK!

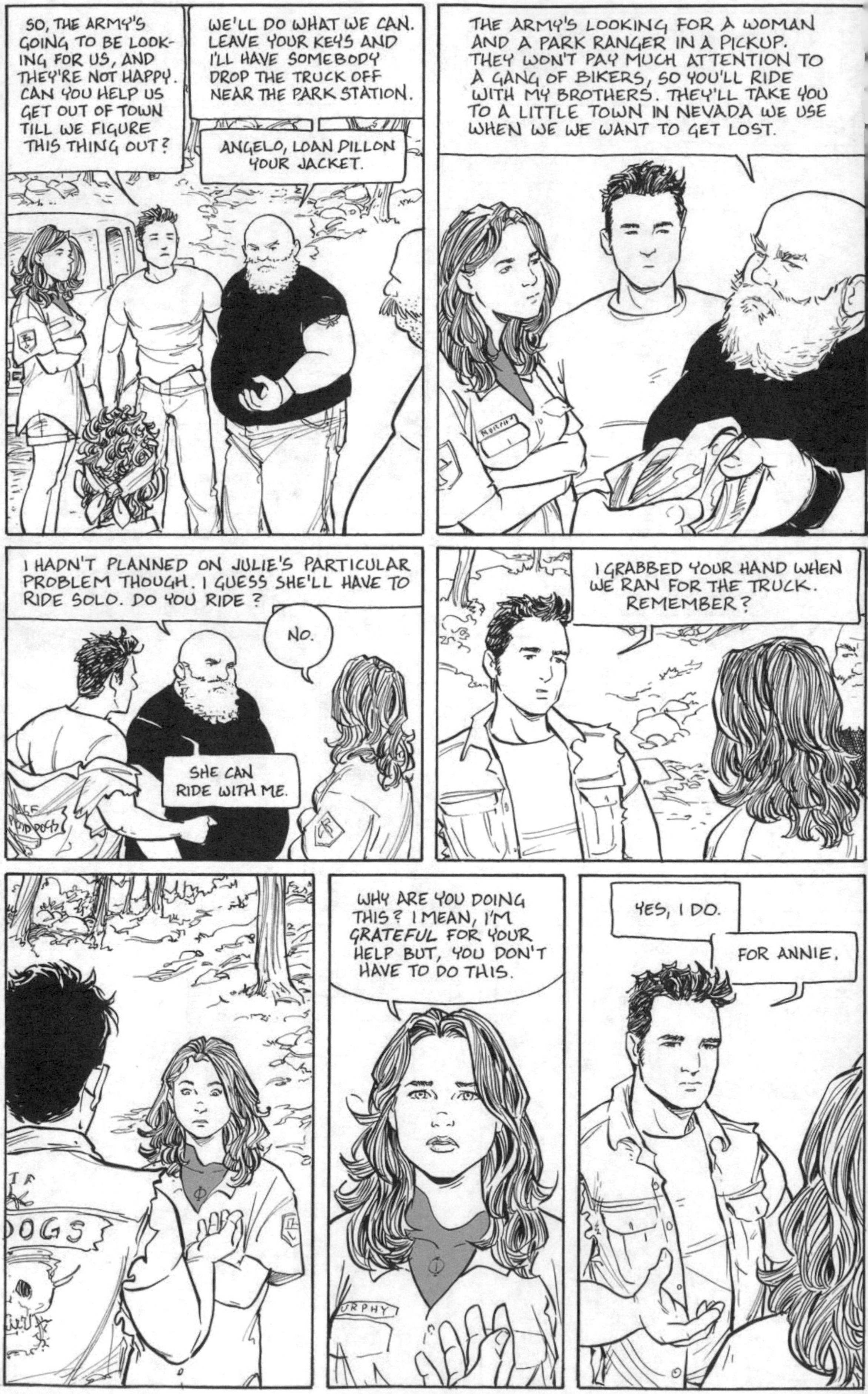
SO, THE ARMY'S GOING TO BE LOOKING FOR US, AND THEY'RE NOT HAPPY. CAN YOU HELP US GET OUT OF TOWN TILL WE FIGURE THIS THING OUT?
WE'LL DO WHAT WE CAN. LEAVE YOUR KEYS AND I'LL HAVE SOMEBODY DROP THE TRUCK OFF NEAR THE PARK STATION.
ANGELO, LOAN DILLON YOUR JACKET.
THE ARMY'S LOOKING FOR A WOMAN AND A PARK RANGER IN A PICKUP. THEY WON'T PAY MUCH ATTENTION TO A GANG OF BIKERS, SO YOU'LL RIDE WITH MY BROTHERS. THEY'LL TAKE YOU TO A LITTLE TOWN IN NEVADA WE USE WHEN WE WE WANT TO GET LOST.
I HADN'T PLANNED ON JULIE'S PARTICULAR PROBLEM THOUGH. I GUESS SHE'LL HAVE TO RIDE SOLO. DO YOU RIDE?
NO.
SHE CAN RIDE WITH ME.
I GRABBED YOUR HAND WHEN WE RAN FOR THE TRUCK. REMEMBER?
WHY ARE YOU DOING THIS? I MEAN, I'M GRATEFUL FOR YOUR HELP BUT, YOU DON'T HAVE TO DO THIS.
YES, I DO.
FOR ANNIE.

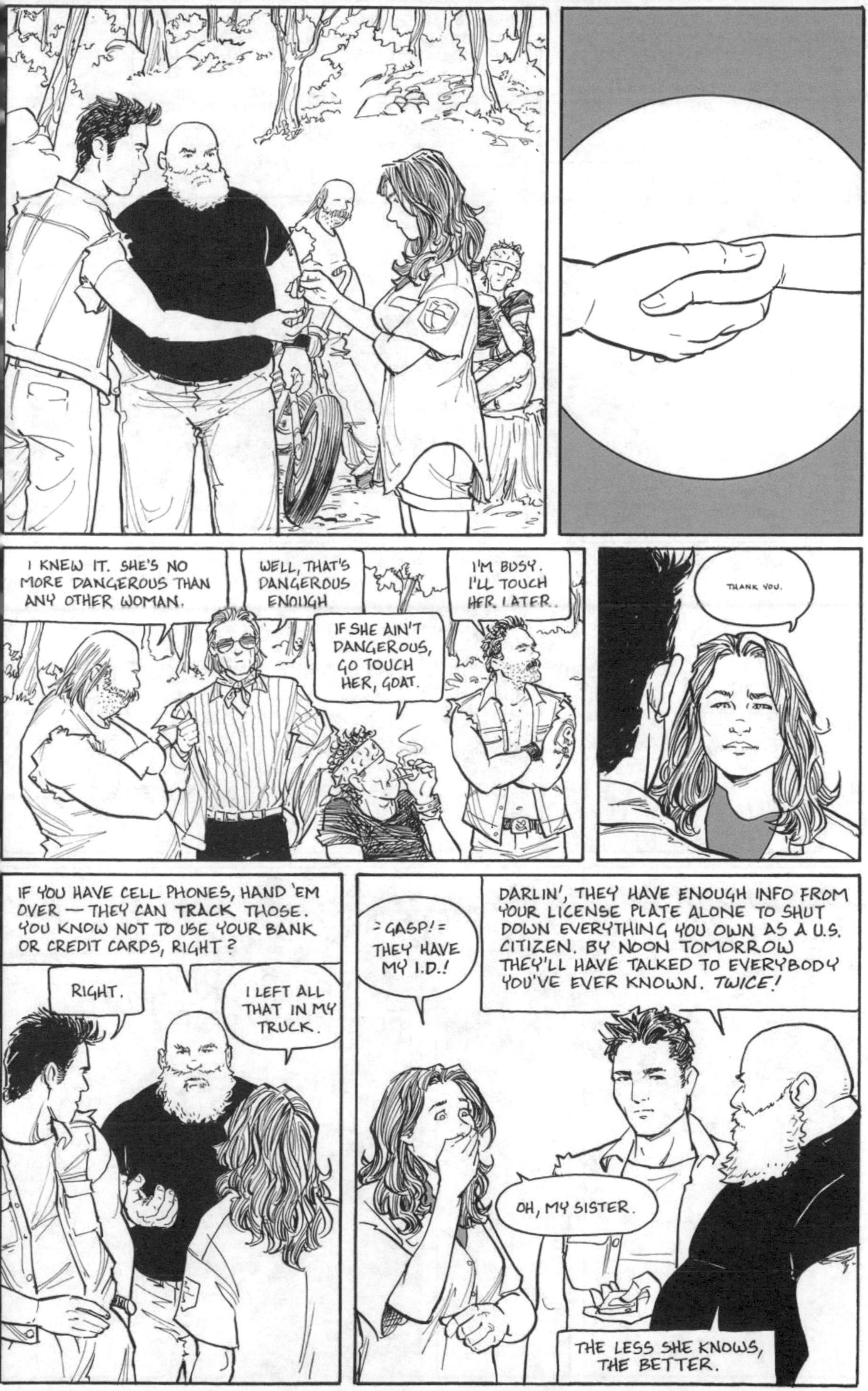
I KNEW IT. SHE'S NO MORE DANGEROUS THAN ANY OTHER WOMAN.
WELL, THAT'S DANGEROUS ENOUGH.
IF SHE AIN'T DANGEROUS, GO TOUCH HER, GOAT.
I'M BUSY. I'LL TOUCH HER LATER.
THANK YOU.
IF YOU HAVE CELL PHONES, HAND 'EM OVER — THEY CAN TRACK THOSE. YOU KNOW NOT TO USE YOUR BANK OR CREDIT CARDS, RIGHT?
RIGHT.
I LEFT ALL THAT IN MY TRUCK.
=GASP!= THEY HAVE MY I.D.!
DARLIN', THEY HAVE ENOUGH INFO FROM YOUR LICENSE PLATE ALONE TO SHUT DOWN EVERYTHING YOU OWN AS A U.S. CITIZEN. BY NOON TOMORROW THEY'LL HAVE TALKED TO EVERYBODY YOU'VE EVER KNOWN. TWICE!
OH, MY SISTER.
THE LESS SHE KNOWS, THE BETTER.

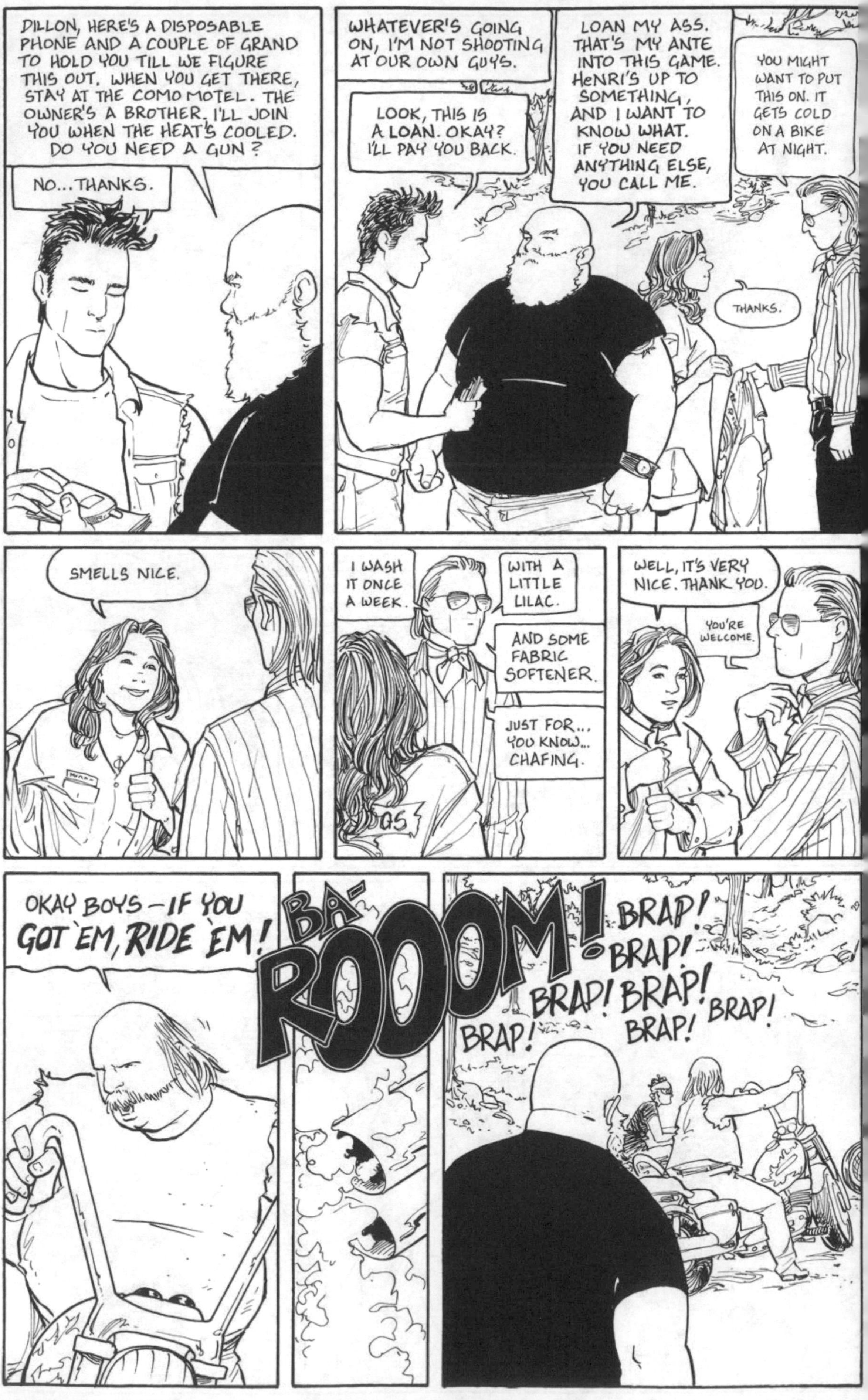
DILLON, HERE'S A DISPOSABLE PHONE AND A COUPLE OF GRAND TO HOLD YOU TILL WE FIGURE THIS OUT. WHEN YOU GET THERE, STAY AT THE COMO MOTEL. THE OWNER'S A BROTHER. I'LL JOIN YOU WHEN THE HEAT'S COOLED. DO YOU NEED A GUN?
NO... THANKS.
WHATEVER'S GOING ON, I'M NOT SHOOTING AT OUR OWN GUYS.
LOOK, THIS IS A LOAN. OKAY? I'LL PAY YOU BACK.
LOAN MY ASS. THAT'S MY ANTE INTO THIS GAME. HENRI'S UP TO SOMETHING, AND I WANT TO KNOW WHAT. IF YOU NEED ANYTHING ELSE, YOU CALL ME.
YOU MIGHT WANT TO PUT THIS ON. IT GETS COLD ON A BIKE AT NIGHT.
THANKS.
SMELLS NICE.
I WASH IT ONCE A WEEK.
WITH A LITTLE LILAC.
AND SOME FABRIC SOFTENER.
JUST FOR... YOU KNOW... CHAFING.
WELL, IT'S VERY NICE. THANK YOU.
YOU'RE WELCOME.
OKAY BOYS — IF YOU GOT 'EM, RIDE 'EM!
BA-ROOOOM!
BRAP! BRAP! BRAP! BRAP! BRAP! BRAP! BRAP!

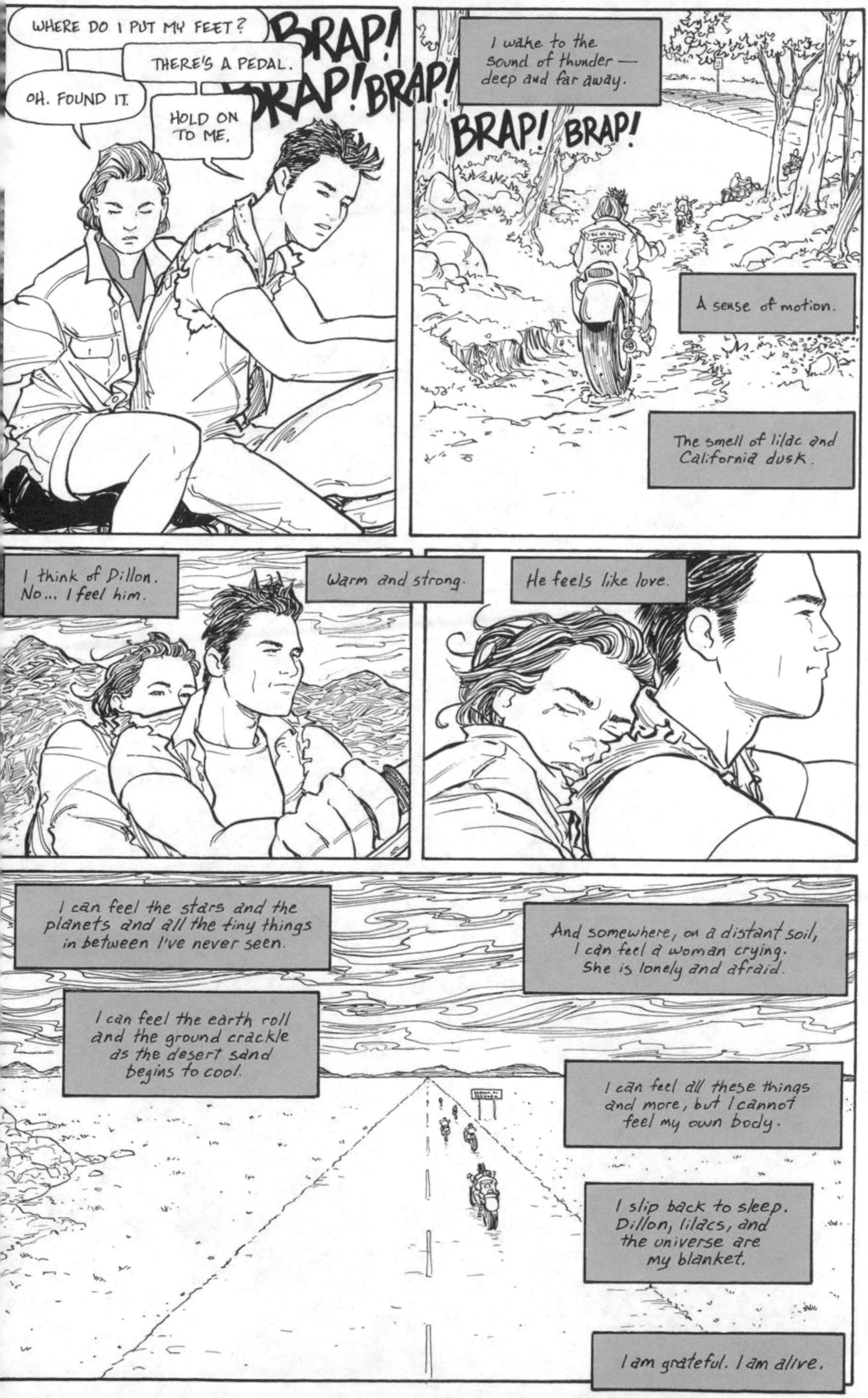
WHERE DO I PUT MY FEET?
THERE'S A PEDAL.
OH. FOUND IT.
HOLD ON TO ME.
BRAP! BRAP! BRAP!
I wake to the sound of thunder — deep and far away.
BRAP! BRAP!
A sense of motion.
The smell of lilac and California dusk.
I think of Dillon. No... I feel him.
Warm and strong.
He feels like love.
I can feel the stars and the planets and all the tiny things in between I've never seen.
And somewhere, on a distant soil, I can feel a woman crying. She is lonely and afraid.
I can feel the earth roll and the ground crackle as the desert sand begins to cool.
I can feel all these things and more, but I cannot feel my own body.
I slip back to sleep. Dillon, lilacs, and the universe are my blanket.
I am grateful. I am alive.

# ECHO

Sketchbook

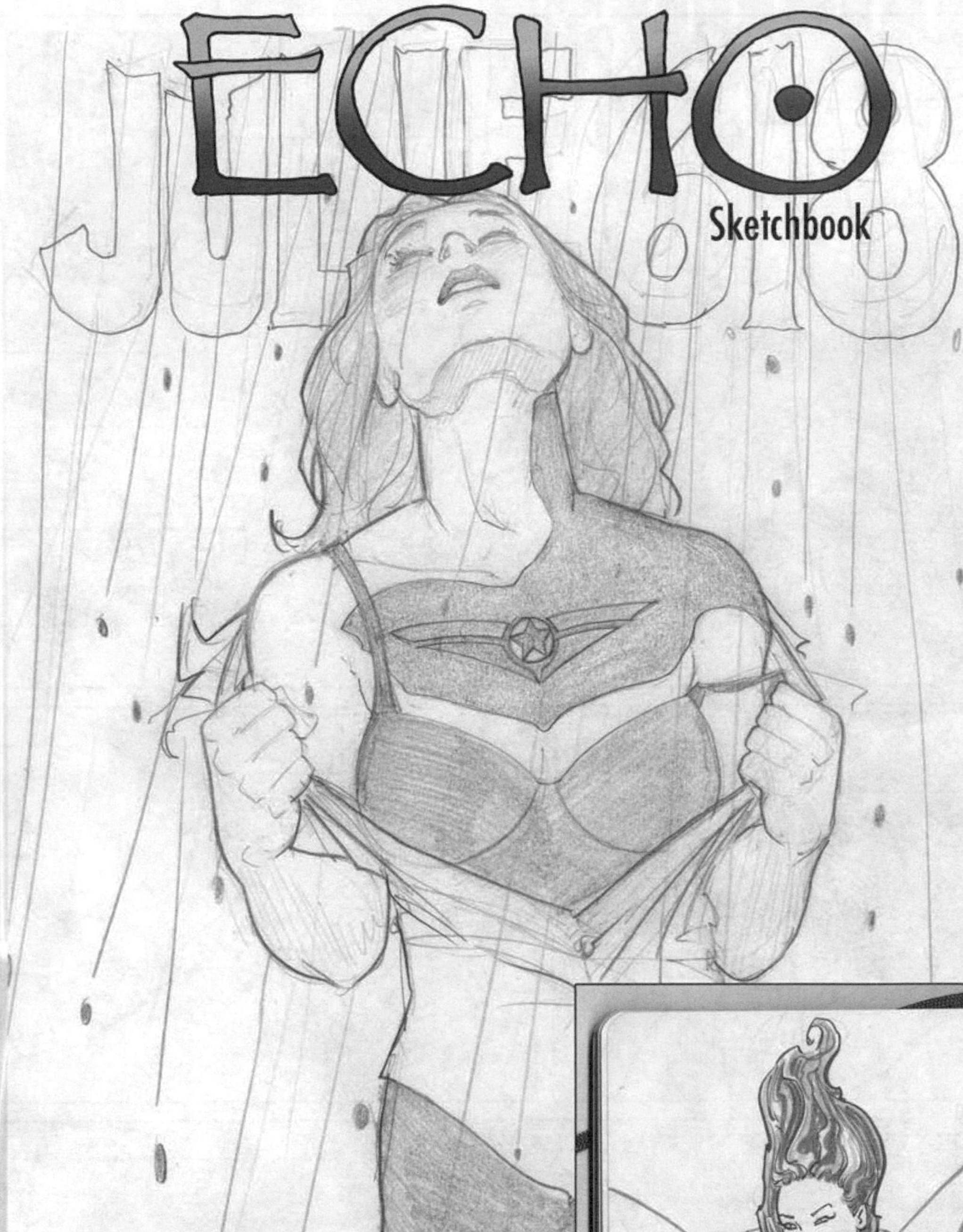

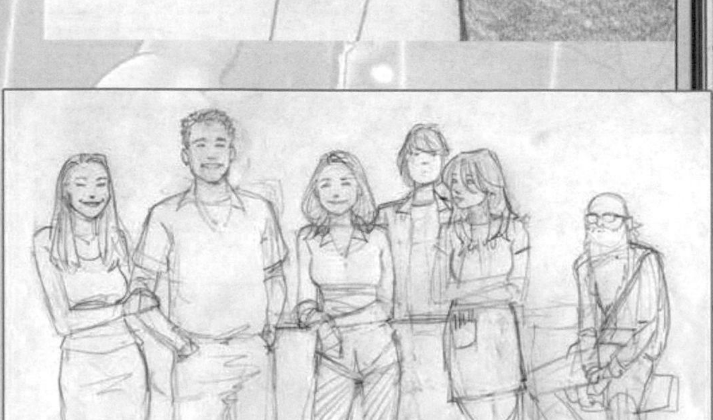

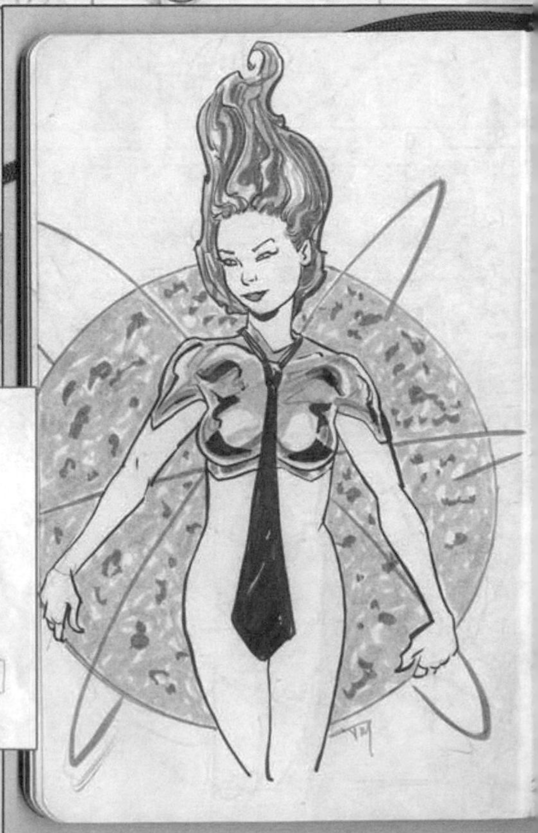

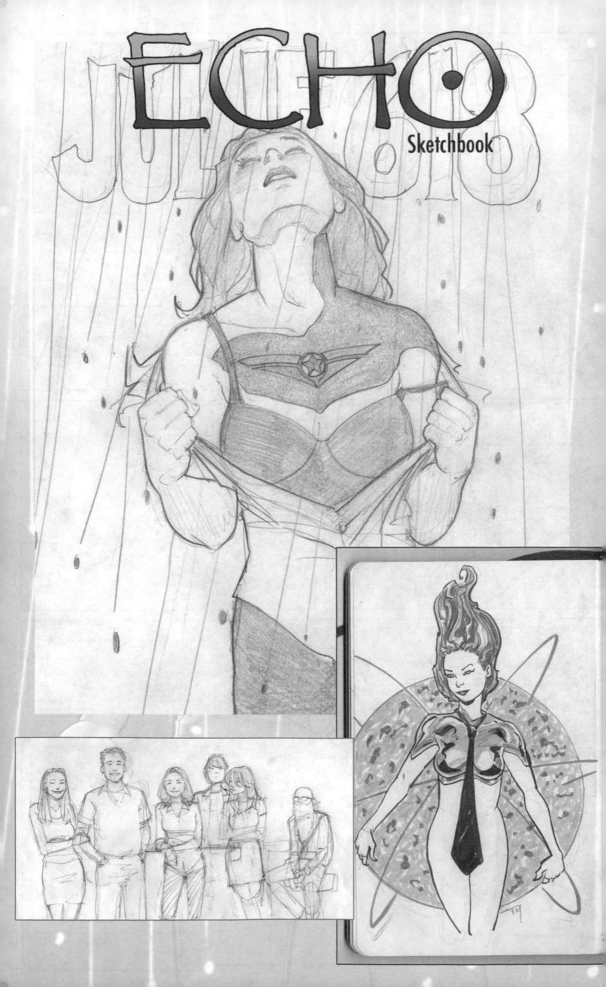

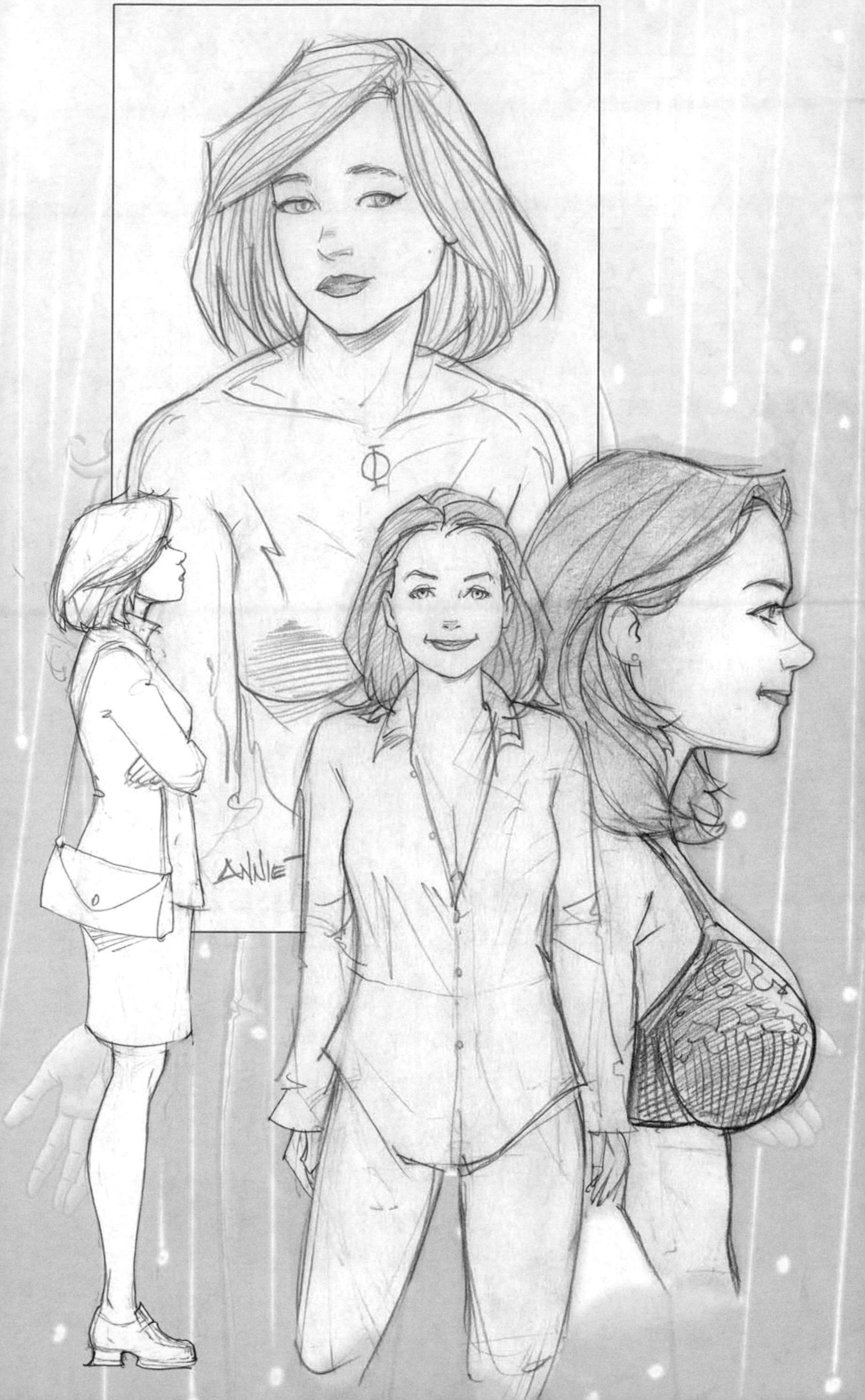
ANNIE

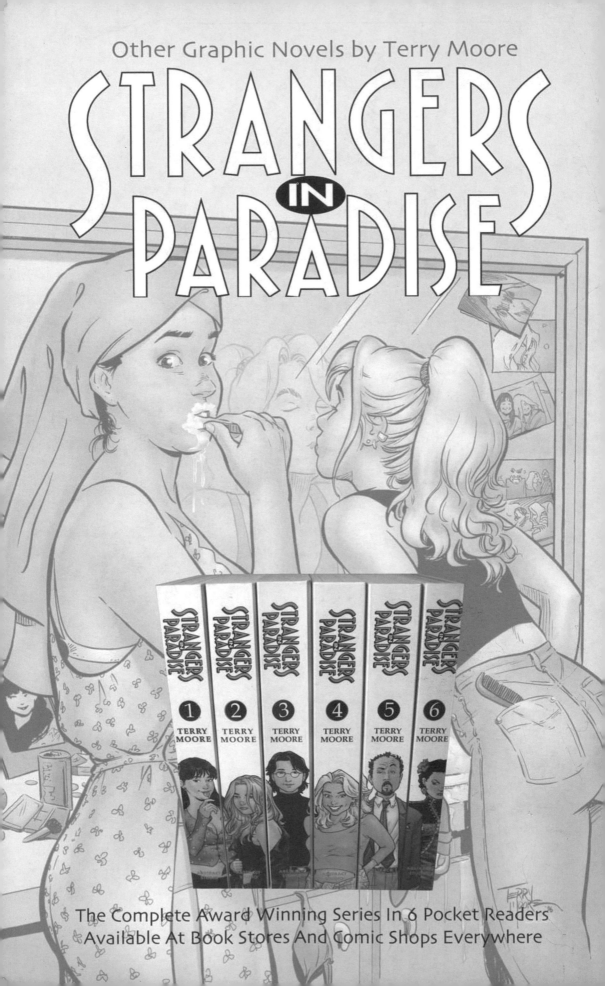